BRI ...

... tory Critical Studies

General Editor: Robin Mayhead

JOSEPH CONRAD

In this series

JOSEPH CONRAD
The major phase

JACQUES BERTHOUD

Lecturer in English, University of Southampton

CAMBRIDGE UNIVERSITY PRESS

CAMBRIDGE

LONDON · NEW YORK · MELBOURNE

Published by the Syndics of the Cambridge University Press
The Pitt Building, Trumpington Street, Cambridge CB2 IRP
Bentley House, 200 Euston Road, London NW1 2DB
32 East 57th Street, New York, NY 10022, USA
296 Beaconsfield Parade, Middle Park, Melbourne 3206, Australia

First published 1978
Reprinted 1979

Set, printed and bound in Great Britain by
Fakenham Press Limited, Fakenham, Norfolk

Library of Congress cataloguing in publication data
Berthoud, Jacques A 1935–
Joseph Conrad: the major phase.
(British authors introductory critical studies)
1. Conrad, Joseph, 1857–1924 – Criticism and interpretation.
PR 6005.04z562   823'.9'12   77-8242.
ISBN 0 521 21742 3 hard covers
ISBN 0 521 29273 5 paperback

General Preface

This study of Joseph Conrad is the ninth in a series of short introductory critical studies of the more important British authors. The aim of the series is to go straight to the authors' works; to discuss them directly with a maximum of attention to concrete detail; to say what they are and what they do, and to indicate a valuation. The general critical attitude implied in the series is set out at some length in my *Understanding Literature*. Great literature is taken to be to a large extent self-explanatory to the reader who will attend carefully enough to what it says. 'Background' study, whether biographical or historical, is not the concern of the series.

It is hoped that this approach will suit a number of kinds of reader, in particular the general reader who would like an introduction which talks about the works themselves; and the student who would like a general critical study as a starting point, intending to go on to read more specialized works later. Since 'background' is not erected as an insuperable obstacle, readers in other English-speaking countries, countries where English is a second language, or even those for whom English is a foreign language, should find the books helpful. In Britain and the Commonwealth, students and teachers in universities and in the higher forms of secondary schools will find that the authors chosen for treatment are those most often prescribed for study in public and university examinations.

The series could be described as an attempt to make available to a wide public the results of the literary criticism of the last thirty years, and especially the methods associated with Cambridge. If the result is an increase in the reading, with enjoyment and understanding, of the great works of English literature, the books will have fulfilled their wider purpose.

ROBIN MAYHEAD

Contents

Acknowledgements

I would like to express my warmest thanks to Kenneth Graham and John Swannell, for reading the manuscript and making all kinds of invaluable suggestions; to Anthony Palmer, whose powers of philosophical argument have been a source of general stimulus throughout the writing of this study; and to my mother, who once upon a time persuaded me to read 'Heart of Darkness'.

NOTE

The *Collected Edition of the Works of Joseph Conrad* (22 vols., J. M. Dent, 1946–54) has been used throughout.

1

A Personal Record

The facts gleaned from hearsay or experience were but opportunities offered to the writer. What he has done with them is matter for a verdict which must be left to the individual conscience of readers.

Last Essays, p. 145

I

While an author is planning, writing, and revising a novel, the work may be said to be part of his life, in the sense that what he is doing is one of the many ongoing activities that make up his life. But once he has decided that his novel is finished – which means, in practice, that it is ready for publication – then it assumes a different status: it now stands outside his life and must make its way independently of him. Whether it survives or not is a question beyond his control – one ultimately to be determined not by himself but by his public. Having left the life of its author, the new novel depends for its fate on whether it enters the life of its readers.

When, therefore, we raise the question of the relationship of art and life, it would seem that we are asking how a work is related to its author and to its readers. Thus we could proceed in two directions: backwards, as it were, into the conception and genesis of the work, or forwards into its reception and survival. If we decided to move backwards, we could ask an increasingly complex series of questions. What biographical event (if any) occasioned the work? What research (if any) went into its creation? What psychological or social factors determined its meaning? So, taking *Lord Jim* as an example, we could find with Norman Sherry that the very existence of the novel depended on Conrad's having come across the story of the First Mate of the *Jeddah* while visiting Singapore in 1883 (or 1887); or we could learn with J. D. Gordan that Jim would not have been sent to Patusan had Conrad not become interested in the career of the imperialist adventurer, Sir James Brooke; or we could be taught by Gustav Morf to consider Conrad's obsession with the subject of betrayal as the expression of the unconscious guilt of a renegade Pole.[1] This sort of inquiry could, no doubt, be pursued almost indefinitely. Yet, however impressive its eventual results, the question with which it began – the nature of the relationship between art and life – would remain unresolved. We would have learnt a good deal about Conrad's biography; we would have acquired a number of facts about his work. But as to the relationship between the two, we would remain as ignorant as when we started.

On this matter Conrad himself is quite unambiguous. 'Your praise of my work', he writes to a young admirer, Richard Curle, who had sent him in 1922 an article entitled 'Joseph Conrad in the East', 'your praise of my work, allied to your analysis of its origins (which really are not its origins at all, as you know perfectly well), sounds exaggerated by the mere force of contrast.' And again a year later, *à propos* of another article:

I was in hopes that on a general survey it could also be made into an opportunity for me to get freed from that infernal tail of ships, and that obsession of my sea life which has about as much bearing on my literary existence, on my quality as a writer, as the enumeration of the drawing rooms which Thackeray frequented could have had on his gift as a great novelist.[2]

For Conrad, inquiry into the biographical origin of a work is not only misconceived and irrelevant but also (since he claims that the 'praise' it produces sounds 'exaggerated') reductive. There can be no mistaking the extent of his objection: he is not simply saying that his readers' infatuation with his sea-life diverts attention from that portion of his work not concerned with the sea; he is also saying that it is damaging to his work as a whole, the sea-stories included.

We cannot feel the full force of this attack on biographical criticism unless we make some attempt to understand the otherwise banal truth that a novel derives its life from its author and its readers. The majority of Conrad's critics have simply assumed that a quasi-mechanical process of cause and effect is involved: that is to say, that a work is, as it were, 'caused' by its author, and its

---

[1] See N. Sherry, *Conrad's Eastern World* (Cambridge, 1966) on *Lord Jim*, *Almayer's Folly*, *The Outcast of the Islands*, 'The End of the Tether', *The Shadow Line*, and 'The Secret Sharer'; J. D. Gordan, *Joseph Conrad: the Making of a Novelist* (Camb. Mass., 1940) on the sources of Conrad's early work; G. Morf, *The Polish Heritage of Joseph Conrad* (London, 1931). Norman Sherry's *Conrad's Western World* (Cambridge, 1971) does for *Nostromo*, *The Secret Agent*, 'Heart of Darkness' and various tales what its predecessor did for the eastern narratives.

[2] R. Curle (ed.), *Conrad to a Friend: 150 Selected Letters from Joseph Conrad to Richard Curle* (reissued New York, 1968), pp. 113 and 147.

effects are 'registered' on its readers. However, the language of cause-and-effect is not intelligible in every context – least of all in relation to what it is to write or to read a novel like *Lord Jim*. Why this is so can perhaps best be brought out by reference to the well-known distinction between *causes* and *reasons*. According to this distinction, it is a logical error to treat reasons in terms of causes. For instance, if a reader decides that the Patusan episode as narrated in the novel *Lord Jim* (to keep to our example) is melo-dramatic, or irrelevant, or absurd, he cannot establish that it is so by invoking causes. It won't help him to study Conrad's biography in the hope of discovering, say, that he was suffering from malaria while composing the chapters in question. Such a fact, if it turned up, might explain *why* the episode was absurd; but it wouldn't show *that* it was absurd. This would have to be established first, and it could only be done by providing reasons. Similarly, the episode is not invalidated by an appeal to effects: the mere fact that it produced irritation or boredom in certain readers would not in itself constitute a demonstration or a refutation.

So, if we ask the question 'why did Conrad write *Lord Jim*?', the answer may come up in the form of 'causes' or it may come up in the form of 'reasons', depending upon the assumptions we make. In the former case we will reply: 'Because of the biographical, psychological and social conditions that determined his actions', and we will undertake a programme of research into his life and times. In the latter case we will answer: 'Because he saw, felt, understood, imagined something which he wished to explore and communicate', and we will address ourselves to the work in order to discover what it is. When, therefore, Conrad told Richard Curle that his article had failed to take 'an opportunity for [him] to get freed from that infernal tail of ships' he was claiming nothing more or less than the right to be understood as a writer.

There is little doubt that for Conrad himself the question of the relationship of art and life was a particularly urgent one. 'The nature of my writing', he noted in the same correspondence, 'runs the risk of being obscured by the nature of my material.'[1] He was intensely concerned that the life which provided the material should not be identified with the mind that made sense of it. This was not, of course, to claim that life and material had nothing to do with art and writing. The fact that, before settling down as a novelist, Conrad led an active, exposed, and adventurous exis-tence, first as the orphaned son of a revolutionary Polish patriot,

[1] *Ibid*, p. 147.

3

then as a naturalized British sailor and master-mariner, means that he had at his disposal a range of experience available only at second-hand to most other novelists. That this was a source of strength there can be no doubt; but it was also a source of weakness. Having had to acquire his craft late, as a man of mature experience, he found it easy to resist the appeal of the ivory-tower aestheticism to which so many of his younger contemporaries of the 1890s succumbed; but by the same token he remained till the end of his life unable to practise his craft without continuous strain: he came to his chosen craft and language too late ever to achieve the fluency of a James or a Bennett. Such factors are undeniable, and Conrad acknowledged them.[1] Nevertheless, he remained unwavering in his conviction that it was not the experience as such that mattered, but the experience as understood by the mind and rendered significant by the art.

It is understandable that a life such as Conrád's should have arrested the attention, often at the cost of the novels themselves, of men belonging to an age still inspired by the imperial adventure. What is less clear is why later critics should have found the intentions of his work, and even its quality, so difficult to determine. During his life-time Conrad was considered alternatively a realist and a romantic. Since then, he has been cast in an almost absurd number of more or less incompatible roles: as an impressionist, as a *symboliste* of sorts, as an allegorist (Jungian or Freudian), and more recently as a political moralist of reactionary, conservative, organicist, existential, and even revolutionary tendencies.[2] Such arbitrariness in diversity cannot be attributed solely to a concern for the life at the expense of the work. There is something about the work itself – in part related to the fact that it was produced at two removes (at least) from its author's native environment – which makes it specially prone to irresponsible criticism. This means that any new attempt to comment on the novels finds itself faced at the outset with the problem of relevance. There would be little point in adding yet another item to the

---

[1] The best biography of Conrad is Jocelyn Baines, *Joseph Conrad: a Critical Biography* (Weidenfeld and Nicolson, 1959). All references in this study are to the 1971 Penguin edition. The best work on Conrad's Polish life is Z. Najder (ed.), *Conrad's Polish Background: Letters to and from Polish Friends* (Oxford University Press, 1964).

[2] Substantiation would require reference to virtually the entire critical canon. For contemporary reception of the novels, see N. Sherry, *Conrad: the Critical Heritage* (London, 1973); for convenient summaries, see *Modern Fiction Studies*, x (1964–5) and the preface to the 2nd ed. of D. Hewitt, *Conrad: a Reassessment* (London, 1969).

growing list of studies analysing Conrad in relation to a seemingly arbitrary set of assumptions, or explaining his work in terms of ideas wholly unnatural or foreign to it. But what is the test of relevance in his case? One cannot take reliable bearings from the tradition within which he wrote, for it is precisely that tradition that is in question. What was his relationship to Victorian–Edwardian literature? How far was it affected by his veneration for the French novelists of the second half of the nineteenth century? To what extent was his adherence to the cultural norms of Western Europe undercut by the more fundamental influence of Polish culture? These are only some of the more intractable questions raised by the Conrad 'phenomenon' when one tries to understand it in terms of its cultural context. Given these difficulties,therefore, I see no alternative but to approach the work from, so to speak, the opposite direction, and to attempt to understand it, at least to begin with, *in terms of his own understanding of himself.* Normally, the question of how an author understands himself is as fraught with difficulties as the question of how he relates to his environment: often one is obliged to hypothesize on the basis of deduction from scanty or inadequate evidence. In Conrad's case, however, one is on firmer ground, for he has left us a major work, produced at the height of his creative powers, devoted in its entirety to an effort of self-discovery. I refer to the autobiography, *A Personal Record*, written in 1908,[1] at the age of fifty-one.

II

We have just seen that Conrad energetically repudiated all attempts to reduce his work to its biographical origins. Isn't the writing of a personal record, therefore, an act of flagrant inconsistency? If the purpose of an autobiography is to assemble a sequence of chronological facts, then Conrad stands condemned. Some such assumption seems to have been made by the very few critics who have examined the book. Conrad's biographer, Jocelyn Baines, is of the opinion that *A Personal Record* shows 'no analysis, no probing below the surface';[2] and one of his most favourable interpreters, Albert Guerard, although alone in calling it 'a true work of art', finds it 'most evasive'.[3] Yet there are at least two

---

[1] Published serially, December 1908–June 1909; as a book, 1912.

[2] *Joseph Conrad*, p. 354.

[3] A. J. Guerard, *Conrad the Novelist* (Camb. Mass. and Oxford, 1958), p. 3. This is a vivid and elegant study, tending to psychological extravagance.

reasons for believing that the assumptions that prompt these judgements are mistaken in the present case.

The first arises out of Conrad's own discussion, in the fifth chapter of *A Personal Record*, of the motives for which auto-biographies are produced. Comparing his own memoirs with those of Rousseau, he writes: 'The matter in hand is to keep these reminiscences from turning into confessions, a form of literary activity discredited by Jean-Jacques Rousseau on account of the extreme thoroughness he brought to the work of justifying his own existence' (*A Personal Record*, p. 95). The purpose of this attack against Rousseau is to enable Conrad to distinguish clearly be-tween 'reminiscences' and 'confessions': the former are prompted by the question, 'What do I remember?', the latter by 'What do others think of me?' On this basis, Conrad proceeds to differentiate between those who examine themselves from motives of vanity – the 'megalomaniacs who rest uneasy under the crown of their unbounded conceit' – and those who do so from motives of egoism – those 'ambitious minds always looking forward to some aim of aggrandisement'. What these two types share is a common incapacity for sparing a 'detached impersonal glance upon them-selves' (pp. 91–2). To undertake to write about oneself, therefore, is a project fraught with risk, and redeemable only through the purifying virtue of disinterestedness.

The second reason arises out of a consideration of the structure of *A Personal Record*. As a conventional autobiography, the book is inadequate, not only because it makes no intimate or private disclosures, but also because it confines itself to a handful of episodes set out in complete disregard of chronological order. A glance at Conrad's disposition of his material will make this clear. Chapter 1 begins with Conrad on board his last ship at work on his first novel, *Almayer's Folly*, then turns back to the previous autumn when he was making his final visit to his uncle and guardian in the Polish Ukraine (1893, 1892); Chapter 2 refers to events in his Polish past, especially to a great-uncle's participation in the Napoleonic retreat from Moscow (1812), then moves forward to Conrad's long struggle to go to sea (summer 1873); Chapter 3 describes Poland's distress under Russian occupation, largely through a dramatic account of the same great-uncle's life, and of Conrad's mother's last visit to her family before her death in exile (1863); Chapter 4 describes the very beginnings of Conrad's work on *Almayer's Folly* in London (autumn 1889), then recalls his first meeting with the original Almayer in Borneo a year before; Chapter 5 opens with some general remarks on life and literature, and ends with an account of the composition of *Nostromo* (summer 1904); Chapter 6 recalls the three examinations leading to his master's ticket (1880–6); and then evokes his first experience of the sea at Marseilles (autumn 1874); the final chapter provides a vivid account of his first glimpse of a British merchant-ship during a night-excursion with the Marseilles pilots.

Brief as this summary is, it is sufficient to show that the impression of confusion is only superficial. Once chronological expectations are relinquished, it becomes clear, as the preface to *A Personal Record* itself suggests, that 'these memories have [not] been thrown off without system or purpose' (p. xxi). The narrative is organized around the two major events of Conrad's life: his decision to go to sea, and his decision to become a writer. The first is set against the background of his Polish origins, the second in the context of his commitment to the Merchant Service. Furthermore, these two events do more than determine selection: they also determine structure. 'In the purposely mingled resonance of this double strain', says Conrad in his preface, 'a friend here and there will perhaps detect a subtle accord.' The making of the seaman and the making of the writer are treated in such a way that they become mutually illuminating. *A Personal Record* is not primarily a source of explanatory fact; it is an exploration of the relationship between Conrad's two professions. In that the book is concerned with events that actually took place and men and women who really lived, it is an historical work. But it is also the product of a man's prolonged meditation on the significance of his past. It is not merely a 'record' but a 'personal' one. It represents not simply a life, but a life understood. And in its concern to explore the parallels between Conrad the seaman and Conrad the writer, it gradually formulates a view of the relationship between life and art.

That Conrad did not envisage this relationship in causal terms is confirmed by a rather difficult passage towards the beginning of Chapter 5. Conrad begins by stating that conceited and ambitious minds 'together with the much larger band of the totally unimaginative, of those unfortunate beings in whose empty and unseeing gaze . . . the whole universe vanishes into a blank nothingness' may well miss 'the true task of us men whose day is short on this earth, the abode of conflicting opinions'. He goes on:

The ethical view of the universe involves us at last in so many cruel and absurd contradictions, where the last vestiges of faith, hope, charity, and even of reason itself, seem ready to perish, that I have come to suspect that the aim of creation cannot be ethical at all. I would fondly believe that its object is purely spectacular: a spectacle for awe, love, adoration, or hate, if you like, but in this view – and in this view alone – never for despair! Those visions, delicious or poignant, are a moral end in themselves. The rest is our affair – the laughter, the tears, the tenderness, the indignation,' the high tranquillity of a steeled heart, the detached curiosity of a subtle mind – that's our affair! And the unwearied self-forgetful attention to every phase of the living universe reflected in our consciousness, may be our appointed task on this earth. A task in which fate has perhaps engaged nothing of us except our conscience, gifted with a voice in order to bear true testimony to the visible wonder ... of the sublime spectacle.

A Personal Record, p. 92

This sombre utterance may become more intelligible if we remember its context: Conrad's return, after the vicissitudes of nineteen years' absence, to Poland, the place of his origins. Such an event would overwhelm most of us with a sense of the remorse-lessness of change. For Conrad, the sole survivor of a vanished past, the question whether there is *anything* permanent in the affairs of men must take on a special immediacy. His journeys over the face of the globe – 'the abode of conflicting opinions' – have taught him to reject the idea of 'an ethical universe': that is to say, a universe created to sustain and endorse the good. The virtuous and vicious alike suffer the ravages of time and chance; the very idea of the good is subject to the accidents of period and place. Can anything survive this universal wreckage? Despite his experience of loss, Conrad is not yet ready to give up. He stakes his hopes on a single hypothesis: that of 'a spectacular universe', that is to say, of a world that requires of man only one task – to make his experience of it real to himself. Of all the variety of men's duties, the command to see and to hear is the only one that is not self-appointed, the only one whose authority is not 'our affair'.

This philosophical position has been described, notably by Jocelyn Baines,[1] as 'impressionistic'. But this label seems to me to be seriously misleading. First of all it implies that the act of perception required of us is essentially passive and fragmentary. On the contrary, Conrad insists that the attention we have to direct to 'every phase of the living universe' must be 'unwearied' and 'self-forgetful'. Secondly, 'impressionism' is a morally neutral term, and therefore it disregards what is perhaps the most striking

---

[1] *Joseph Conrad*, p. 231: with respect to the 'Preface' to *The Nigger of the 'Narcissus'*, Conrad's most explicit – though incomplete – statement of the artist's aim. Baines adds that, *in practice*, Conrad was never an impressionist.

turn in Conrad's argument: that the rejection of the 'ethical universe' in favour of the 'spectacular universe' has *moral* consequences. To the spectacle which offers itself to our senses he
permits every response except that of despair: 'in this view there is
room for every religion except for the inverted creed of impiety, the
mask and cloak of arid despair'. The reason for this, of course, is
that the law which bids us take an imaginative interest in the world
in which we find ourselves presupposes that life is worth living. To
'despair imaginatively' would, for Conrad, constitute a contradiction in terms. If it were not so, he would not be able to claim
that 'those visions ... are a moral end in themselves'. Far from
producing impressionism, the rejection of the 'ethical' in favour of
the 'spectacular' creates the basis of moral action, for moral action,
as far as Conrad is concerned, is not justifiable in terms of abstract
principle or revealed dogma, but in terms of imaginative understanding.

III

This view of man's task on earth forms the foundation of Conrad's
artistic creed. 'Only in men's imagination does every truth find an
effective and undeniable existence', he writes at the end of his first
chapter. 'Imagination, not invention, is the supreme master of art
as of life' (p. 25). The distinction between imagination and invention enables Conrad to safeguard such activities as the writing and
reading of fiction from the charge of escapism. For while invention
may be, and often is, an irresponsible faculty, imagination is
censored by the very reality it perceives, interprets, or recreates. A
work produced by the imagination cannot, by definition, merely
express the self-born fantasies of the mind; it has to do justice to the
reality of a world that exists beyond the self.

Thus considered, a work of imaginative fiction is not something
that merely happens, and so an object for research, but something
achieved, and so an object of judgement. In one form or another,
this idea runs right through the autobiography. Chapter 5, for
example, refers to 'the prose artist of fiction, which after all is but
truth often dragged out of a well and clothed in the painted robes of
imaged phrases', and to 'the novelist, whose first virtue is the exact
understanding of the limits traced by the reality of his time to the
play of his invention' (p. 93). This 'truth' is quite plainly not the
truth of fact, and therefore cannot be verified in the manner in
which, for instance, legal or historical or biographical evidence is
tested. But it is not – otherwise it would be difficult to see how the

9

idea of truth could be invoked at all – a truth that has nothing to do with fact. The novelist's invention is not a blank cheque: what he can write is limited by 'the reality of his time' – that is, the reality directly accessible to him. I have suggested that the auto-biographer's concern is not with the facts but the meaning of the facts: but this meaning, whatever it may be, depends at least on not getting the facts wrong. So, it is impossible to see a man who habitually misrepresents to himself every detail of his experience of others ever achieving the understanding required for even as imperfect a novel as *Almayer's Folly*. Alternatively, it is impossible to imagine a novelist without a memory. Although the meaning of an author's work cannot be reduced to the facts of his life, the work is strictly inconceivable without these facts. As Conrad said to Richard Curle: 'Without mankind, my art, an infinitesimal thing, would not exist.'

The opponents of the 'intentional fallacy' have rightly stressed that professed intentions are not necessarily identical with realized intentions, and hence that the task of the biographer is not the same as that of the critic. However, they have opened such a gap between the work of art and 'mankind' that they have made it very difficult to see what a novel could have to do with truth. Unlike these critics, Conrad refuses to treat the novel as some sort of 'self-sufficient' object. He regards it instead as the intelligible product of the imagination of one man appealing to the imagi-nation of his fellow-men. Yet by so doing he seems to me to be endorsing the insights of this critical school while avoiding the hazards it creates. He clearly recognizes that since, by definition, a work of fiction cannot exhibit the facts and events from which it derives its reality, it depends for its truth on the good faith of its author – on his 'sincerity' or 'conscience', as Conrad indifferently calls it. In his preface, Conrad writes: 'I know that a novelist lives in his work. He stands there, the only reality in an invented world, among imaginary things, happenings, and people. Writing about them, he is only writing about himself.' The truth of a novel, then, would seem to be guaranteed solely by the subjective or private integrity of the novelist. 'In that interior world', Conrad goes on, 'where his thoughts and his emotions go seeking for the experience of imagined adventures, there are no policemen, no law, no pres-sure of circumstances or dread of opinion to keep him within bounds. Who then is going to say Nay to his temptations if not his conscience?' (p. xiii). And *A Personal Record* does full justice to this phase of the creative process. Seldom has the solitary struggle of the artist been evoked with more sardonic insight than in the few pages at the end of Chapter 5 devoted to the composition of *Nostromo* – a struggle ironically described as 'the perfect delight of writing tales where so many lives come and go at the cost of one which slips imperceptibly away'. Yet this is only part of the story. Private integrity may be a necessary condition for truth, but it is not a sufficient one. *A Personal Record* also makes it quite clear that if writing a novel were not an act of communication, drawing on the shared conventions of a language and the collective traditions of a culture – if the novel were not *in principle* destined for the test of public recognition – then all talk of the truth of fiction would be pointless.

The first chapter describes with considerable subtlety the state of mind of a man at a moment of transition, when the reality of the familiar is beginning to yield to the demands of the new. Reluctantly holding on to an appointment he did not seek, to a ship destined not to leave harbour, Conrad finds himself increasingly absorbed by the composition of his first novel. Working in his cabin, he recalls being interrupted by a young officer with 'What are you always scribbling there if it's fair to ask?', and turning over the pad 'with a movement of instinctive secrecy' (p. 4). This response prepares the way (logically if not chronologically) for another incident in which Conrad, now outward bound on the clipper *Torrens*, brings himself to show his manuscript for the first time. The significance of this moment is heavily underlined by the sentences that introduce it.

What is it that Novalis says? 'It is certain my conviction gains infinitely the moment another soul will believe in it.' And what is a novel if not a conviction of our fellow-man's existence strong enough to take upon itself a form of imagined life clearer than reality and whose accumulated verisimilitude of selected episodes puts to shame the pride of documentary history?

The ensuing dialogue has almost the form of an elementary demonstration: 'Is it worth finishing? – Distinctly; Were you interested? – Very much! Now let me ask you one more thing: is the story quite clear to you as it stands? – Yes! Perfectly' (pp. 15–18). What is being demonstrated is that an imaginative truth is one capable of being recognized as such by another mind.

IV

We have seen that *A Personal Record* sets up a parallel between the beginnings of Conrad's sea-life and the start of his novelist's career.

This parallel enables him to make a number of striking individual points. For example, about the obsessiveness of the novelist's vocation: 'I dare say I am compelled, unconsciously compelled, now to write volume after volume, as in past years I was compelled to go to sea, voyage after voyage' (p. 18). Or about the uncertainty of the novelist's quest: 'A certain latitude, once won, cannot be disputed. The sun and stars and the shape of your earth are the witnesses of your gain; whereas a handful of pages, no matter how much you have made them your own, are at best but an obscure and questionable spoil' (p. 99). However, its general purpose is to develop the view that 'imagination, not invention, is the supreme master of art and life' (p. 25). And this it does by establishing three major common denominators, and drawing out their implications.

The first of these common factors is the idea of *restraint*. In his sixth chapter, Conrad informs us that every one of the 'characters' or testimonials he has earned as an officer 'contain [s] the words "strictly sober"'. And his comment is emphatic: 'That august academical body of the Marine Department of the Board of Trade takes nothing for granted in the granting of its learned degrees. By its regulations ... the very word SOBER must be written, or a whole sackful, a ton, a mountain of the most enthusiastic appreciation will avail you nothing' (p. 111). In a craft in which the merest slip can produce a catastrophe it is not difficult to see why this demand should be made. But what of the novelist's vocation, where the test is not the impartial ocean but a notoriously deceivable public? Responding to a French critic's description of him as *un puissant rêveur*, he is equally emphatic:

Yet perhaps not such an unconditional dreamer as that ... There is more than one sort of intoxication. Even before the most seductive reveries, I have remained mindful of that sobriety of interior life, that asceticism of sentiment, in which alone the naked form of truth, such as one conceives it, such as one feels it, can be rendered without shame. It is but a maudlin and indecent verity that comes out through the strength of wine.

A Personal Record, pp. 111–12

Conrad recognizes in these sentences that the view of art as truth is incompatible with the view of art as the *exhibition* or the *arousal* of emotion. 'An historian of hearts is not an historian of emotion', he says in his preface (p. xix), thereby implying (in context) that understanding a feeling is not the same thing as yielding to it. 'I too', he goes on, 'would like to hold the magic wand giving that command over laughter and tears which is declared to be the highest achievement of imaginative literature.' But he renounces that alternative on the grounds that it would weaken his hold on his perceptions: 'Only to be a great magician one must surrender oneself to occult and irresponsible powers, either outside or within the breast' (pp. xvi–xvii). For Conrad, restraint is as important in art as in life, and always for the same reason: that a man cannot serve truth *and* power, insight *and* enchantment. The effort to bring into play 'the extremities of emotion' may in the end tempt the writer 'to despise truth itself as something too cold, too blunt for his purpose – as in fact not good enough for his insistent emotion' (p. xviii). Does this mean then that he considers head and heart to be incompatible? Uncertain as our grasp of the concept of emotion is, I think we may safely distinguish between possessing a feeling, and being possessed by a feeling. To possess a feeling is not necessarily to deny or to repress it; it is to understand it, to be conscious of its source and object, to be able to relate it to the world within and the world without. Conrad subordinates emotion to imagination and intelligence; but this does not mean that he rejects emotion. On the contrary: such scrupulousness may well safeguard its springs from the aridities of sensationalism, insincerity, and sentimentality.

'It may be my sea training acting on a natural disposition to keep good hold on the one thing really mine, but the fact is that I have a positive horror of losing even for one moving moment that full possession of myself which is the first condition of good service' (p. xvii).[1] This declaration may serve to explain some of the less accessible aspects of Conrad's character as a writer. It seems to me that even his most personal work never establishes a relationship of intimacy with the reader. We can never finally relax, never unreservedly abandon ourselves to the movement of the narrative, or yield uncritically to the life of the characters. Yet by the same token, we as readers are never cajoled, nudged, flattered or insulted, but treated with unfailing decorum and dignity. Again, Conrad's writing (the flavour of his English is only partially ascribable to his foreignness) is never wholly spontaneous or natural; even at its most fluent, it retains a sense of difficulty overcome. Yet this too has its compensatory virtues: at his best he achieves a power, fullness, and precision of utterance quite beyond the scope of a more casual style; and even his more magniloquent pages are seldom without at least an echo of the brooding sobriety which he has made so particularly his own.

[1] Cf. p. 112.

Conrad's range as a novelist has its limitations. A writer who confesses to a positive phobia for loss of self-possession is unlikely to be reliable on the subject of love or passion. It is not surprising that a man like D. H. Lawrence, for example, whose strengths and weaknesses are the exact opposite of Conrad's, should have thought of him as one of 'the Writers among the Ruins' and been unable to forgive him 'for being so sad and for giving in'.[1] Conrad is not a man to put much faith in nature's powers of restoration and renewal. On the other hand, on the problems of personal identity and conduct, he seems to me to have no rival among English novelists.

V

The second of these factors common to the life of the seaman and novelist is the idea of *solidarity*. The last chapters of *A Personal Record* are devoted to two episodes. The first, in a style at once affectionate and humorous, recalls Conrad's threefold ordeal as a Port of London examinee; the second sumptuously evokes a night expedition with seasoned mariners in the bay of Marseilles. We find, as we would expect, that both convey a strong feeling of delight, the first in achievement, the second in discovery. But these are not our final impressions. Beyond them, there lingers the suggestion of some sort of process or ceremony of initiation. The reason for this is that the seaman's life, as Conrad conceives it, is more than merely functional. To be admitted to it is to enter a confraternity sustained and defined by a special tradition of service. By contrast, the activity of the novelist might seem self-regarding and solitary. Yet for Conrad it is inspired by an analogous ideal. In his first chapter, for example, describing the beginnings of the process that was to transform him into an author, he remembers some of the people met in the course of his journeys in the Far East.

They came with a silent and irresistible appeal – and the appeal, I affirm here, was not to my self-love or my vanity. It seems now to have had a moral character, for why should the memory of these beings, seen in their obscure sun-bathed existence, demand to express itself in the shape of a novel, except on the ground of that mysterious fellowship which unites in a community of hopes and fears all the dwellers of this earth?

A Personal Record, p. 9

The meaning of the artist's life, as that of the sailor's, must be sought in the ideal of human solidarity. This ideal is impersonal, in

[1] D. H. Lawrence, *Collected Letters*, ed. H. T. Moore (Heinemann, 1962), p. 152.

that it is not motivated by a concern for the self; but it is human, for it seeks to express and develop man's latent capacity for comradeship and reciprocity.

The idea of solidarity receives extensive treatment in Chapter 4, where Conrad describes the circumstances of his meeting with the historical Almayer – without whom, he tells us, 'it is almost certain there would never have been a line of mine in print' (p. 87). This Almayer Conrad presents very much as his fellows would have known him: a comic–pathetic failure, his eccentricities a source of gossip throughout the East Indies. Conrad ends, however, by imagining a meeting with Almayer in the Elysian Fields, where he is called to task for having so shamelessly put a fellow-creature to the service of art. His excuse is characteristic.

Since you were always complaining of being lost to the world [he tells him], you should remember that if I had not believed enough in your existence to let you haunt my rooms ... you would have been much more lost ... I believed in you in the only way it was possible for me to believe ... It was not worthy of your merits? ... Nothing was ever quite worthy of you. What made you so real to me is that you held this lofty theory with some force of conviction and with an admirable consistency.

A Personal Record, p. 88

The point of this imaginary encounter is not Conrad's compunction at misrepresenting the facts of the historical Almayer's existence, but the grounds on which he makes his excuse. In life, Almayer seems to have been an outsider, even an outcast – the fated victim of the malice of the community – yet one who retained a self-estimation wildly at variance with the popular image of him. In the novel, which does not soften his self-deceptions, this interior life is given an irresistible reality. Conrad explains himself to the reproachful ghost in terms of the nature of the novelist's art, which persuades us to accomplish what the real Almayer's acquaintances had failed to achieve: the recognition, which is the basis of human solidarity, that another man's world is as real to him as ours is to ourselves.

In attributing a moral character to his inspiration as a novelist Conrad implicitly repudiates two well-known ethical positions. The first is the view that the moral life depends on abstract principles or Utopian visions. 'I have never been able to love what was not lovable or hate what was not hateful out of deference for some general principle', he writes in the preface (p. xvii); and in this he is perfectly consistent, for the imaginative view requires, as we have seen, that feelings be inspired by known objects, not by abstract imperatives. Similarly, he attacks moral concerns derived from Utopian visions. Of Rousseau, whom he calls 'an artless moralist' – that is, one without imagination – he remarks: 'Inspiration comes from the earth, which has a past, a history, a future, not from the cold and immutable heaven' (p. 95). Moral action not inspired by a living context must remain dangerous or unreal. The second view that Conrad repudiates is what can be loosely described as 'individualism' – the idea that individual man should be a self-sufficient unit acting from motives of competitive success. This emphasis on the independence of the self – which produces utilitarianism in ethics, liberalism in economics, and aestheticism (the cultivation of 'the thrill') in art – is incompatible, of course, with the ideal of service. Conrad's account of his ancestral traditions in *A Personal Record* is a consistent refutation of both these general views. His position is succinctly summed up in the author's note:

An impartial view of humanity in all its degrees of splendour or misery, together with a special regard for the rights of the unprivileged of this earth, not on any mystic ground but on the ground of simple fellowship and honourable reciprocity of services, was the dominant characteristic of the mental and moral atmosphere of the houses which sheltered my hazardous childhood: – matters of calm and deep conviction both lasting and consistent, and removed as far as possible from that humanitarianism which seems to be merely a matter of crazy nerves or a morbid conscience.

A Personal Record, p. vii

Conrad reserves his special scorn for those altruists who seek their inspiration in the treacherous exaltations of mysticism (Conrad certainly had in mind the various Messianic cults that swept Eastern Europe in the course of the nineteenth century), or for those humanitarians whose 'crazy nerves' are the penalty they have to pay for doing good for the sake of the doer. In the light of this it is not surprising that he should have been so hostile to Dostoevsky. He may have been incapable of the great Russian's experience of damnation and salvation, but there is more than Polish Russophobia in his rejection of the abnormal tensions and shrillnesses of Dostoevsky's fictional world.

VI

The last of the three major factors common to the seaman and novelist is the idea of *fidelity*. 'Those who read me know my conviction that the world, the temporal world, rests on a very few simple ideas; so simple that they must be as old as the hills. It rests notably, among others, on the idea of Fidelity.' These famous lines from the preface to *A Personal Record* (p. xix) have been held up as a flagrant example of self-deception. Douglas Hewitt, for instance, argues that Conrad's great novels treat 'ideas and beliefs which are very far from simple and to which any naïve moralizing is irrelevant'.[1] This seems to me to betray a simple-minded notion of what simplicity involves. The idea of simplicity has commonly been set as the final goal not only of the moral life (for example, Eliot's 'condition of complete simplicity costing not less than everything'[2]) but also of the intellectual life (where the only simple problems are those that have been resolved). It is surely not difficult to see that Conrad is not using the word 'simple' as a synonym for 'easy' or 'elementary'. When he declares that the 'temporal world' of human society as it exists rests on the idea of fidelity – for instance, fidelity to a contract – he is not indulging in naïve moralizing, but stating one of the basic conditions of social existence. By ideas 'so simple that they must be as old as the hills', Conrad means fundamental ideas; and it is on fundamental ideas that the most formidable works of literature are built up.

For a man to whom temporal life presents itself as unreliable, and even destructive, the idea of fidelity must take on a particular importance, for it is his main bulwark against the drift of dissolution – the point on which he can make his stand and declare 'This is the kind of man I am.' To be faithful is to make a lasting commitment. But what are the conditions for a lasting commitment? The first is that the choice must be more than personal, for (as we have seen) no permanence can be founded on the gratification of appetite or desire. The second is that it must be active, for merely private decisions have no substance until they have issued out in deeds. Conrad's two main commitments amply satisfy both these conditions. Consider, for example, his reiteration throughout *A Personal Record* that the impulses that drove him to his two careers were as unexpected as they were inexplicable. Of his desire to go to sea, he says in Chapter 6: 'I understood no more than the people who called upon me to explain myself. There was no precedent. I verily believe that I was the only case of a boy of my

---

[1] Hewitt, *Conrad*, p. 4. Hewitt's forceful little study, together with J. I. M. Stewart's more balanced *Joseph Conrad* (London, 1968), constitute perhaps the best two introductions to Conrad's work.

[2] In 'Little Gidding', Section v.

nationality and antecedents taking a, so to speak, standing jump out of his racial surroundings and associations' (p. 121). Of his decision to write, he says in Chapter 4: 'The necessity which impelled me . . . was not the famous need for self-expression which artists find in their search for motives', but 'a hidden obscure necessity, a completely masked and unaccountable phenomenon' (p. 68). This emphasis must not be taken as a covert invitation to solve a puzzle; it is a recognition, rather, of the genuineness of the impulses – of the fact that they were not fabricated to satisfy vanity or ambition. To take another example: Conrad's assertion that fidelity to the traditions of seamanship has to be active (whence his pride in his accumulated certificates and testimonials, 'those few bits of paper' that constitute unassailable proof of twenty years' active service at sea) is paralleled by his conviction, powerfully illustrated in his account of what the writing of *Nostromo* cost him, that a novel is 'an achievement of the active life . . . as much as the conquest of a colony'.[1] Or again, by insisting that the writer's primary task is the imaginative exploration of the world, he is able to suggest that the desire to go to sea was also an imaginative impulse, to be understood not in terms of causes but in terms of goals. In *A Personal Record* the call of the sea, like the call of letters, is not presented as a means of advancement (or a means to any other end), but as the challenge of the unknown, as the summons, inaudible to the unimaginative, of the variety and possibility of life. In general, then, Conrad affirms that the reality of the worlds we create, whether in the forms of voyages accomplished or of books written, is not founded on self-seeking but on our capacity for fidelity.

How far this is from naïve moralizing is demonstrated by Conrad's recognition that, as an ideal of conduct, fidelity is not a panacea. The reason why his struggle to go to sea occupies a central place in his autobiography is that it forced him to learn, at an age younger than most, that fidelity to one principle may mean infidelity to another. This struggle cannot be understood as anything other than a crisis of conscience. In Chapter 5 he defines conscience as 'that heirloom of the ages, of the race, of the group, of the family, colourable and plastic, fashioned by the words, the looks, the acts, and even by the silences and abstentions surrounding one's childhood' (p. 94); and also as a man's 'deeper sense of things lawful and unlawful' (p. 95). In other words, conscience is what makes a man belong most deeply to himself, and

[1] 'A Glance at Two Books' in *Last Essays*, p. 132. Cf. *The Mirror of the Sea*, p. 33.

at the same time what makes him belong most deeply to others. The reason why the decision to go to sea provoked what can only be called a crisis of identity is that it set these two elements, both of them equally valid, at odds with each other. That the contradiction was an internal one is shown by the fact that he was opposed not by some uncomprehending family tyrant but by his young tutor, an idealistic medical student, able to urge him by his own example to weigh against his 'sincerity of purpose' the 'claims of affection and conscience'. Hence when, at the moment of his victory, Conrad is told, 'You are a hopeless, incorrigible Don Quixote' (p. 44), he acknowledges the aptness of the title. 'The sublime *caballero* ... rides forth, his head encircled by a halo – the patron saint of all lives spoiled or saved by the irresistible grace of imagination. But he was not a good citizen ...' (p. 37). As Conrad could see even then, his dilemma consisted in the fact that fidelity to his vision was not compatible with fidelity to his community.

Conrad's detailed account, in Chapter 3, of his great-uncle Nicholas B.'s career can be considered an attempt to show why for Poles of their generation these two imperatives were mutually incompatible. Unlike Conrad, Nicholas chose the patriotic alternative. But this choice, too, constituted no escape from contradiction, and Nicholas, much more bitterly even than Conrad, spent the rest of his life suffering its consequences. Systematically dispossessed of his inheritance by a step-father, Nicholas joined Napoleon in an attempt to free his country from Russian occupation. After Napoleon's fall, he enlisted in the army of the new Polish kingdom, and in the 1831 revolt led his regiment against Russia. He was defeated and exiled to the tenancy of a country estate, only to have his house looted and destroyed in the 1863 uprising. What were the rewards of life-long commitment to the cause of a baffled and disorientated nation? Honour and respect certainly – but also all the bitterness of a damaged identity. In later life his character was marked by a 'taciturnity' which was symptomatic, as Conrad saw, of 'a most painful irresolution in all matters of public life'. By devoting himself to his country he gradually made himself incapable of serving it. Nicholas chose Poland; Conrad did not. From the patriotic point of view the uncle's choice condemns the nephew's. But if one remembers his fate, it also vindicates it.

Conrad's early exposure to the contradictions latent in the ideal of fidelity marked him for life. It taught him once and for all that the individual is a product of the community, but at the same time that he cannot be identified with it. The importance of this discovery for his writing is not difficult to demonstrate. His claim that he would probably not have become a novelist had he not met Almayer is not capricious. His attention was caught and held by this tragi-comic figure because of one crucial trait – Almayer's refusal, in the face of the justified mockery of his fellows, to abandon his conviction of the 'inner marvellousness' of his life. In other words, Conrad recognized in this shabby and querulous trader, so different from the aloofly courteous officer he himself then was, a fellow Don Quixote. So when we turn to the novel we find that its theme is the paradoxical ambiguity inherent in the idea of the self. In depicting the fictional Almayer's 'anguish of paternity' Conrad dramatizes the love for his daughter that betrays Almayer's most contemptible weaknesses – his irresponsibility, his snobbery, his evasiveness – but which also affirms, because of its unreserved intensity, his essential dignity as a man.

The idea of fidelity common to both phases of Conrad's life can be shown, on his own account, to have a major bearing on his novels. When looking back at the circumstances surrounding his departure from Poland, he is sometimes tempted to imagine that his choice of a sea career involved no disloyalty to the land of his birth. 'The fidelity to a special tradition', he writes in Chapter 3, 'may last through the events of an unrelated existence, following faithfully, too, the traced way of an inescapable impulse' (p. 36). In so far as he tried to remain true to the conscience that was virtually his only inheritance, this assertion is valid enough, and his book – the record of this conscience – must remain his answer to the reproaches of his compatriots: to *ad hominem* arguments, *ecce homo* is the only reply. Yet such justifications are not wholly satisfactory, and Conrad knows it, for he goes on at once to suggest that conscience itself may sometimes involve paradoxes too complex for resolution. 'It would take too long to explain the intimate alliance of contradictions in human nature which makes love itself wear at times the desperate shape of betrayal. *And perhaps there is no possible explanation*' (p. 36). [My italics.] Surely this is an acknowledgement that the ideal of fidelity, if upheld seriously enough, may lead directly to problems that can only be described as tragic?

A good deal of recent criticism has tried to argue that Conrad must be regarded as a fundamentally political novelist. If this means that his work is concerned not with individuals alone, but with individuals in their relation to society, then what serious novelist does not deserve to be called political? On the other hand, the argument may be that most of his novels – certainly all his major ones – concern themselves with man as a political being caught up in events and situations of a political character. But even this is not enough to earn him the epithet 'political' in any strict sense. For one thing, he never offers, as Balzac or Zola sometimes do, detailed social and historical documentation. For another, his fiction never advances, as that of Dickens or Tolstoy sometimes does, any specific political programme, or any particular solution to social or political problems. This is not to say that he is not politically aware: after all, a man who cannot unreservedly call himself a Pole or an Englishman is in a position to question political assumptions or ideologies that native-born citizens take for granted. Perhaps for that very reason, however, he cannot be described as politically committed in any real sense. Consider, for instance, his notorious statement that 'political institutions, whether contrived by the wisdom of the few or the ignorance of the many, are incapable of securing the happiness of mankind'. Looked at politically this might brand him as an arch-reactionary. Looked at in the context of the essay from which it comes – a tribute to the achievement of the socialist writer Anatole France – it acquires a very different meaning. In that context, the fact that men's aspirations – 'the very strength of their humanity' – can neither be realized nor relinquished becomes the 'almost incredible misfortune of mankind'.[1] The argument as to the precise shade of Conrad's political complexion must remain inconclusive, for in terms of such tragic insights, it becomes irrelevant.

The political novelist concentrates on those ills that are capable of alleviation, the tragic novelist on those that are not. This is of course an oversimplification, for at his best the former is no mere optimist, the latter no mere pessimist. Yet it remains broadly true that, confronted by the fact of suffering, the one passes judgement in the interests of reform, while the other endures his fate with whatever steadiness and dignity he can muster. Nor is such resignation a form of indifference: the tragic vision is vouchsafed only to those capable of moral commitment. One must at least possess the concept of fidelity to understand the meaning of infidelity; one has to be capable of fidelity to experience infidelity as tragic.

Conrad's belief in a 'spectacular universe' and his defence of the novel as a form of truth – his affirmation of lucidity in art and in life – make him a sceptic and an ironist. Few novelists are more convinced of the boundlessness of man's capacity for

[1] *Notes on Life and Letters*, p. 33.

2

The Nigger of the 'Narcissus'

... the crew of a merchant ship, brought to the test of what I may venture
to call the moral problem of conduct.

from Last Essays, p. 95

I

It has long been recognized that *The Nigger of the 'Narcissus'*
and 'Heart of Darkness' (published in *Youth: a Narrative; and Two
Other Stories*)[1] stand out from the rest of Conrad's early work for
their concentration and intensity. As my purpose in this study is
not to characterize Conrad's output as a whole, but to try to show
something of the intellectual power and consistency of the major
phase of his creative life, I have no hesitation in confining my
examination of his early writing to these two narratives. Before I
begin, however, I must briefly refer to a preliminary difficulty
which no student of Conrad can afford to ignore: the peculiarities
of his English. The charge of over-writing which Dr Leavis has
levelled at 'Heart of Darkness'[2] is a just one; it also applies to *The
Nigger of the 'Narcissus'*. Indeed, a great many English readers have
felt that Conrad's style as a whole is all too often unnaturally
congested and over-wrought. It is, of course, not surprising that
the English of a foreigner should in some respects be found wanting. What does require explanation, however, is that these oddities
of expression should rarely inhibit the power and coherence of his
meaning.

Although the full-scale analysis of Conrad's language would
obviously demand a separate study, it is worth emphasizing here
that his 'bad writing' is not unsatisfactory in the way in which that

---

[1] *The Nigger of the 'Narcissus'* published serially August–December 1897; as a book,
1898; 'Heart of Darkness' published serially February–April 1899; as a book,
1902.

[2] F. R. Leavis, *The Great Tradition*, originally published 1948 (Penguin, 1962), pp.
196–7. The section on Conrad in this classic study, amplified by two further
essays on *The Shadow Line* and 'The Secret Sharer' (in *'Anna Karenina' and other
essays* (Chatto, 1967)), constitutes the most powerful definition of Conrad's
greatness.

of a native speaker would be. Generally speaking, his stylistic lapses are of three kinds. First, there are the straightforward failures in idiomatic usage. 'There was yet a visit to the doctor. "A simple formality," assured me the secretary.'[1] A native Englishman, remembering that there *remained* a visit to be paid, would have been *told* that it was a *mere* formality. Yet solecisms of this sort (which are much more difficult to find than one expects) seldom, if ever, obscure the sense. In a native speaker, a grammatical lapse makes for unintelligibility; if in Conrad it does not do so, the reason is that it is never the result of his inability to follow a rule, but of his unfamiliarity with some of the rules. Then there are the blemishes that spring from over-anxious attempts to do too much: 'The ship rose to it as though she had soared on wings, and for a moment rested poised upon the foaming crest as if she had been a great sea-bird' (*The Nigger of the 'Narcissus'*, p. 57). The second simile, it seems to me, weakens the effect of the first. After the 'as though ...', which so vividly conveys the sensation as well as the movement desired, the 'as if ...' (an inelegant variation which merely underlines the syntactical repetition) spoils 'rested poised ...' by adding nothing to it, and it reduces the drama of the moment by taking the reader off the ship. Such defects, which are more artistic than grammatical, are typical of the work of a man still in the process of mastering his craft. One must remember that if Conrad came to English late, he came to fiction even later. Moreover, in an inexperienced writer, blunders of excess are a better augury than blunders of deficiency; and a predilection for metaphor is more easily forgiven than a reliance on cliché. Finally, there are the failures in stylistic decorum – in particular the magniloquence, often so absurd to English ears, imported out of Polish and French. 'And in the hush that had fallen suddenly upon the whole sorrowful land, the immense wilderness, the colossal body of the fecund and mysterious life seemed to look at her, pensive, as though it had been looking at the image of its own tenebrous and passionate soul.'[2] It is scarcely possible for an English writer to produce a sentence as inflated as this (nine adjectives, eight of them polysyllabic, seven latinate) without incurring the charge of vacuousness. Conrad has indeed subjected it to a good deal of rhetorical engineering: for instance, he has tried to make it suggest, at one and the same time, that the woman's entrance, like that of a

---

[1] 'Heart of Darkness', p. 57. I owe this example to an unpublished article on foreigners' English by R. T. Jones.
[2] 'Heart of Darkness', p. 136.

prima donna on a stage, silences every other activity, and also that she is being watched as by some omnipotent, brooding monster. Yet if the sentence doesn't come off, it is not because nothing is said. The words never quite lose touch with the reality to which they refer. For example, Conrad thinks of the 'life' of the 'wilderness' in terms of the 'soul' of a 'body': the body is 'colossal' because it represents the immensities of the virgin forest; its life or soul is 'fecund and mysterious' because these are the qualities of the great tropical unknown; and this soul is further called 'tenebrous and passionate' because its nature is reflected in the superbly barbaric black queen who is the subject of the description. I am not trying to justify the style of what is (perhaps with the concluding scene) the most artificial episode of 'Heart of Darkness'. What I am suggesting is that even Conrad's most unsatisfactory failures remain the failures of an intelligent man.

In any case, very little linguistic acclimatization is required to begin to respond to the vividness and power which fill the pages of *The Nigger of the 'Narcissus'* and 'Heart of Darkness'. Whatever their occasional defects of expression, these two great narratives are conspicuous for their extraordinary urgency. A fierce exploratory zest drives through the writing; an intense excitement keys up each successive episode. We know of course that both tales – but especially 'Heart of Darkness' – were inspired by important autobiographical events. *The Nigger of the 'Narcissus'*, composed during the period September 1896 – January 1897, when Conrad was thirty-nine, looks back to a voyage from Madras to Dunkirk accomplished twelve years earlier. 'Heart of Darkness', written some twenty-two months after the first story (December 1898 – February 1899), deals with the fateful Congo expedition of the second half of 1890. It can be safely assumed, therefore, that they owe something of their quality to a confessional, and even a cathartic, function. Certainly they exhibit an exploratory intensity found only in works concerned with the central problems of their author's life. And there can be no doubt that they establish a moral and intellectual foundation on which Conrad was to build for the next ten years of his creative career.

II

The Nigger of the 'Narcissus' is a tale of the sea. In view of the swarm of symbolic or allegorical interpretations that are now threatening to envelop Conrad's texts, even this simple proposition needs to be explained. It implies that if the sea acquires any special significance in the story as a whole, it is *not* because it stands for something other than itself. In this account of the return voyage of an English merchant ship from the Far East, the sea remains what it has always been – the element on which the ship sails. To venture on to it is to forsake the unfamiliar and the secure for the unknown and the untamed. Hence its significance in the novel, which it can only acquire by remaining what it is, is that of a test – a putting to the proof of the mettle of men who have chosen to deal with its power. When, for example, the old mariner Singleton is awakened by the violence of thirty hours of wind and wave to a consciousness of his mortality, this is how Conrad renders his perceptions:

He looked upon the immortal sea with the awakened and groping perception of its heartless might; he saw it unchanged, black and foaming under the eternal scrutiny of the stars; he heard its impatient voice calling for him out of a pitiless vastness full of unrest, of turmoil, and of terror. He looked afar upon it and he saw an immensity tormented and blind, moaning and furious, that claimed all the days of his tenacious life, and, when life was over, would claim the worn-out body of its slave.[1]

The Nigger of the 'Narcissus', p. 99

The sea is in every respect immeasurably bigger than the men who sail on it. Its 'vastness' contracts man's stature to a particle, its 'immortality' shrinks his life to a moment, its 'heartless might' reduces his will, his pride, his very independence, to the attributes of a 'slave'. But above all the sea is 'blind' – that is, utterly indifferent to man's fate. In this passage, Conrad's use of rhetorical personification, far from having a humanizing effect, conveys powerfully the sea's essential unintelligibility. 'Unapproachable ...', 'mysterious ...', 'impenetrable ...': such epithets, deployed almost like a litany throughout the novel, serve to remind us that the sea preserves an august neutrality in relation to human affairs.

Man does not master the sea: he can only serve it. But even this is an inaccurate statement. One cannot serve an elemental force; one can only serve an instrument designed to cope with that force. In this narrative, of course, the instrument is the sailing-ship; but the demands it makes are so exacting that only two members of the ship's company are fully adequate to them. One is the old sailor Singleton, who devotes all his strength and tenacity to the performance of those physical tasks on which a ship's survival

[1] Cf. pp. 82, 114, 155.

depends; the other is the captain, Alistoun, who, through his officers Baker and Crighton, is the interpreter and the embodiment of the Merchant Navy's practical traditions.

In an essay in *The Mirror of the Sea* Conrad suggests that dealing with sailing-ships is like dealing with men, in that in both cases it is fatal to rely blindly upon rules. Individual flair and judgement are essential, for, as he says, both men and ships 'live in an unstable element, are subject to powerful and subtle influences, and want to have their merits understood rather than their faults found out'.[1] However, unlike men, who have an 'extraordinary knack for lending themselves to deception', ships, being mere instruments, are unconscious, and thus infallibly register not only the public character but also the secret weaknesses of the men who use them. At sea, therefore, integrity of purpose is an inflexible requirement of long-term survival. What this integrity involves is demonstrated by Singleton and by Alistoun. At the beginning of the narrative Singleton defines the priority that must be the law of the seaman's life. Asked by James Wait, a negro who has just enlisted, what the ship is like, he replies: 'Ships are all right. It is the men in them.' This laconic utterance suggests that any attempt to treat a ship as an excuse for failure is already a symptom of failure. Nothing less than an unswerving singleness of purpose will do. Later in the narrative, Alistoun demonstrates the same truth. When the fury of the storm lays the ship on her side, he flatly refuses to cut her masts, despite the desperate appeals of certain members of his crew. Why? When we first meet him, we are informed that 'he loved his ship, and drove her unmercifully; for his secret ambition was to make her accomplish some day some brilliantly quick passage (pp. 30–1). In *The Mirror of the Sea* Conrad notes that a steamer's performance can be measured and the duration of its voyage predicted; hence punctuality is the criterion of success. A sailing-ship, however, is wholly dependent on the variables of wind and weather; so the criterion can only be the greatest speed possible. A man accustomed to regard every voyage as a race would instinctively refuse to cut the masts prematurely. In his instinctive decision to put his ship quite ruthlessly above every other consideration, Alistoun joins Singleton as a true representative of service at sea.

This service Conrad describes as an 'austere servitude', for it is hard and uncompromising, and the labour it exacts is unremitting and unrecognized. What then is its justification? This basic ques-

[1] 'The Fine Art'. p. 27.

tion is raised in the very opening pages of the novel. Of the sailors of Singleton's generation we are told:

> They had been strong, as those are strong who knew neither doubts nor hopes ... Well-meaning people had tried to represent those men as whining over every mouthful of their food; as going about their work in fear of their lives. But in truth they had been men who knew toil, privation, violence, debauchery – but knew not fear, and had no desire of spite in their hearts. Men hard to manage, but easy to inspire; voiceless men – but men enough to scorn in their hearts the sentimental voices that bewailed the hardness of their fate.
>
> *The Nigger of the 'Narcissus'*, p. 25

To men like Singleton, 'voiceless' because incapable of doubt or hope, the question of the meaning of their lives is an unreal one. Instinctively at one with the conditions of their existence, they keep back no element of themselves to goad them into consciousness. Our very first glimpse of Singleton reveals him sitting in the forecastle, oblivious of the babel of voices around him, deep in a novel by Bulwer-Lytton. Intrigued by this author's popularity among seamen, the narrator asks: 'What meaning their rough, inexperienced souls can find in the elegant verbiage of his pages?'(p. 6). Of all the novels Singleton could have picked up, *Pelham* is perhaps the least relevant to his life. But this is the very point Conrad is making. To the man incapable of the question 'Why am I what I am?' or 'What is the justification of my life?' reading must necessarily be an activity without content. For Singleton, then, the basic problem of self-justification is an unreal one, because there is no gap between himself and his work. For the sentimental voices that pity him, the problem of justifying his life is unreal for exactly the opposite reason: the gap between their own and the sailor's existence is so wide that they cannot imagine *any* justification of its privations and dangers. Acutely conscious themselves, they can only conceive of the seaman's task as intolerable, and of the seaman himself as the most abject of victims. What we have here are two antithetical views, consistently represented throughout the novel as the rival 'ethics' of the sea and of the land. Of the old sailors, the narrator says: 'They were the everlasting children of the mysterious sea' – children because incapable of adult consciousness, and everlasting because continuously tested by the element on which they lived. Then he adds: 'Their successors are the grown-up children of the discontented earth.' These new sailors are adult because they have become capable of thought; but they remain 'children', for they are incapable of

coping with the ideas of an alien philanthropy. Caught between
land and sea, they make up a class of person to whom the problem
of justifying their lives is a real one. And as they constitute almost
the entire crew of the *Narcissus*, their problem becomes the novel's
central concern.

If *The Nigger of the 'Narcissus'* can be said to have a protagonist,
it is the ship's company. Conrad's technique in this novel – the use
an anonymous seaman as informal narrator whose attention,
moving from one individual to another, gradually creates an
impression of unity out of diversity – is admirably adapted to
conveying the collective life of a merchant crew. The organization
of the narrative – the first chapter, for instance, begins with the
variegated confusion of the forecastle and ends with the formal
mustering of the men – reinforces the same effect. Unlike their
counterparts on warships, merchant seamen, whose 'sense of
hierarchy is weak', are not dominated by a mechanical discipline,
but bound by 'the unspoken loyalty that knits together a ship's
company' (p. 16). It is the function of the First Mate, Mr Baker, to
keep alive this sense of comradeship. Conscious of his task – we
hear him calling the names of the men 'distinctly, in a serious tone
as befitting this roll-call to an unquiet loneliness' – he knows that it
is useless for him to behave like a martinet. With his mock ferocity,
his rough retributions, his disregard of trivial offences, and his
unselfconscious participation in the life of the forecastle, he is a
man who takes every situation on its own merits. He is perfectly
aware that (as we have seen) 'there may be a rule of conduct; there
is no rule of human fellowship'.

One of the main reasons why the voyage of the *Narcissus* can be
said to constitute a test is that this fellowship is not something
given but something that has to be achieved – to be wrested out of
the instinctive egoism that appears as soon as men become conscious of themselves. This is perhaps the main point of the novel's
central episode, the storm and its aftermath. Conrad's handling of
the awe-inspiring tumult of a storm at sea is justly famous – and not
least for the fact that he resists the temptation of painting a mere
seascape, but registers the unchained fury of the elements on the
minds and bodies of human beings. His rendering of the exposure
of the crew to night-long cold, shock, thirst, exhaustion, and terror
banishes all illusions about the romance of sail. And when the
night is at last over, the pressure is not relieved: the stricken ship
has to be righted. Whether lashed to the railings for their protection, or wearily hoisting up the sail that will finally save them,

the men endure not because they choose to, but because they must. In due course, the storm blows itself out, and gradually gives way to a calm. Relieved of their recent stress, they now have leisure to meditate. What they discover, however, is not a chastening sense of their mortality, or even the simple fact that they have had a narrow escape, but that they have conducted themselves like heroes. They begin to dramatize themselves: 'We boasted of our pluck, of our capacity to work, of our energy ... We remembered our danger, our toil – and conveniently forgot our horrible scare (p. 100). Hardship recollected in tranquillity, it would seem, becomes an opportunity for conceit. To reflect on one's own virtue is to transform it into a vice. By itself, the storm can be considered a test of the qualities necessary for immediate survival; in relation to the calm that follows it, it must also be seen as a test of the moral value of a life at sea.

III

The crew of the *Narcissus* can be said to be caught between two antithetical ideas of what a community should be. The first, upheld by Alistoun and Singleton, is inspired by the specific requirements of a common task. The second, inculcated by two new members of the crew, the sickly negro from St Kitts, James Wait, and the shifty and rancorous cockney, Donkin, is based on a demand for individual rights. The fact that the apologists of the second view are either dishonest or vicious – to the point that if any fraternity is involved it is (in the words of 'The Fine Art') on the principle that 'no matter how earnestly we strive against each other, we remain brothers on the lower side of our intellect and in the instability of our feelings'[1]– might create the impression that Conrad is weighting his scales. However, in this novel, these two communities are dependent on each other, and cannot profitably be considered apart. Their representatives are distinguished in terms of each other: a forceful, taciturn, and self-sufficient pair against an evasive, articulate and gregarious one. And in their struggle to control the crew, they are individually matched: Wait, who operates psychologically, is opposed by Singleton, the only man wholly proof against his subtle demoralization; Donkin, who operates politically (he tries to foment a mutiny), is opposed by Alistoun, the embodiment of authority on the ship.

To the men, James Wait is a source of bafflement from the start.

[1] *Ibid*, p. 29.

Everything about him is ambiguous. His looks (he is at once powerful and diseased), his manner (he is simultaneously dignified and over-sensitive), and even his name (it creates a mis-understanding when it is first heard coming out of the darkness of the muster) all defy steady definition and make it impossible for the men to adopt a consistent attitude towards him. When, after his half-hearted attempts to participate in the common task, he is finally laid up, they cannot decide whether he is a malingerer who deserves their contempt, or a sick man entitled to their com-passion. He exacerbates this uncertainty by loudly complaining of their selfishness: 'He made us feel we had been brutes', says the narrator, 'and afterwards made us suspect we had been fools.' Why are they so vulnerable to his moral bullying? – 'We lovingly called him Jimmy in order to conceal our hate of his accomplice.' (His accomplice is, of course, the figure of Death.) This subtly turned sentence not only suggests the falsity of an affection inspired by fear, but also hints at the complexities of Wait's collusion in the process. (He collaborates with what terrifies him in order to exor-cise it by means of the attention he thus secures.) The men are caught in a mesh of emotional sophistry. The more sentimental they become, the less they are able to identify the true object of their dismay; the more they evade their secret fear, the further they sink into self-regarding introspection. Wait's spectral accomplice 'seemed to have blown with his impure breath undreamt-of subtleties in our hearts'. It takes Singleton, of course, to interrupt this spell. 'Are you dying?' he asks 'a horribly startled and con-fused' Wait. And when he obtains an affirmative answer: 'Well, get on with your dying; don't raise a blamed fuss with us over that job. We can't help you.' Such directness brings instant relief: 'At last we knew that our compassion would not be misplaced.' But deliverance is short-lived. All Donkin has to do is to interpret Singleton's intervention as implying that everyone, themselves included, must die sooner or later, and they are back on the treadmill of their anxiety and bafflement (pp. 36–43).

The complexity of Conrad's treatment of the men's relationship with Wait is essentially a complexity of insight. That is to say, it requires to be understood on its own terms, not to be decoded like a symbolic system. An example of what seems to me to be the wrong kind of interpretation is provided by the always lively Albert Guerard. He rightly chooses one of the most remarkable incidents of the novel – the crew's rescue of Wait at the height of the storm (pp. 63–74) – for special commentary, but all he provides is a flight of allegorical speculation. In the confusion that follows the disabling of the ship, someone suddenly remembers that the sick negro, who has been isolated in a deck-cabin, is trapped, and perhaps drowned. Five men instantly volunteer to fetch him out, and after frenetic efforts, drag him out through a gap smashed in the bulkhead of his cabin. Guerard's first move is to see the actual rescue in terms of 'a difficult childbirth'[1] – an idea which, if applied literally to Wait as he is pulled out of his hole, becomes simply comic, and if applied metaphorically in order to suggest that the men 'have assisted at the *rebirth* of evil on the ship' is patently wrong. After this initial flourish, his second move is to argue that the carpenter's shop, through which the men have had to lower themselves in order to get to the wall of the cabin, is 'the messy pre-conscious' above 'the deeper lying unconscious', and hence that the rescue dramatizes a 'compulsive psychic descent'.[2] I do not wish to suggest that the doctrines of Freud have no part to play in the interpretation of literature; or even that Guerard's particular brand of Freudianism is wholly worthless. But I want to insist that the kind of 'reading off' Guerard indulges in is suspect, for it assumes that the complexity of an episode stands revealed, once it has been shown to be transposable into terms to which it makes neither direct nor indirect reference. A satisfactory demonstration of complexity, it seems to me, would have to proceed on the assumption that the meaning of a literary episode was not something 'behind' what happens, but 'in' what happens; and that the interpretation of a scene could not be brought ready-made to it, but had to be discovered within it. In this particular example, Conrad has devised an incident which exhibits, with considerable audacity, the fact that the men adhere to the principles of *both* the communities I have defined. To risk their lives for the sake of a comrade in danger, as they do, is a declaration of human solidarity. But the high-pitched frenzy with which they do it indicates the persistence of their morbid obsessions. Their efforts to save Wait are prompted at one and the same time by a selfless concern for a fellow seaman, and by a self-regarding tenderness for him. If the rescue is symbolic, it is symbolic *to them*: the survival of the negro has acquired, for them, the almost magical property of keeping his sinister 'accomplice' at bay. A trace of cowardice persists at the centre of their most daring act of courage. Thus Conrad treats us to the spectacle, itself a profound commentary on the complexities of

[1] Guerard, *Conrad the Novelist*, p. 112.
[2] *Ibid.*, p. 113.

human action, of five men defying the imminent threat of concrete death about them while yielding to the insubstantial fears of imaginary death within them.

After the storm has abated, it becomes increasingly clear to everyone that Wait is indeed doomed. Yet Wait himself steadfastly refuses to countenance his fate; and the crew, who now completely share his 'untruthful attitude in the face of the inevitable truth', become increasingly demoralized – that is, 'highly humanized, tender, complex, excessively decadent'. They deliberately connive at his various pretences, sympathizing with 'all his repulsions, shrinkings, evasions, delusions', and making 'a chorus of affirmation to his wildest assertions, as though he had been a millionaire, a politician, or a reformer' (pp. 99–103). At this point we may be tempted to wonder whether the novel is not mounting an attack on compassion itself. Is this in fact the case? As Wait's illness worsens, there occurs a subtle change in Conrad's presentation of him. For the first time we are admitted into his mind, made to see and hear what he can see and hear from his bunk, and permitted to participate in his half-delirious dreams and memories. Thus prompted to use our imaginations, we begin to feel a measure of real sympathy for him, and in so doing begin to recognize the falsity inherent in the compassion of the crew. We are made to identify more clearly what Conrad calls 'the latent egoism of tenderness to suffering' – that is, a sympathy poisoned by the bad faith of self-pity. That disinterestedness is a pre-condition of true compassion is established in a minor episode which contrasts the cook Podmore's handling of Wait with the captain's (pp. 115–21). The cook, who makes a great show of solicitude for the dying man's soul, seems more humane than the captain, who has peremptorily forbidden him the deck. But the opposite is the case. Podmore, intoxicated by the memory of how, during the worst of the storm, 'he went walking on the sea to make coffee for perishable sinners', extinguishes the last spark of pity 'in the infernal fog of his supreme conceit' and lets loose on the terrified Wait his visions of hell-fire and damnation. The resultant hubbub brings the captain on to the deck, and Wait is ordered back to his cabin. To the men, this seems sheer tyranny; but Alistoun's mutterings, overheard by the officers, suggest something very different: 'When I saw him standing there, three parts dead and so scared – black amongst that gaping lot – no grit to face what's coming to us all – the notion came to me all at once, before I could think. Sorry for him.' These simple phrases imply a keener recognition of the black man's loneliness and terror than all the spurious fascination felt by the crew. And the reason is obvious: he is thinking of Wait; they are thinking of themselves.

IV

Donkin's attempts to subvert the crew are much more open than Wait's, and his self-concern is much more blatant, yet the two men's deeper purposes are not unrelated. If Wait is unable to face the imminence of death, Donkin cannot face the demands of service. The former instinctively infects the crew with his evasiveness; the latter tries to contaminate them with his rancour. Like Wait, too, Donkin tries to replace the community of the common task with a false community – that of the gang, which defines itself not by what it affirms or performs, but by what it rejects. Donkin's impudence has a venomously national and racial bias. His talk is laced with such remarks as 'these damned furriners should be kept under', 'bloody Yankees', 'fat-headed Dutchman' (this to a Finn), 'black-faced swine' (to Wait: that Wait seems 'positively to revel in that abuse' however, is a sign that he has recognized an ally). Again, like Wait, he makes his appeal to the weaknesses of the crew: to their pride, by making them believe that work is unmanly; to their self-pity, by reminding them of the hardness of their lives; to their conceit, by praising their conduct in the storm; to their sentimentality, by presenting first himself, then Wait, as victims of injustice. And finally, like Wait, he has an insidiously ambivalent effect on his listeners. 'He talked with ardour, despised and irrefutable', says the narrator. 'Our contempt for him was unbounded – and we could not but listen to that consummate artist.'

Even Conrad's most sympathetic critics have felt that the figure of Donkin betrays a certain prejudice against social reform. But this objection is largely misconceived. The impersonal majesty of sky and sea, which the novel never allows us to forget, gradually persuades us to view the *Narcissus* from an ever more remote vantage-point, until we see her voyage itself as unfolding *sub specie aeternitatis*.[1] From such a perspective, the question of what is improvable in human life loses its urgency, and the novel reveals its deeper intention, which is to explore the subterfuges (one of the most subtle of these being a false humanitarianism) which men resort to when confronted by an irremediable reality. Taken by

[1] Cf. pp. 29, 77, 82, 99, 124, 155.

itself, Donkin's appeal to his 'rights' might quite legitimately raise the question of social reform. The novel, however, compels us to connect his rejection of the demands of maritime service with Wait's refusal to countenance his inevitable end. The implications of this connection are revealed in the scene with which Conrad brings his narrative to its climax: the formal confrontation between the captain and the crew (pp. 132–7).

Conrad prepares this crisis by allowing the two separate currents of dissatisfaction to flow together. This he achieves by means of the simple but effective device of making Donkin take up Wait's case. When, as we have just seen, the apparently dictatorial Alistoun orders the dying Wait back to his bunk, Donkin seizes the opportunity which the crew's reaction gives him, leads a half-hearted rush in the darkness against the captain, and in the confusion hurls a belaying-pin in his direction. The men stop, momentarily shocked by the outrage; whereupon Alistoun regains the initiative and summons them to the deck for the following morning.

The confrontation itself begins with a blunt challenge by the captain.

I haven't till now found fault with you men. And I don't now, but I am here to drive this ship and keep every man-jack aboard of her up to the mark. If you knew your work as I do mine, there would be no trouble. You've been braying in the dark about 'See to-morrow morning!' Well, you see me now. What do you want?

The men's response, at once wholly unexpected and wholly inevitable, is one of Conrad's master-strokes.

What did they want? They shifted from foot to foot, they balanced their bodies; some, pushing back their caps, scratched their heads ... They wanted great things. And suddenly, all the simple words they knew seemed to be lost for ever in the immensity of their vague and burning desire. They knew what they wanted, but they could not find anything worth saying.

The captain's challenge and the crew's response respectively embody the two antithetical conceptions of life on which the novel is based. The captain stands squarely for the collaborative performance of concrete tasks; his questions are accordingly specific. Are they complaining about the food? About the work? About his treatment of Wait? Yet the more he probes, the more they feel at a loss, for the real source of their dissatisfaction is not something outside them (even Wait is now forgotten) which could be

identified and named. It is the legacy of consciousness, the knowledge that life offers only to take away, and promises what it cannot
fulfil – whether it be relief from labour or deliverance from mortality. To sense the irremediable poignancy of life, as the men do
under the captain's battery of questions, is one thing; to try to erect
it into a principle of action is quite another. What, then, *is* the
proper principle of action? The crew, in their complexity, may be
more representative of human experience, but it is to the captain
that we must turn for an answer. His men having failed to find
anything to say, Alistoun decides to deal with the *agent provocateur*.
Significantly, he shows no sign of wanting to turn the previous
night's attack into a cause of personal resentment, or a reason for
abstract discipline. Instead, he suddenly produces the belaying-
pin and, bearing down on Donkin, forces him step by step to return
it to its rightful place. For Donkin, this object (with which, incidentally, Alistoun had already threatened him, when he refused to
help during the storm) is nothing but a projectile; for the captain it
is a functional part of the ship's equipment. Alistoun's treatment of
Donkin is more than the public humiliation of a wrongdoer. It is a
practical demonstration of why the men are on board the *Narcissus*:
they are there to drive the ship.

Alistoun defeats Donkin by direct confrontation. In the conflict
between Singleton and Wait, however, no such resolution is possible. The dying man lingers on in the becalmed ship, allowing
himself to be distracted, as far as he can, by his shipmates' con-
tinuing solicitude. His deliberate disregard of his approaching
death is matched by a new development in the crew's evasiveness.
They now begin to play games with his death: 'We wanted to keep
him alive till home – to the end of the voyage.' Only Singleton
keeps aloof; but he is not indifferent. On the one and only occasion
he pauses to look into Wait's cabin (pp. 141–2), the crew immediately become aware of an invisible tension.

We kept very quiet, and for a long time Singleton stood there as though he
had come by appointment to call for someone, or to see some important
event. James Wait lay perfectly still, and apparently not aware of the gaze
scrutinizing him with a steadiness full of expectation. There was a sense of
a contest in the air.

This unseen struggle is in complete contrast to Alistoun's open
collision with Donkin. The point at issue between Alistoun and
Donkin – the authority of the tradition of service – must in principle be publicly validated. The point at issue between Singleton

and Wait, however, is the question of whether the negro will die. This question, of course, has moral implications; but its outcome is out of their hands. Hence their conflict can only take the form of an antagonism of expectations. Wait's refusal to believe in the fact of his approaching death (a refusal which persists, in a manner of speaking, even after this death has occurred, when his corpse seems reluctant to slip off the plank committing it to the sea) is opposed by Singleton's steadfast conviction that the negro will die at the first sight of land, and in so doing break the calm in which the ship has been stagnating. In the event, Singleton is proved right: Wait does die at the first sight of land and the winds do suddenly spring up. Yet this resolution, with its hint of occult powers, seems strange in a writer who has repeatedly declared himself to be 'too firm in [his] consciousness of the marvellous to be ever fascinated by the mere supernatural, which ... is but a manufactured article, the fabrication of minds insensitive to the intimate delicacies of our relation to the dead and to the living'.[1] One can understand that the protraction of Wait's illness should be represented as a hindrance to the ship's progress, for it prolongs the crew's unprofessionalism. One could even accept that a landfall might credibly provoke the death of a man kept alive only by the expectation of the journey's end. But the idea that Wait's death actually makes the breeze return takes us into the realm of the bizarre. Is it then an invitation to recognize the occult as an operative force in the tale? The question, it seems to me, has to be left open: we cannot decide whether the coincidence is to be explained in terms of chance, or of magic. Yet, in so far as the supernatural does enter into the narrative, it does so not mainly to provoke a debate on the question of its reality, but to establish that, in relation to what is beyond man's control (such as death, or the weather), Singleton's superstitious fatalism is infinitely preferable to Wait's irrational evasiveness. For while the first is compatible with the requirements of maritime service, and indeed often facilitates their fulfilment, the second incapacitates the sailor from performing even the simplest of his appointed tasks.

The victories of Alistoun and Singleton are, of course, an endorsement of the kind of community they represent. Although they have to put up a fight, what they defend possesses its own inherent strength, for it is founded not on a theory or an emotion but on the objective requirements of a practical task. The rival community implied in the collaboration between Wait and

[1] 'Author's Note' to *The Shadow Line*, p. v.

Donkin, on the other hand, has no such strength, for it is based on nothing more substantial than the demands of mutual egoism. Hence, left to itself, this association can only collapse into paradox and contradiction. After he had been foiled of his designs on the crew, Donkin withdraws into himself. However he starts to pay regular visits to Wait's cabin and, gradually gaining the sick negro's confidence, watches over his decline. But the tacit alliance between the two men, established at the beginning of the journey, is now brought to a vicious conclusion (pp. 147–55). When Wait, utterly helpless but still conscious, is at last balanced on the very brink of death, Donkin silently robs him of his life's savings. By placing this infamous scene beyond the reach of his narrator – it is the only one in the novel so treated – Conrad manages to suggest that it takes place outside the pale of human fellowship. In this furtive context, Donkin's act finally reveals the ironies implicit in the community of egoism. Wait, who has corrupted the crew in order to escape the solitude of death, expires in a condition of moral isolation far more dreadful than any he could have anticipated. Donkin himself, who has shirked his appointed task in the name of the rights of man, ends by spurning the most sacred of these rights – the claims of the dying. Yet no obvious retribution falls on *him*. His uneasy feeling, as he emerges from the death cabin, that he has been 'judged and cast out' soon wears off; and, when the ship finally berths at its home port, he is the richest man to step ashore.

To demand that malefactors should be punished in ways they can understand, however, is to disregard the spirit of moral realism in which *The Nigger of the 'Narcissus'* has been written. The novel undertakes an unflinching examination of human evasiveness – to the point, indeed, of suggesting that to think is to err. Yet its effect is not finally pessimistic. On the contrary, it keeps up a tone of hard, keen, even austere exultation. And it can do so because at its heart is the discovery that the vast, impersonal reality of the sea, of which men are so much afraid, ends by becoming the means by which they achieve their redemption.

On men reprieved by its disdainful mercy, the immortal sea confers in its justice the full privilege of desired unrest. Through the perfect wisdom of its grace they are not permitted to meditate at ease upon the complicated and acrid savour of existence. They must without pause justify their life to the eternal pity that commands toil to be hard and unceasing, from sunrise to sunset, from sunset to sunrise; till the weary succession of nights and days tainted by the obstinate clamour of sages, demanding bliss and an empty heaven, is redeemed at last by the vast silence of pain and labour, by

the dumb fear and the dumb courage of men obscure, forgetful, and
enduring.

The Nigger of the 'Narcissus', p. 90

This strangely powerful paragraph, which forms the link between the disruption of the great storm and the return to the routine
of ordinary labour, tries to answer the question with which the novel
began: how are men's lives justified? The answer, of course, is in
accord with what has been demonstrated by the narrative itself –
that human existence is justified not by words, but by deeds; not by
demands, but by duties. This is a truth, however, which most men,
caught as they are between the imperatives of the land and of the
sea, are unlikely to learn by themselves. As self-conscious beings,
they are vulnerable to the blandishments of land-inspired
'clamour', and expect that a life of unremitting ease should be
theirs by right. But the sea they serve soon puts an end to these
self-regarding reveries. By the very labour it exacts, it not only
stops them from falling heavily back upon themselves, but it also
teaches them the truth on which their redemption depends – that
the life which they will not forgo at any cost consists of the 'unrest'
of perpetual toil. This paragraph articulates the alternatives with
which the entire novel has been concerned. To be tested as the crew
of the *Narcissus* has been is to be made to choose between the
salvation of sages who proffer an 'empty heaven', and the salvation
dependent on the 'immortal sea'.

What does that salvation consist of? It is part of the point of the
novel that only a false prophet will try to provide a direct answer.
But we must not conclude that the question is meaningless. Consider the narrator's appeal, as the novel closes, to his now vanished
shipmates: 'Haven't we, *together and upon the immortal sea*, wrung out
a meaning from our sinful lives?'[My italics.] Although he does not
disclose what this 'meaning' is, he indicates, with incomparable
precision, the twin conditions for its achievement. These are the
community ('we ... together') and the sea – that is to say, collaborative labour. The meaning thus achievable is not, like the
money they earn, something that can exist apart from their efforts;
but it is not identical with these efforts. It is like the *expressiveness* of a
musical phrase, neither independent of the notes, nor reducible to
them. 'Good-bye, brothers! You were a good crowd. As good a
crowd as ever fisted with wild cries the beating canvas of a heavy
foresail; or tossing aloft, invisible in the night, gave back yell for
yell to a westerly gale' (p. 173). This shared exultation, which is the

meaning of collaborative labour, can only be achieved indirectly, like grace. But it is not granted automatically. If Conrad's august cadences have sometimes seemed to invest the sea with the attributes of divinity itself, it is not because he considers it capable of dispensing salvation on its own account, but because, in exposing men to the dangers and hardships of a struggle against elemental powers, it offers them the opportunity, not merely to survive, but to live.

3
'Heart of Darkness'

I confounded the beat of the drum with the beating of my heart.

Marlow in 'Heart of Darkness', p. 142

I

It is appropriate that 'Heart of Darkness' should begin in the Thames estuary – the very place where *The Nigger of the 'Narcissus'* ended – for it is, in a special sense, a continuation of that novel. 'Heart of Darkness' takes up the affirmations of its predecessor, and exposes them to a process of systematic questioning. The test of the sea generates values which are submitted to the test of the wilderness.[1]

In respect of the positives it discovers, the world of *The Nigger of the 'Narcissus'* is a self-sufficient one. This does not mean that its inhabitants are unrepresentative, particularly in the weaker side of their nature; or that the redemption they achieve together cannot be sought in other forms of service. On the contrary, the voyage of the *Narcissus* – particularly in its final phase – is susceptible of wider application. As the ship approaches England, a sudden glimpse of the coast leads the narrator to imagine the island as some mighty vessel in its own right, which its subjects can serve much as its crew serves the *Narcissus*. And later, after the ship has berthed, and a swarm of strangers has taken possession of her 'in the name of the sordid earth', and the narrator sees the men, now paid off, drifting in front of London's historic Tower, he immediately associates them with their 'fighting prototypes' – the great line of English maritime heroes. Yet for all this wider relevance, *The Nigger of the 'Narcissus'* achieves its affirmation at the cost of a certain abstraction. By deliberately contrasting the ethic of service at sea with the principle of self-seeking on land, Conrad suggests that service is intrinsically meaningful, an end in itself – irrespective of

[1] This famous narrative has provoked a mass of critical material, a good deal of which is irrational and self-indulgent. Some of it has been collected by L. F. Dean, *Joseph Conrad's 'Heart of Darkness': Backgrounds and Criticisms* (Englewood Cliffs, 1960); and by B. Harkness, *Conrad's 'Heart of Darkness' and the Critics* (San Francisco, 1960).

the further purposes it may advance. He does not, of course, disregard the commercial interests that send sailing-ships out on their voyages. As early as the second chapter, he remarks: 'The august loneliness of her path lent dignity to *the sordid inspiration* of her pilgrimage'.[1] [My italics.] The inspiration of the ship's journey may be sordid; but once she has shaken herself free of the land she acquires a solitary beauty that neither her origin nor her destination seems to be able to affect. And there can be no mistaking the meaning of our last sight of the 'dark knot of seamen' drifting away in a pale shaft of English sunlight. 'The sunshine of heaven fell like a gift of grace on the mud of the earth . . . And to the right of the dark group the stained front of the Mint, cleansed by the flood of light, stood out for a moment, dazzling and white.'[2] The work of men who take no thought beyond their immediate task – and who by virtue of that, and that alone, achieve a purifying disinterestedness – cannot altogether abolish the taint of minted currency; but, like a sudden gleam from heaven, it can momentarily transfigure it.

If no such shaft of light interrupts the gloom brooding over Marlow's London, it is essentially because his tale forgoes all pretence of a distinction between land and sea. The men on the deck of the yawl *Nellie*, like their predecessors of the *Narcissus*, share the bond of the sea. But three of them are also landsmen – and businessmen to boot: a director, an accountant, and a lawyer, each serving commercial interests in his own way. As for the fourth, Marlow (if we ignore the anonymous narrator who opens and closes the narrative), he is a tested seaman who has stepped out of the circle that insulates the sailor's life. For ordinary sailors, 'there is nothing mysterious . . . unless it be the sea itself'; hence, 'a casual spree on shore suffices to unfold . . . the secret of a whole continent'. In this respect, Marlow does not represent his class. Although he has learnt the lesson of the sea and is wholly committed to integrity in word and deed, he is also a 'wanderer', urged on by a most unseamanlike curiosity about life on land, which takes him (as he is about to disclose) into a region where the values he upholds are deprived of most of their moral effectiveness.

The four men who constitute Marlow's audience are uncritical products of a powerful maritime civilization. It is not surprising, therefore, that, as they talk among themselves, waiting for the tide to turn, they should offer a view of English history which uncon-

[1] *The Nigger of the 'Narcissus'*, p. 30.
[2] *Ibid.*, p. 172.

42

sciously elaborates the idea of the 'ship of state' evoked in the closing pages of *The Nigger of the 'Narcissus'*. We have seen that life at sea depends on a number of factors: the sea itself, of which the rigours have to be faced; the ship, of which the demands have to be met; and the tradition of service, of which the requirements have to be observed. As Marlow's companions contemplate the waterway 'leading to the uttermost ends of the earth', they discover analogous qualities in England's imperial past. The selfless mariners are now 'the great knights-errant of the sea', the challenge they face is 'the mystery of the unknown earth', and the cause they serve is the 'torch' or 'sacred fire' of their inherited civilization.

Marlow's initial response to this grandiose prospect ('Heart of Darkness', pp. 48–51) is a profoundly disturbing one. 'Light came out of this river since – you say knights? ... But darkness was here yesterday.' For the vision of a heroic England bearing the torch into unknown lands he substitutes another and earlier picture: England herself an unknown territory, receiving the attentions of a Roman invader. In this perspective English civilization begins to look much less permanent – the 'flicker', as he calls it, of 'a running blaze on a plain, like a flash of lightning'; and imperialism, which is the expansion of this civilization, begins to seem much less glamorous. The imagined invader, dismayed and demoralized by the surrounding wilderness, loses his chivalric zest; his struggle with exhaustion, disease and death tarnishes whatever ideal of service he may have brought in with him. In this predicament, says Marlow, 'what saves us is efficiency'. The significance of this wry comment should not be missed: what in the context of the sea had become redemptive labour is now reduced to a merely mechanical means of survival. Taken all in all, 'the conquest of the earth, which mostly means the taking it away from those who have a different complexion or slightly flatter noses than ourselves, is not a pretty thing when you look into it much.' The imperialist is obviously even more in need of justification than the merchant seaman. But what justification *can* there be? 'What redeems it is the idea only ... An idea at the back of it; not a sentimental pretence, but an idea – something you can set up, and bow down before, and offer a sacrifice to.' This seems to be a return to the solution of *The Nigger of the 'Narcissus'*. But even here resemblances are deceptive. The sailor who serves his ship is governed by a practical tradition; the imperialist, at best, has to rely on the justification of an abstract idea – an idea which, moreover, acquires in Marlow's presentation of it the connotations of a dubious idolatry.

43

The elaborate preamble to Marlow's narrative with which 'Heart of Darkness' opens does more than provide an appropriate physical setting for the telling of the tale. It also raises the questions which the tale will explore. Considered as a test, Marlow's venture into the African jungle can be compared to the ocean voyages he has accomplished. In its scale, power, aloofness, and inscrutability, the virgin forest bears a certain resemblance to the sea. Marlow, for example, can describe it in terms that recall the storm scenes of *The Nigger of the 'Narcissus'*.

The great wall of vegetation, an exuberant and entangled mass of trunks, branches, leaves, boughs, festoons, motionless in the moonlight, was like a rioting invasion of silent life, *a rolling wave of plants, piled up, crested, ready to topple over the creek, to sweep every little man of us out of his little existence.* [My italics.]

'Heart of Darkness', p. 86

But there is one essential difference. Whereas the sea is an absolutely alien element, the land-locked jungle is part of man's abode. It contains human beings who are not unrelated to the ancestors of the modern Englishmen listening to Marlow's story. This means that as we move from one work to the next, we have to change our bearings. Whereas a voyage on the 'immortal sea' can be seen as taking place under the gaze of eternity, a journey into the jungle is also a descent into man's history, a return to his primordial origins. The darkness into which Marlow ventures has a heart which can be found within his own breast.

II

We have seen that *The Nigger of the 'Narcissus'* dramatizes a conflict between fidelity to a defined tradition of service and the temptation of self-regarding individualism. What is in question in 'Heart of Darkness' is man's fidelity to the general tradition of civilization. But whereas the crew of the *Narcissus* could rely on objective structures and imperatives – that is, on a tradition embodied, independently of themselves, in such tried veterans as Alistoun and Singleton – the imperialist invaders of Africa, sundered as they are from the regulating context of their society, are left wholly to their own devices. There is, to be sure, an essential difference between Marlow, who has passed the test of the sea, and so can distinguish between words and deeds, professions and performances, and the agents of the exploitative company he encounters in the Congo. But the Marlow who takes up his appointment as captain of the river-steamer has not yet undergone the ordeal of the jungle – and in having to do so, he is as cut off as everybody else.

'Heart of Darkness', then, can be considered as an inquiry into how strong the hold of civilization is on its members. It is therefore necessary to note the degree to which this tale, particularly in its initial phase, exhibits the consequences of abstracting men from their native contexts. One of the salient features of Marlow's narrative is his insistence on the 'unreality' of his experience. This is more than a matter of what he says; it is also implied in the presentation of his story. That 'Heart of Darkness' makes extended, and sometimes obtrusive, use of non-naturalistic devices has been widely recognized. Mythical correspondences (the journey as a quest), literary allusions (the Dantesque grove of death), symbolic oppositions (light/darkness, white/black), anthropomorphism (the forest as 'an implacable force brooding over an inscrutable intention'), and the like, are not solely or even mainly (as some critics have complained) means of inflating significance; they also express – and on the whole with remarkable success – the sense of dream, of phantasmagoria and nightmare, which Marlow claims is of the essence of his experience. But if such devices help to convey Marlow's feeling of unreality, it is because they work within the context of a much more directly mimetic use of language.

Let us consider a justly famous example of this. Marlow is sailing down the coast of West Africa.

Once, I remember, we came upon a man-of-war anchored off the coast. There wasn't even a shed there, and she was shelling the bush. It appears the French had one of their wars going on thereabouts. Her ensign dropped limp like a rag; the muzzles of her long six-inch guns stuck out all over the low hull; the greasy, slimy swell swung her up easily and let her down, swaying her thin masts. In the empty immensity of earth, sky, and water, there she was, incomprehensible, firing into a continent. Pop, would go one of the six-inch guns; a small flame would dart and vanish, a little white smoke would disappear, a tiny projectile would give a feeble screech – and nothing happened. Nothing could happen. There was a touch of insanity in the proceeding, a sense of lugubrious drollery in the sight; and it was not dissipated by somebody on board assuring me earnestly there was a camp of natives – he called them enemies! – hidden out of sight somewhere.

'Heart of Darkness', pp. 61–2

Why Marlow feels there is a touch of insanity about these

proceedings is because what should be a recognizable human action presents itself as an arbitrary event. In this alien environment, where the tepid, echoless air, the sluggish, greasy swell, and above all the sheer scale and emptiness of land and sea defeat the purposes of European precision, the phrase 'to fire a cannon' loses all connotation. The shattering report becomes a 'pop', the death-dealing shell a 'tiny projectile', the target to be destroyed a 'continent'. In other words, we are made to witness an action that claims to be intentional, but can no longer be regarded as such. What this incident brilliantly demonstrates is that the intelligibility of what men do depends upon the context in which they do it. The first important thing that Marlow's journey reveals to him is that what made sense in Europe no longer makes sense in Africa. As he disembarks, for instance, he notices that a railway is apparently being built; but he can make little sense of it. The activity of the engineers reduces itself to 'objectless blasting'; familiar artifacts are transformed into strange beasts: a boiler is 'wallowing in the grass', a truck lies 'on its back with its wheels in the air'. And if displaced action and objects behave peculiarly, displaced concepts go hopelessly adrift. The term 'enemy' is applied to bewildered and helpless victims, the word 'criminals' to moribund shadows, the concept of 'law' to those to whom it comes 'like bursting shells, ... an incomprehensible mystery out of the sea'. Such words as 'worker', 'rebel', 'custom-house', 'seat of government', presuppose the entire social apparatus of European life; sundered from their natural contexts, they can find little purchase in the 'darkness' of the African continent. Most disturbing of all, death itself – the one absolute experience of a man's life – becomes a commonplace triviality. The first information about Africa that Marlow imparts concerns the fate of his predecessor – a man who loses his life over a misunderstanding about two black hens. The insignificance of the cause is matched only by the casualness of the event itself: 'some man ... made a tentative jab with a spear at the white man – and of course it went quite easily between the shoulder blades'. This nightmare disorientation becomes a familiar aspect of his African experience. It is indeed important, for it demonstrates that the sense of reality is not absolutely founded, but the product of a long process of cultural assimilation.

Really to possess a concept is to know when it does not apply. One of the essential differences between Marlow and his fellow-Europeans in Africa is that he can recognize the unreality of the notions that have been arbitrarily imported into the country, whereas they cannot or will not. This of course implies that he is capable of acknowledging the reality of the alien context. How far he does so is indicated by his encounter with some African canoes immediately after sighting the French warship.

> Now and then a boat from the shore gave one a momentary contact with reality. It was paddled by black fellows. You could see from afar the whites of their eyeballs glistening. They shouted, sang; their bodies streamed with perspiration; they had faces like grotesque masks – these chaps; but they had bone, muscle, a wild vitality, an intense energy of movement, that was as natural and true as the surf along their coast. They wanted no excuse for being there.
>
> 'Heart of Darkness', p. 61

Paradoxically, it is because of his firm grasp of the norms and conventions of his own society that Marlow is able to recognize the humanity of the members of a 'primitive' culture. Knowing what he is, he can accurately measure the gap that separates the Europeans in their steamer from the black men in their boat. He does not pretend that the latter are anything but unfamiliar to him: their faces, for example, seem to him to be 'grotesque masks'. Yet this very recognition of difference is an acknowledgement of otherness; the grotesque masks belong to 'these chaps': because he accepts dissimilarity, he is able to affirm a common humanity. Conscious of the fact of cultural relativity, he can contrast the vitality of the 'black fellows' with the flabbiness of the invaders. The blacks are real because they want 'no excuse for being there'. They belong to their environment, and their environment belongs to them.

Marlow's possession of his own reality is complete enough for him not to have to erect it into some kind of absolute. Hence he does not feel compelled to reject what is alien to him as abnormal or absurd. A striking example is his response, as he navigates up the river, to the throb of jungle drums. 'Perhaps on some quiet night', he recalls, 'the tremor of far-off drums, sinking, swelling, a tremor vast, faint; a sound weird, appealing, suggestive, and wild – and perhaps with as profound a meaning as the sound of bells in a Christian country' (p. 71). An even more searching illustration is his discovery of the cannibalism of his native stokers. What would be unspeakable horror in London and Brussels becomes, on the Congo river, an unremarkable topic of conversation. Halted by dense fog near their destination, Marlow and his companions hear an outburst of shrieking from the invisible bank (pp. 102–5). The stokers' headman turns to Marlow:

'Catch 'im ... Give 'im to us.'

'To you, eh?' I asked; 'what would you do with them?'

'Eat 'im!' he said, curtly, and, leaning his elbow on the rail, looked out into the fog.

Marlow's response is typical: 'I would no doubt have been properly horrified, had it not occurred to me that he and his chaps must be very hungry: that they must have been growing increasingly hungry for at least this month past.' Remembering who and where he is, he is not stampeded into indiscriminate revulsion. Indeed, far from casting the cannibals beyond the pale of humanity, he discovers in them a quality which in one important respect sets them above the very moralists who condemn them: their restraint in leaving untasted, despite the 'exasperating torment' of their 'lingering starvation', the defenceless cargo of so-called 'pilgrims' virtually at their disposal. To Marlow, Africa and all it contains may seem strange, mysterious, and even unintelligible: but it is not unreal. And for that very reason he retains, displaced as he is, a sense of his own reality.

It is not the native inhabitants of Central Africa that Marlow regards as unreal, but their European invaders and colonizers. *Their* unreality, moreover, does not arise merely from the fact of geographical and cultural dislocation, but from their failure to recognize it. That is to say, their alienation is an internal one: their inability to understand the values which they are supposed to represent leads them to regard foreign ways as nothing more than illegitimate deviations from their own. And this has sinister repercussions. The fact that the society that sustains them is not merely different from, but also stronger than, the tribal communities they encounter abolishes every external check and makes it possible for them to treat the populations they deal with as if they were exploitable raw material, though of considerably less intrinsic value than the ivory they seek.

The trial of the jungle, therefore, can be considered as a test of the degree to which civilization, understood as the sublimation of primitive energies, is more than a mere word. Within advanced communities like Brussels or London one cannot tell whether the citizen is *really* civilized: whether the values he professes are really his – or his merely by virtue of 'the holy terror of scandal and gallows and lunatic asylums' (p. 116).[1] Transport him, however, into a region where every external control is abolished – not only

[1] Cf. p. 114.

48

the steadying presence of butcher and policeman, but also the regulating effects of good health and a temperate climate – and he may abandon every vestige of the restraint on which civilization is founded, and without which it becomes a mere fraud. It is just such a collapse, of course, that Marlow witnesses on his arrival in Africa. In 'the blinding sunshine of that land' he finds that the whites, far from retaining possession of civilized norms, have themselves become possessed by 'a flabby, pretending, weak-eyed devil of a rapacious and pitiless folly' (p. 65). Thus considered, the trial of the jungle is like the trial of the sea, distinguishing Marlow from his demoralized colleagues very much as service at sea is distinguished from self-seeking on land.

III

Up to this point, then, 'Heart of Darkness' might be said to develop the moral distinction established in *The Nigger of the 'Narcissus'*. However, as soon as we begin to scrutinize Marlow's relations with his fellow-whites, this distinction becomes problematic. Broadly speaking, the company officials with whom he comes into contact fall into two main categories: the established traders, whose task is to exchange worthless trinkets for as much ivory as they can lay their hands on; and a new kind of agent, sent out in deference to the pressure of philanthropic opinion, part of whose purpose is – in the words of Marlow's aunt – to wean 'those ignorant millions from their horrid ways'. After his arrival in the Congo, Marlow – who is assumed to belong to what the brickmaker of the Central Station cynically calls 'the gang of virtue' – quickly starts suspecting that the two groups are engaged in some sort of power struggle; and despite his attempts to remain uninvolved he is willy-nilly drawn into the contest. As this process of engagement forms the central part of his narrative, it is necessary to look more closely at his relationship first with the anonymous Manager of the Central Station, the leader of the 'exploiters', then with Kurtz, the chief agent of the Inner Station, the representative of the 'civilizers'.

The Manager, who is Marlow's immediate employer, reveals himself at once as the very type of the exploiter. His single virtue, invulnerable health, frees him from the sole remaining check operative in Africa – tropical fever; and as none of his rivals is able to withstand this disease, he has had an unprecedented stretch of nine years in which to consolidate his position. In all other respects, however, he is – like the 'pilgrims' who loiter about his run-down station – an unredeemable mediocrity, incapable of any guiding principle other than that of maximum profit for minimum effort. 'He had no genius for organizing, for initiative, or for order even ... He had no learning and no intelligence ... He originated nothing, he could keep the routine going – that's all.' Marlow's contemptuous summing-up of the qualities of his employer seems merely to reinforce the distinction between the two men; his tone makes it clear that at least *he* owes his self-respect to his capacity for efficient service. Yet at the same time it defines the essence of Marlow's dilemma. For serving an employer like the Manager is a very different proposition from serving one like Captain Alistoun. To work for a man for whom the ideal of service has no meaning whatsoever instantly revives the problem which *The Nigger of the 'Narcissus'* seemed to have resolved: can labour in the service of a vicious end retain its redemptive character? 'Heart of Darkness' as a whole makes the evasion of this problem quite impossible. During the whole of his sojourn in the Congo, Marlow meets only a single case of integrity in work – that of the Chief Accountant of the Lower Station whose meticulous bookkeeping, together with his stunning sartorial correctness, strikes him, in the context of the general demoralization, as evidence of real 'backbone'. Yet this exception only raises the problem in a more acute form. The Accountant's competence is achieved at the cost of an inhuman detachment. While he continues to make 'correct entries of perfectly correct transactions' in the Company's ledger, he remains oblivious of the appalling consequences of exploitation that are being enacted outside his door: the monotonous groans of a dying man; the 'rascally grin' of a 'redeemed' black in charge of a chain-gang; and, worst of all, the immobility of the broken slaves thrown out like refuse into the despairing hush of the 'grove of death' (pp. 67–70).

In such a situation, it is obviously impossible for Marlow to suggest that fidelity to the task in hand is any sort of justification. All he can claim is that it preserves him from the worst of the surrounding disintegration. The fact that he has to repair his steamer helps him to retain some sort of hold on his identity. 'No, I don't like work', he confesses '– no man does – but I like what is in the work, – the chance to find yourself. Your own reality – for yourself, not for others – what no other man can ever know' (p. 85). Yet even in this reduced form the ideal of service is not secure. The reason why he has to repair the steamer, Marlow understands, is that it has been accidentally wrecked by the Manager, as he set out to rescue an apparently ailing Kurtz. Yet there remains something disturbing about this incident, although Marlow does not spot it immediately: 'I did not see the real significance of that wreck at once ... Certainly the affair was too stupid – when I think of it – to be altogether natural.' So although the Manager inspires a general sense of uneasiness, Marlow does not suspect him of anything specific. However, the more he learns about Kurtz – about his singular success as an ivory collector, but also about the multiplicity of his talents: as the painter of an allegorical figure of justice, as author of an eloquent tract against 'savage customs', as musician, orator, journalist – the more he becomes aware that Kurtz is universally loathed and envied by his colleagues. He receives his first inkling of an actual conspiracy against him only when he overhears the Manager assent to a proposition that 'anything – anything can be done in this country'. But it is only some months later, when Marlow notices the Manager displaying 'a beautiful resignation' at the fact that their rescue of Kurtz has been delayed yet again, that he becomes fully conscious that 'the essentials of this affair lay deep under the surface'. He is now certain that the Manager did not confine himself merely to *hoping* that delay would let the wilderness finish Kurtz off. The events of the recent past suddenly appear in an entirely new light. For example, when the Manager originally claimed that it would take three months to repair the steamer Marlow had taken him for 'a chattering idiot': how could anyone confidently predict that the work would take so long? But now he adds: 'Afterwards I took it back when it was borne in upon me startlingly with what extreme nicety he had estimated the time requisite for the "affair".' Whatever the meaning of the word 'affair' – whether it refers to the repair of the steamer (which the Manager would have been able to prolong at will since he controlled the supply of rivets), or to the destruction of Kurtz (which with his unprecedented experience of tropical climate he would have been able to calculate to a nicety) – Marlow can now see that the Manager has all along remained in complete control of events. What he has to face is something more disconcerting that the mere fact of perfidiousness: that the rescue operation, a task with which he had been professionally entrusted and from which he had derived a modicum of self-respect, has proved itself to be from beginning to end a cynical masquerade. It is not surprising that he feels himself caught in a situation in which, as he says, 'my speech or my silence, indeed any action of mine, would be mere futility' (p. 100, generally).

IV

If in his relationship with the inscrutable Manager of the Central Station Marlow is brought into contact with moral cynicism, in his relationship with Kurtz he is confronted with the phenomenon of idealistic self-deception. Kurtz seems to be a passionate and eloquent defender of the policy which holds, against the more pragmatic views of the Manager, that every station should be 'a centre of trade of course, but also for humanizing, improving, instructing'. It is understandable that Marlow, surrounded as he is by an exploitation that has 'no more moral purpose at the back of it than there is in burglars breaking into a safe', should find himself drawn towards the idea of a man who, by all accounts, seems to be 'equipped with moral ideas of some sort'. In complete contrast to the Manager, Kurtz seems to be a person of exceptional talents and culture. Indeed he appears to be a very embodiment of that civilization which the African wilderness has so comprehensively annihilated. 'All Europe contributed to the making of Mr Kurtz', says Marlow. His elaborate advocacy of European values, however, turns out to be even more disturbing than the Manager's uncomplicated denial of them.

As Marlow, navigating upstream towards Kurtz, penetrates more and more deeply into the wilderness, his feelings towards it undergo a substantial change. It is no longer a merely alien environment: it acquires the force of a positive presence. 'We are accustomed to look upon the shackled form of a conquered monster', he tells his listeners; '– there you could look at a thing monstrous and free.' He even admits to responding atavistically to the spectacle of unchained nature. The sight and sound of savage dancing, so much a part of its primeval setting, awakens in him the sense of his 'remote kinship with that wild and passionate uproar'. As Lionel Trilling has pointed out,[1] this marks one of Conrad's more striking originalities, for whereas most of Conrad's contemporaries would have been moved by the primitive only as an idyll in the tradition of Rousseau, Marlow responds to it precisely because of its sheer savagery. In it he finds what he calls 'truth stripped of its cloak of time' – that is, a truth which antedates the truth that civilization has brought about, and which is therefore timeless or permanent. But what he goes on to do is even more

---

[1] Lionel Trilling, 'On the teaching of modern literature', in *Beyond Culture*, originally published 1965 (Penguin, 1967), p. 32. The incident referred to is in 'Heart of Darkness', pp. 95–7.

striking. Having acknowledged that the primitive is fundamental, he at once sets up a contradictory truth: a man 'must meet that truth with his own true stuff – with his own inborn strength ... I hear; I admit, but I have a voice too, and for good and evil mine is the speech that cannot be silenced.' In this view, civilization is thought of not merely as a given, but as something achieved – something deliberately constructed and upheld in defiance of an elemental nature. This *antithetical* conception of reality – in which the recognition of a basic truth prompts the affirmation of a counter-truth – is at the centre of 'Heart of Darkness'. Without it one cannot fully understand the spectacular degradation of the Kurtz whom Marlow finally comes upon when he reaches the Inner Station. We have seen that what distinguishes Marlow from the Manager is his refusal to countenance the exploitation of the primitive; we now see that what differentiates him from Kurtz is his refusal to condone a surrender to the primitive. A man cannot shed his inheritance of civilization with impunity, for primitivism, like innocence, once outgrown or lost cannot be recovered. Kurtz has stripped himself of all the cultural values he took so ostentatiously into Africa. But he has not thereby regained the reality possessed by his primitive ancestors. Instead, he has, in Marlow's words, 'taken a high seat among the devils of the land' (p. 116). What exactly does this imply?

Like his meeting with the Manager, Marlow's meeting with Kurtz is preceded by an encounter with a subordinate figure – the Russian sailor who makes an even more unexpected appearance in the remote Upper Station than the Accountant did in the Lower (pp. 122–5 and 126–33). He has, incredibly, managed to survive the jungle – not, like the Accountant, by insulating himself, but by remaining completely incapable of registering experience. He too is defined by his attire – a brilliant harlequin's patchwork which suggests a man without a fixed identity. His extraordinary eagerness, his buoyancy, his childlike spirit of adventure seem to Marlow 'to have consumed all thoughts of self'. But this is not moral strength: it is moral naïveté. Hence, while it may enable him to survive the trials of Africa, it leaves him completely exposed to the influence of Kurtz. Marlow quickly discovers that he has become a kind of neophyte, and he asks him what Kurtz's talk is really like. 'It was in general. It made me see things – things.' This reply (which recalls the inexpressible yearnings of the crew of the *Narcissus*) indicates that the young man's enthusiasm is completely uncritical. Reflecting back on it, Marlow ominously concludes:

'He had not meditated over it.' Thus the disciple has no inkling of what is quite plain to Marlow: that in his reverence for his master he has crawled 'like the veriest savage of them all'. What price fidelity now? The riddle posed by the young Russian's navigation manual – which, when Marlow had chanced upon it downstream, had imparted both a 'delicious sensation' of reality by its content, and a feeling of bewilderment by its marginal glosses in 'cipher' – is now solved. At once recognizable and baffling, it marks the ambiguous condition to which the certainties of maritime service have been reduced.

Some critics have complained that Conrad has been insufficiently specific about the inconceivable ceremonies and nameless lusts to which Kurtz is supposed to have abandoned himself. Yet Marlow's encounter with the young Russian enables us to see that what finally damns Kurtz is not the horror of the shrunken heads which decorate his house, nor even the ferocity of his raiding excursions, but what these things indicate: the appalling fact that he has taken upon himself the role of God. This is tantamount to saying that he has entered into a state of final self-deception. In this, as the interview with the young Russian again suggests, Kurtz is the victim of his own gifts – specifically of the gift of speech. Of itself, expression is a fatally ambivalent power – an instrument of truth or of deceit. When Marlow, before his arrival at the Inner Station, has a premonition that he may not see Kurtz after all, he suddenly realizes the reason for his disappointment.

The point was in his being a gifted creature, and that of all his gifts the one that stood out preëminently, that carried with it a sense of real presence, was his ability to talk, his words – the gift of expression, the bewildering, the illuminating, the most exalted and the most contemptible, the pulsating stream of light, or the deceitful flow from the heart of an impenetrable darkness.

'Heart of Darkness', pp. 113–14

Without what Conrad calls impersonality – the moral capacity for resistance or restraint – the gift of speech can prove catastrophic. It enables Kurtz to establish an ascendancy over the blacks which the Manager, with all his rifles, cannot even remotely approach. At the same time it allows him to continue to believe in himself as the apostle of disinterested altruism. Unquestionable virtue added to inviolable power instantly produces self-deification. But although he may be very dangerous, this new god, being hollow at the core, is a complete sham.

Albert Guerard has argued that there is a contradiction in Conrad's presentation of Kurtz: that he cannot be both an evil man and a hollow man.[1] But this seems based on a misunderstanding. Kurtz is only hollow with respect to what he *says* he is; there is nothing insubstantial about what he *does*. Or, to put the matter in another way, he becomes hollow by virtue of his lack of moral identity; but he does not remain hollow. The vacated space, in obedience to a well-known law, is immediately filled by primitive powers – whether mounting from below or invading from without. Marlow's own diagnosis of the case seems unanswerable: 'Everything belonged to him – but that was a trifle. The thing to know was what he belonged to, how many powers of darkness claimed him for their own.' He who wants to be a god becomes a devil.

It is only in the context of Kurtz's self-deception – of his turning the gift of speech from a 'stream of light' into a 'flow ... of darkness' – that Marlow's special insistence on the virtue of honesty makes proper sense. 'You know I hate, detest, and can't bear a lie, not because I am straighter than the rest of us, but simply because it appals me', he declares. 'There is a taint of death, a flavour of mortality in lies – which is exactly what I hate and detest in the world – what I want to forget (p. 82).' Kurtz is a living incarnation of everything Marlow claims to hate. His condition of dishonesty substantiates the view that lying is related to death, not only because his self-deception is the immediate cause of his collapse (one cannot pretend to be God without running certain risks), but also, more subtly, because it dissolves the substance of his moral identity (one cannot yield to one's instincts without falling into their power). That Marlow, therefore, should find himself obliged to go over to his side is an even stronger shock to his convictions than having to work for the Manager. It does not make him into a self-deceiver – any more than the Manager's incompetence rendered him inefficient. But, without doubt, it calls into question the point or purpose of his commitment to veracity.

It is Marlow's meeting with Kurtz that precipitates the decisive crisis of the book. As in *The Nigger of the 'Narcissus'*, a choice has to be made between two alternatives. But these alternatives no longer consist of men who affirm and men who deny the ideal of service. They are the Manager and Kurtz. Marlow's predicament is not unlike that of a member of the crew of the *Narcissus* who, having been abandoned by Alistoun and Singleton, is obliged to decide between Donkin and Wait. (The parallel is less fanciful than it

[1] Guerard, *Conrad the Novelist*, p. 131.

might seem: for example, one of Kurtz's last remarks, 'This noxious fool [i.e. the Manager] is capable of prying into my boxes when I am not looking', brings to mind the moribund Wait's dispossession by Donkin.) The confrontation takes place after Kurtz has at last been stowed away into his cabin (pp. 137–8). The Manager, who knows now that his opponent is finished, tries to secure Marlow's support.

We have done all we could for him, haven't we? But there is no disguising the fact, Mr Kurtz has done more harm than good to the Company. He did not see the time was not ripe for vigorous action ... I don't deny there's a remarkable amount of ivory – mostly fossil. We must save it, at all events – but look how precarious the position is – and why? Because the method is unsound.

It is this final declaration that brings Marlow off the fence. What he cannot take is the reference to Kurtz's murderous raids. Looking at the shore, he asks: 'Do you call it "unsound method"?' And when he receives a hotly affirmative answer, his sole rejoinder is 'No method at all.' The Manager's complacent nihilism so revolts him that his thoughts turn towards Kurtz 'positively for relief': better moral collapse than sub-moral success. After his attempts to remain free of Company politics, he now feels obliged to declare himself. So, facing the Manager, he deliberately says to him: 'Nevertheless I think Mr Kurtz is a remarkable man.' These words are a sentence of instant banishment. From now on he finds himself ostracized as an advocate of the party of 'unsound' method. This, obviously, is no great loss; however, that the only alternative to the Manager's unfeeling meanness should be Kurtz's megalomaniac raving is a very different matter. Marlow is under no illusions: what has been forced upon him is 'a choice of nightmares'.

Marlow's association with Kurtz produces the final stage of what one could term his ordeal by darkness. What it implies is brought out by an incident that takes place during the evening that follows his conversation with the Manager (pp. 140–5). Unable to sleep, Marlow looks into Kurtz's cabin and finds it vacant. After the first thrill of terror (Kurtz, it seems, can make even Marlow momentarily superstitious), he realizes that the sick man has managed to escape, and that if the expedition is to survive, he must be prevented from rejoining his tribesmen. Without betraying this absence to the sleeping guards ('it was written I should be loyal to the nightmare of my choice'), Marlow slips ashore by himself. 'I was anxious to deal with this shadow by myself alone', he explains,

'– and to this day I don't know why I was so jealous of sharing with anyone the peculiar blackness of that experience.' Marlow may not know why, but Conrad makes sure *we* do. Marlow had been thinking of Kurtz as a potential ally; he now instinctively regards him as a sort of anti-self or inverted double. The essential difference between Kurtz and himself is not that Kurtz has been exposed to a different kind of temptation, but that, for all his gifts, he has proved incapable of restraint, and thus of fidelity to the values he has professed. What has finally counted with him is the gratification of his desires. Even his advocacy of civilized values has had no impersonal or objective foundation, but remained a mere self-indulgence, an expression of vanity or conceit. So in going after Kurtz, Marlow sets off in pursuit of what presents itself to him as his own antithesis; and the ultimate test of the wilderness comes to him as a confrontation, not directly with savagery, but indirectly with a ghastly parody of civilization.

When Marlow finally overtakes Kurtz crawling in the long grass towards the flicker of the camp-fires, he discovers to his horror that there is nothing in him to which he can appeal. Kurtz's solipsism has become so perfect that he seems to have 'kicked himself loose of the earth' – that is, to have lost contact with everything outside himself. Marlow is left with one last possibility: to 'invoke him – himself' directly, as one would invoke a god. Incapable as Kurtz is of seeing any contradiction between his words and his deeds, between his professed values and his actual practices, he remains a creature in conflict, torn between his 'European' ambitions and his 'African' lusts. Depending, for example, on the ebb and flow of his 'European' fantasies, he alternately adores and abominates his barbaric existence, first launching his tribesmen into an attack against the steamer coming to deprive him of it, then persuading them to allow the rescuing party to take him away from it unmolested, then again – as now – irresistibly possessed of a fiery thirst for its lawless gratifications. So in the absence of any reason or morality in Kurtz, Marlow is obliged to appeal directly to that aspect of his self-love which makes him recoil from the primitive. He encourages him to indulge dreams of his 'immense plans'; he flatters him with the prospect of his success in Europe which 'in any case is assured'. Marlow has no doubt of what is really at issue in this struggle: it is more than survival – it is salvation.

If anybody had ever struggled with a soul, I am the man [he tells his auditors]. Believe me or not, his intelligence was perfectly clear – concentrated, it is true, upon himself with horrible intensity, yet clear . . . But his soul was mad. Being alone in the wilderness, it had looked within itself, and, by heavens! I tell you, it had gone mad. I had – for my sins, I suppose – to go through the ordeal of looking into it myself. *No eloquence could have been so withering to one's belief in mankind as his final burst of sincerity.* [My italics.]

Up to the moment of Marlow's encounter with Kurtz, it is Marlow's strength, that is, his capacity to serve a moral idea, that the wilderness has challenged; what it now calls into question is his faith, that is, his capacity to believe in the value or meaning of such an idea. The very sincerity of Kurtz's belief in his humanitarian mission – in other words, the very completeness of his self-deception – provides an insane parody of the values for which Marlow stands. Faith in humanity, as it were, must look into a deranged mirror – and overcome the mocking image. For Marlow, to prevent Kurtz from returning to the jungle is not only necessary for his physical survival; it is also a last-ditch affirmation of the reality of the civilized against that of the primitive. His success in bringing Kurtz back to his cabin, therefore, is some sort of spiritual victory.

V

In thus committing himself to Kurtz, of course, Marlow is unable to affirm civilized values unequivocally. He has wrested Kurtz out of the clutches of the wilderness, but only in the name of his insane egoism. The humanitarian he now holds is a mere fake, sealed up in his self-deception by his self-generated eloquence. 'He could get himself to believe anything', says an admiring journalist after Marlow's return to Europe. But to believe anything is to believe nothing. What Kurtz endlessly says, whether to Marlow or to himself, is flatly contradicted by what he is. What then does Marlow gain by this nightmare alliance? Is an essentially empty affirmation of value, like Kurtz's, really preferable to the Manager's open cynicism? Is Marlow's claim that Kurtz is 'a remarkable man' really defensible? Just as Marlow is to remain faithful to Kurtz in his fashion to the last, so Kurtz finally vindicates Marlow's faith in him – although he keeps him in suspense, as it were, until his ultimate moment. The scene of Kurtz's death, and particularly his last cry, has become perhaps the most notorious crux of interpretation in modern literature; it is, however, not as problematic as it is commonly supposed to be.

Anything approaching the change that came over his features I have never seen before, and hope never to see again. Oh, I wasn't touched. I was fascinated. It was as though a veil had been rent. I saw on that ivory face the expression of sombre pride, of ruthless power, of craven terror – of an intense and hopeless despair. Did he live his life again in every detail of desire, temptation, and surrender during that supreme moment of complete knowledge? He cried in a whisper at some image, at some vision – he cried out twice, a cry that was no more than a breath –

'The horror! The horror!'

I blew the candle out and left the cabin.

'Heart of Darkness', p. 149

It has sometimes been forgotten that this is not the only, or indeed the first, death that Marlow witnesses in 'Heart of Darkness'. There is the earlier killing of the careless and excitable steersman during the skirmish in the approach to the Inner Station (pp. 111–13). The parallel is quite explicit: as an 'improved specimen' – culturally disorientated too, in his way – the steersman 'had no restraint, no restraint – just like Kurtz – a tree swayed by the wind'. And although as he dies he does not actually say anything, he casts on Marlow a 'lustrous and inquiring glance ... like a claim of distant kinship'. The moment of death, it would seem, has a meaning that is relevant to all mankind. So that what the dying Kurtz perceives may not only be true of himself as an individual; it may also be significant for humanity at large.

We have to take the moment of death, then, as Marlow presents it: not as a cause of terror, but as a condition for insight. As far as Kurtz is concerned, it is the instant in which, for the first and last time, he sees his past for what it has truly been; it is the point at which, in a rending flash, his values at last connect with his life and reveal it to be a 'darkness'. Retrospectively, Marlow finds this ultimate summing-up, in contrast to his own indifference as fever brings him close to extinction himself, 'an affirmation, a moral victory'. And he is right to do so, for by recognizing that the values to which he had paid lip-service apply to himself, Kurtz has made them real at last. The words with which he passes judgement on 'the adventures of his soul on this earth' are no longer merely pronounced, but meant.

But there is more. Kurtz has achieved self-knowledge: but thereby he has also achieved knowledge of mankind. His verdict against himself is also a verdict against human life. Looking back on Kurtz's death, Marlow concludes that the reason he can now affirm – and not merely gamble or speculate – that Kurtz was indeed a remarkable man is that 'he had something to say': that his final appalled stare 'was wide enough to embrace the whole universe, piercing enough to penetrate all the hearts that beat in darkness'. And what was it that Kurtz had to say? – 'He had summed up – he had judged. "The horror!"' Problematic as the further meaning of Kurtz's cry has proved, there are two things that can be confidently said about it. The first is that it records some sort of 'ultimate truth' about man; the second is that it implies that this truth is morally abhorrent.

One of the major assumptions on which 'Heart of Darkness' rests is that if we want to find out the 'real' truth about man – what his 'essential' nature is – we must inquire into his origins. This basically evolutionary view holds that civilization is something merely imposed on man's essential nature – that culture does not eradicate, but merely keeps in check, his primitive instincts. In this sense, Marlow's journey to the Inner Station – to the heart of the African darkness – is a voyage into his ancestral past; and what Kurtz in the end discovers for himself is what Marlow has already grasped: that the ideals of European life form no part of man's essential self – that the heart of the European citizen, for all the endeavours of his education, remains an abode of darkness. But this is only part of Kurtz's meaning. The rest is that this truth is a terrible one – that is to say, that the values it denies survive the denial, in the sense that they remain supremely important. According to this view, teleological rather than evolutionary, the 'real' truth about man is not merely where he comes from, but where he is going to: his 'essential' nature is not found merely by uncovering his past but also by defining his future. Thus civilization cannot be dismissed, as it were, as a defective actuality: it should more properly be regarded as a potential to be sustained, or a destination to be pursued. The criterion for reality is no longer existence, but possibility. Man's goals do not have to be realized in order to be made 'real': it is enough that they be taken seriously. That Kurtz's last cry should not have been 'a word of careless contempt' is, as Marlow emphasizes, a fact of supreme importance to him, for it proves that Kurtz – and again in this like Marlow before him – has felt the need, in the face of what he has at last recognized as darkness, for an alternative reality.

In a brilliant paragraph in his essay 'The Teaching of Modern Literature', Lionel Trilling suggests that Kurtz, in contrast to Marlow whom he calls 'the ordinary man', must be considered 'a hero of the spirit', for he has dared to venture beyond the security of permitted experience and thereby earned the right to pronounce judgement.[1] This comparison is suggestive, but it does not seem to me to be precise enough. Both Marlow and Kurtz end by perceiving the same thing: that so-called 'civilized' man, unlike (as we have seen) savages in a state of nature or (as we shall see) women in a state of innocence, is trapped between two antithetical realities. But their mode of perception is quite different. It is only in his relation to Kurtz that Marlow might be taken for the ordinary man; in relation to everyone else in the story he represents, surely, the moral man. For him, the dual reality revealed by the test of the jungle poses a problem of conduct: in its aspect of primitive truth, it demands his courage, for it has to be outfaced; in its form of civilized goal, it requires his fidelity, for it has to be upheld. For Kurtz, on the other hand, this duality is not so much something to be dealt with, as something to be embodied or enacted. He *is*, on his death-bed, the horror he perceives. His last cry, like that of Faustus, is the cry of a man who can only learn what his soul is worth as he discovers that it is irretrievably lost, or of one who can only affirm moral value as he perceives that it cannot exist. If Marlow is the moral hero, Kurtz becomes, for a visionary instant, the tragic hero.

It would be a mistake, however, to conclude that 'Heart of Darkness' is an essentially tragic narrative, for it is finally Marlow, not Kurtz, who retains the centre of the stage. Marlow's story is one of survival. He has successfully endured the immediate onslaught of the jungle. But how is he going to adapt to its consequences? And in particular, how will he cope with the duality that has been revealed to him? It seems at first as if he opts for a cynical discounting of one of its imperatives. For almost a year after his return to Europe, he can scarcely endure the complacent certainties of his fellow-citizens. Their very normality, based as it must be on wholly untested assumptions of security and superiority, strikes him as derisory in its blindness. He seems well on his way to spurning every claim on behalf of civilization, when he is abruptly halted by an unexpected event – his interview with Kurtz's 'Intended' (pp. 154–62).[2] What disturbs him most about her is not that she is deceived about what Kurtz really is, but that her faith in him should be so disinterested, and her fidelity so unswerving. 'I perceived', says Marlow, with scarcely concealed consternation, 'she was one of those creatures who are not the

[1] Trilling, 'Modern Literature', p. 33.
[2] See p. 115.

playthings of time.' He cannot dismiss her with her compatriots as an 'irritating pretence'. Indeed, she constitutes, in what she is, a living reproof of every kind of cynical evasiveness.

Whether or not Conrad has sacrificed reality to symbol in his portrayal of Kurtz's Intended – as many have felt – there is no uncertainty about the problem she poses for Marlow. Her trustfulness earns her the right to be told the truth; yet the only truth there is for him to tell must destroy the basis of that trust. This is a knot that cannot be untied, but only cut. And this Marlow does by telling her a lie: by making her believe that Kurtz's fidelity to her – and so to the ideals she embodies – has shone untarnished to the very last.

All attempts to explain this act merely in terms of Marlow's compassion for her must remain unsatisfactory, for they fail to take into account its central irony – that the lie which concludes 'Heart of Darkness' is uttered by a man whom the entire narrative has taught us to regard as the very apostle of veracity. Marlow himself tells us that if he deceives her, it is not simply out of concern for her, but also out of concern for himself. This, rather than vulgar male protectiveness, is the real point of his subsequent reflections on the event. 'I laid the ghost of his gifts at last with a lie . . . Did I mention a girl? Oh, she is out of it – completely. They – the women I mean – are out of it – should be out of it. We must help them to stay in that beautiful world of their own, *lest ours gets worse.*' [My italics.] For all his tone of retrospective – and offensive – self-indulgence, Marlow here presents his lie as the guarantor of a certain truth: it preserves intact the innocence of Kurtz's Intended. For a moment, as he senses the depth of her grief for the man she has loved, he sees two antithetical truths overlap: 'I saw her and him in the same instant of time – his death and her sorrow – I saw her sorrow in the very moment of his death.' Kurtz's vision of horror is not replaced by her pity, but it is in some sense exorcised by it. Kurtz's Intended offers Marlow an image of that ideal reality which his despair had latterly threatened to deny. But she can only continue to do so as long as she remains innocent of the actuality. As the narrative draws to its conclusion, this paradox is given an almost schematic representation. Marlow notices that, in all the purity of her sorrow for the ideal Kurtz, she unconsciously mimics the equally passionate grief of the savage mistress to whom the real Kurtz gave himself in the depths of the African wilderness. Should the Intended once suspect this truth, she would instantly be deprived of all redemptive virtue, and find herself on a level with Marlow under the shadow of Kurtz's legacy. Marlow's lie, arguably itself an act of darkness, is also a means of keeping back the darkness.

The concluding episode of Marlow's narrative measures the full extent of the gap that separates the man who set out for his African ordeal, and the man who returned from it. The difference isn't that the latter renounces the principle of service, but that he now knows that it cannot be simply affirmed. If the world we propose to serve is found to be comprehensively corrupted, there would seem to be only two alternatives left to us, each equally unsatisfactory: to give way to the corruption and cynically abandon all notion of service; or to ignore the corruption and continue to uphold a now vacuous ideal. Faced by this choice, however, Marlow is able to discover a third alternative, perhaps less desperate than the other two in that it can preserve what we are and what we should be in some sort of connection with each other. Characterizing his attitude to Kurtz's Intended, he describes himself as 'bowing my head before the faith that was in her, before that great and saving illusion that shone with an unearthly glow in the darkness'. If service is to be vindicated, it can only be in terms of the concept of what may be called *positive illusion*. The girl's belief in the essential virtue of mankind, as instanced by her faith in her betrothed, is an illusion, for it is contradicted by the facts; yet it is not unreal, for it is held with all the force of a truly unselfish conviction. It serves to keep alive, in the darkness of Marlow's experience of actuality, the light of visionary purpose.

What the concept of positive illusion allows Marlow to do is to survive tragic knowledge without incurring self-deception – that is to say, to affirm the values of the active life without blurring his sense of its underlying contradictions. But it is more than the culminating idea of an extraordinarily complex and concentrated work of fiction. It is also one of the central preoccupations of the major works of the first half of Conrad's career as a novelist, enabling him to do full justice to the paradoxes within his own nature – to his urge towards scepticism and to his need for faith.

4

Lord Jim

Il n'y a pas d'expiation. Chaque acte de la vie est final et produit fatalment ses consequences malgré tous les pleurs et les grincements des [*sic*] dents.

(There is no atonement. Every action in life is final and produces its inevitable consequences despite all the tears and gnashings of teeth.)
(from a letter of 15 September 1891 to Marguerite Poradowska)

I

'Heart of Darkness' stands at the threshold of Conrad's major creative phase. Before producing that narrative he had been unable to make any progress on *Lord Jim*, a novel he had been trying to get under way from some months. After it, however, he was able to work uninterruptedly on the new project, completing it in just under one year. *Lord Jim* was published in book form in 1900; it was followed, if not quickly at least steadily, by the two great masterpieces *Nostromo* (published 1904) and *The Secret Agent* (published 1907); these in their turn were succeeded by *Under Western Eyes* (published 1911), which fittingly brought to a close the most productive decade of Conrad's life.

The reason why 'Heart of Darkness' occupies a special place in the Conrad canon is that it was the first of his works fully to disclose the possibilities of tragedy. In *The Nigger of the 'Narcissus'*, to be sure, the crew had been torn between incompatible claims, but the conditions of their life had induced them to choose right: Conrad had been able to turn his back on acknowledged complexity in the name of a moral positive. In 'Heart of Darkness', however, Marlow found every escape route blocked; and Conrad was inexorably brought into collision with the contradictions inherent in his deepest beliefs. Thereafter, every affirmation in his work became something of a pyrrhic victory, every positive something of a deliberate illusion. The shock of this collision continued to reverberate for at least ten years. The four great novels of that period are richly, even extravagantly, textured. Yet for all their mimetic range and

---

[1] *Lettres de Joseph Conrad à Marguerite Poradowska* ed. René Rapin, Université de Lausanne, Publications de la Faculté des Lettres, 12 (Genère, 1966, p. 92).

stylistic variety they remain part of a single, comprehensive, exploratory process. This process was launched by the writing of 'Heart of Darkness'; and there can be little doubt that without that work it would not have come into being at all – or at least not in the form in which we now have it.

Even in its externals, *Lord Jim* is more closely related to its predecessor than is commonly supposed. Like 'Heart of Darkness', it is concerned with the relationship between two men – Marlow, older and subtler than the navigator of the Congo, but recognizably faithful to his maritime values, though with a fidelity tempered by experience; and the young naval officer Jim who recalls Kurtz in at least one essential respect: his failure to live up to the ideal he professes. In the new work, however, Conrad makes a decisive change: he shifts the emphasis from the narrator to the protagonist. This has the effect of bringing the tragic conflict into the foreground. By and large, in 'Heart of Darkness' Marlow had overshadowed Kurtz. In *Lord Jim* he is unquestionably subordinated to Jim. Moreover, a structural alteration of this sort entails a corresponding thematic change, as a closer comparison of Kurtz and Jim reveals. Kurtz may have at the last moment achieved a fleeting self-knowledge; but for the most part he remains a study in self-deception, tragic in potential rather than in fact. Jim, on the other hand, is early awakened to the significance of his failure; he is not allowed to linger in the dream of omnipotence; his convulsive attempts to 'master his fate' – to transcend the contradictions into which his initial error has plunged him – take up most of the book's action. His is not so much a case of self-deception as of self-discovery. *Lord Jim* is a much more classically tragic work than its predecessor; it is also much less sombre. What Kurtz discovered about himself snuffed him out instantly: Jim's discoveries produce defiance, indeed revolt, and thus impart a heroic resonance to the story of his life and death.

There exists, however, another and perhaps even more significant difference between the two men. Jim, unlike Kurtz, is a member of the Merchant Navy. Arguably, Kurtz fails the test of the wilderness because he is a mere landsman, untrained in the 'unthinking and blessed stiffness before the outward and inward terrors' that Marlow considers a pre-condition of successful sea service. But Jim is no outsider to that tradition. He is, as Marlow insists again and again, 'one of us' – a man initiated in the craft of the sea and committed to its standards. In this respect too, *Lord Jim* can be considered an advance on 'Heart of Darkness'. The ambiguities of service now invade the Merchant Navy itself. Its contradictions are no longer revealed merely in the darkness of the jungle, but in the very place of its origins – on the quarter-deck of a ship at sea, within the breast of the officer of the watch. As a result of this, the protagonist's error demands to be regarded in a new way: Jim's leap from the *Patna* is much more than an act of failure; it is an act of betrayal.

With all its vividness of scene and incident, and the breadth and detail of its human panorama, *Lord Jim* as a whole remains focussed on the significance of this single action. The novel is divided into two main parts: the first half, taken up with Jim's reaction to the Court of Inquiry appointed to look into his conduct, dramatizes his jump's immediate effects; the second, devoted to his attempts at rehabilitation in a remote inland province, traces its further consequences. Moreover, this jump instantly becomes the object of universal curiosity and speculation. So systematically does Conrad assemble the judgements and opinions of his characters that the novel could almost be described as a collage of verdicts. The central point of view, around which all the others are organized, is of course Marlow's, which is developed through his struggle to understand Jim. Like the novel itself, this struggle falls into two successive phases. In the first, Marlow tries to solve the problem posed by Jim's betrayal largely by means of moral judgement, in the second, more by means of imaginative sympathy. This is not to say that these phases are mutually exclusive – that Marlow is at first only a judge, and later only a friend. But that they are distinct is indicated by the fact that each is, as it were, sponsored by an appropriate secondary figure who embodies an aspect of Marlow's complex point of view. The 'realistic' French lieutenant who takes charge of the ship Jim abandons and whose conversation with Marlow brings the case against Jim to its climax is balanced by the German 'romantic' Stein who, by offering Jim his second chance – the opportunity of remaking his life in Patusan – launches the novel on its redemptive second movement. Generally speaking, Conrad's novels, like those of his nineteenth-century French masters, are subjected to a process of unobtrusive but systematic patterning. In this *Lord Jim* is no exception. The young English officer who so disastrously betrays the code to which he has committed himself is brought into some kind of contact with no less than three major father-figures who have not failed it: the Englishman Marlow in the centre, a Frenchman on one side, a German on the other. Such structural regularity must not be taken as a symptom of obsessional tidiness on Conrad's part; it represents a determined attempt to achieve overall intellectual coherence. It has to be taken into account, therefore, in any serious analysis of the work as a whole.

II

In the course of describing his long evening's conversation with Jim, Marlow compares him to a number of persons he has known or heard of: with the two Malay steersmen of the *Patna* who stick to their task, for example, or with little Bob Stanton of the *Sephora* who is drowned trying to save a lady passenger. These, however, merely prepare for the appearance of the French lieutenant who, unlike them, has meditated on the problem of courage and cowardice and has something to say. Significantly, Conrad postpones all mention of him until the first phase of his narrative is nearly over. The encounter actually occurs in an ordinary Sydney café, about three years after Jim's fall (*Lord Jim*, pp. 137–49). The heavy, ageing, impassive, anonymous man whom Marlow engages in conversation is Jim's complete antithesis, not only in that he has done without fuss what Jim could not, but also in that he does not need Jim's excited rhetoric or fine linen in order to make the weight of his authority felt. As they talk, Marlow is suddenly impelled to consult him about his young protégé: it would be like 'taking professional opinion on the case'. Having listened to the story with the utmost attention, the lieutenant remarks that one does not die 'of being afraid'.

'That is so,' he resumed, placidly. 'Man is born a coward (*L'homme est né poltron*). It is a difficulty – *parbleu*! It would be too easy otherwise. But habit – habit – necessity – do you see? – the eye of others – *voilà*. One puts up with it. And then the example of others who are no better than yourself, and yet make good countenance ... '

His voice ceased.

'That young man – you will observe – had none of these inducements – at least at the moment,' I remarked.

He raised his eyebrows forgivingly: 'I don't say; I don't say. The young man in question might have had the best dispositions – the best dispositions,' he repeated, wheezing a little.

'I am glad to see you taking a lenient view,' I said. 'His own feeling in the matter was – ah! – hopeful, and ...'

The shuffle of his feet under the table interrupted me. He drew up his heavy eyelids. Drew up, I say – no other expression can describe the steady deliberation of the act – and at last was disclosed completely to me. I was confronted by two narrow grey circlets, like two tiny steel rings around the profound blackness of the pupils. The sharp glance, coming from that massive body, gave a notion of extreme efficiency, like a razor-edge on a battle-axe. 'Pardon,' he said, punctiliously. His right hand went up, and he swayed forward. 'Allow me ... I contended that one may get on knowing very well that one's courage does not come of itself (*ne vient pas tout seul*). There's nothing much in that to get upset about. One truth the more ought not to make life impossible ... But the honour – the honour, monsieur! ... The honour ... that is real – that is! And what life may be worth when' ... he got on his feet with a ponderous impetuosity, as a startled ox might scramble up from the grass ... 'when the honour is gone – *ah ca! par exemple* – I can offer no opinion. I can offer no opinion – because – monsieur – I know nothing of it.'

I had risen, too, and, trying to throw infinite politeness into our attitudes, we faced each other mutely, like two china dogs on a mantelpiece. Hang the fellow! he had pricked the bubble.

Lord Jim, pp. 147–8

The fact that a conversation that began by promising so much should founder into futility must not be taken as a mark of its irrelevance. Conrad, it is true, deftly evokes the embarrassment of a breakdown in communication, and demonstrates that once the point of an exchange has gone, all that the participants are left with is their empty roles. But this does not mean that he registers an adverse verdict against the lieutenant. If we examine the passage we discover that communication between the two men ceases the moment Marlow attempts to exonerate Jim on the grounds of his good intentions. The lieutenant's response – a reminder of the distinction between the subjectivity of 'disposition' and the objectivity of 'dishonour' – is quite unanswerable. And when Marlow goes on to suggest 'with a disconcerted smile' that honour might perhaps 'reduce itself to not being found out', we cannot condemn the lieutenant for putting an end to the discussion: there is little point in talking morality to a man who cannot see that there is more to guilt than the fear of detection. Faced by the problem of Jim's betrayal, Marlow seems to have assumed that it could be dealt with by some uncomplicated process of exoneration. But this is to treat Jim's case as if it were a question of a miscarriage of justice. The problem is not that the verdict against Jim is wrong, but that it is *right*. Of course, the lieutenant's one-sided severity is no more of a solution than Marlow's leniency: but it is not cancelled; it is only placed. At a critical point in the story, when our sympathies might begin to swing a little too easily behind Jim, the lieutenant reminds us once and for all that the facts of the case cannot be altered by wishful thinking. No wonder that after the ruffled French officer has taken his leave Marlow 'sits·down again alone and discouraged'.

Far from being dismissed, this ruthless point of view has been repeatedly endorsed by everything that precedes it. The claim that by 'running away with the others' Jim has betrayed his honour is echoed in one form or another by every person qualified to comment on a case of naval misconduct. For Brierly, the exemplary captain who presides over the Court of Inquiry, what Jim has betrayed is his trust.

This is a disgrace [he tells Marlow]. We've got all kinds among us – some anointed scoundrels in the lot; but, hang it, we must preserve professional decency or we become no better than so many tinkers going about loose. We are trusted. Do you understand? Trusted! Frankly, I don't care a snap for all the pilgrims that ever came out of Asia, but a decent man would not have behaved like this to a full cargo of old rags in bales.

Lord Jim, pp. 67–8

In this view, what counts in guaranteeing professional contracts is neither the nationality of the employer, nor the nature of the cargo, nor the prospect of commercial profit. It is the pride of the man who has accepted the trust. For Marlow, the instructor of generations of sea cadets, Jim has betrayed his craft. 'I tell you I wanted to see him squirm for the honour of the craft' (p. 46),[1] he declares, stung by the young man's devil-may-care nonchalance the first time he sees him. To be admitted into a craft and to be instructed in its 'little mysteries' (its skills and techniques) and its 'one big secret' (the law of selflessness) is ultimately to be granted the means of self-respect.

In seeing Jim's action as a betrayal of honour, therefore, the lieutenant only reiterates the verdict of his professional colleagues. But he does more than this. He shows that honour (or pride, or self-respect) depends on the existence of a fixed code of conduct. This code demands only that it be obeyed; but in that it admits of no exception. If Jim has thrown away his honour – that is, his sense of his own worth as a man – he has done so irretrievably. Even this conclusion is, at least in part, confirmed by Marlow. At the end of Jim's long confession he too is obliged to say: 'He was guilty – as I had told myself repeatedly, guilty and done for' (p. 152). What divides Marlow and the lieutenant is not the truth of this statement, but its significance. For the lieutenant, it is the end of the

[1] Cf. p. 45.

story; for Marlow, it is only the beginning. In *Lord Jim* Conrad is not after all merely asking, 'What does this fixed ideal consist of?' but 'What status does it have in the affairs of men? What does it mean for it to exist in human life?'

For all his deficiencies in imaginative sympathy, the lieutenant is not intransigent out of abstract idealism, but out of its opposite – moral realism. He sees with the clarity of experience that the code has to be a fixed one because it must withstand the assault of the most powerful impulse of our nature: the instinct of self-preservation. The problem of courage and cowardice, therefore, can be interpreted in terms of the opposition between the code and this instinct. The lieutenant tells Marlow that true courage is not a matter of what one feels, or thinks, or intends, but of what one does. *How* one gets oneself to perform one's duty does not matter, as long as it is performed. If this is so, then there can be no disgrace in admitting one's fear. 'Man is born a coward.' For all its laconic simplicity, this fact has not been easily established. It is the realistic assessment of a man who has learnt the meaning of essential fear. But by facing his fear, he has been able to demythologize it – to scale it down to controllable proportions. When he is tested by danger, therefore, he does not have to rely on some improbable fit of heroism. Instead, he has at his disposal something at once more humble and more reliable: a technique of courage. 'But habit – habit – necessity – do you see? – the eye of others – *voilà*. One puts up with it. And then the example of others who are no better than yourself, and yet make good countenance ...' This deceptively unpretentious utterance is in fact – to quote Marlow – 'as full of valuable thoughts as an egg is with meat'. It implies that courage is not the product of operatic attitudes, but of 'necessity' – of having to do no more, but also no less, than one has to do; that it is not exhibited in the spectacular and isolated deed, but in 'habit' – the piecemeal, patient accumulation of small victories; that it is not achieved by a self-sufficient individual, but 'under the eye of others', and with their example in mind.

One cannot fail to notice here that the characteristic Conradian opposition between feeling and action merges into the equally characteristic contrast between individualism and solidarity. The reason for this is the nature of the code of conduct. It has, as Marlow recognizes, all the ambivalence of a convention – 'only one of the rules of the game, nothing more, but all the same so terribly effective by its assumption of unlimited power over natural instincts' (p. 81). From the point of view of individual survival, of course, the code cannot but seem an arbitrary and artificial constraint, wholly at the disposal of one's choice or will. But by virtue of its very conventionality, it is not the creation of the individual, but of the community, and therefore out of the individual's hands. That acts of courage can only be guaranteed 'in the ranks' (to use one of the novel's recurring phrases) is a perfectly consistent claim, for the code is essentially social, both in its origins (as the product of the community), and in its purposes (as the protector of the community). From this point of view, it is the code that is real ('honour ... that is real – that is!'), while the instinct of fear is nothing worse than 'one truth the more' that 'ought not to make life impossible'. In his intransigence, the French lieutenant cannot understand that there is more to human life than the demands of the code. But, however partial it may be, what he does see constitutes one of the two fundamental moral premises of the novel.

III

It is not in the degree, but in the nature, of his commitment to the code that Jim distinguishes himself from the lieutenant. Unlike many of the characters he comes to associate with, he does not have his being 'outside the law'; but he cannot be described as being squarely 'within the law' either. As the novel opens, he is discovered on a naval training-ship, acquiring a technical competence in the practice of his craft that will make him First Mate by the age of twenty-four (pp. 5–9). Yet what we can glimpse of his inner life reveals the insecurity of his professional foundations. As with all youths of his age, his dreams of adventure at sea must be unreal, for he can as yet have no first-hand experience of his future vocation; but he betrays an unusual incapacity to learn. The reason is that he regards the code not as something to be obeyed, but as something to be used. His concern is not with what it demands – steadiness in the face of danger – but with what it sometimes provides – glory at danger overcome. In effect, this means that he does not take danger seriously enough. A man whose profession regularly exposes him to danger will prepare himself against it by doing all he can to reduce the risk.[1] Far from trying to keep it at bay, however, Jim actually invites the idea of it, and in

---

[1] This point is tellingly developed in a thesis in philosophy for the University of London, 'The Nature of Morality' (now published under the title *Morality and the Self* (Blackwell, 1975)) by Michael Weston, who was kind enough to let me read a personal draft. He uses *Lord Jim* as his example throughout.

imagination regularly rehearses feats of audacity and daring. Instead of practising his drill or checking his equipment, he dreams of events in which he is always 'an example of devotion to duty and as unflinching as a hero in a book'. Since his commitment to the code is inspired by self-regarding emotion, it is not surprising that it should have a counter-productive effect. Far from strengthening him for service, it demoralizes him, for it blurs the distinction between intention and action, between wanting to do one's duty and actually doing it. In a word, it unfits him for reality.

Jim's habit of individualistic reverie ominously isolates him from his comrades, on whom he looks down (from the foretop of the mast) 'with the contempt of a man destined to shine in the midst of dangers'. And when the time comes, it is not they who are found wanting. A violent storm suddenly sweeps across the harbour and throws two men into serious difficulties. The cadets are summoned to launch the cutter. Rushing on to the deck from below, Jim is abruptly stopped by 'the brutal tumult of earth and sky', and loses his place in the life-boat. He is ignominiously condemned to watch his alleged inferiors rescue the two half-drowned sailors from the lashing water. Once the danger is over, however, he undergoes a complete change of mood. His original feeling of awe is replaced with a sense of the spuriousness of 'the menace of wind and seas', and he begins to find fault with *them* for 'checking unfairly a generous readiness for narrow escapes'.

It is not the elements that have played a treacherous part in this episode, but his imagination, which, having given him his vision of heroism, has also given him his vision of fear. In all essentials, indeed, his two imaginative acts are indistinguishable from each other. They are equally deceptive, in that what they anticipate (whether heroic rescue or death by drowning) is contradicted by the event; they are equally passive, in that they are incapable of lasting beyond the stimulus of their immediate cause (whether security or danger). Jim's imagination, ceasing to engage with reality, has started to spin freely. What he has done is to exchange his real self for an ideal self, and simultaneously to invent the mechanism required to safeguard it. Thus it is not his fear (the existence of which an ideal self cannot admit) that is responsible for his failure to act, but the trickery or malice of the weather. Instead of feeling guilty, he feels cheated. He persuades himself that failure is a better preparation for the heroic life than the 'paltry' success of his fellows. He concludes that 'he [has] enlarged his knowledge more than those who [have] done the work'. But what kind of

knowledge is it that depends on not doing the work? Jim seems to
be arguing on the premise that failure is like vaccination: a single
dose of emergency, so to speak, will immunize him against all
emergencies to come. But there can be no guarantee against surprise, for, by definition, that which is foreseeable can no longer be
surprising. When Jim complains to Marlow, after his disgrace,
that he has been preparing himself for years 'to face anything',
Marlow wryly retorts: 'It is always the unexpected that happens'
(p. 95). The kind of foresight that consists in trying to draw
unexpectedness out of the unexpected is nothing more than a
preparation for failure. Jim's eventual jump is no merely impulsive
mistake, but the result of a prolonged habit of self-deception.

One of the most striking insights of *Lord Jim* is the recognition
that heroic reverie is not essentially different from blind panic.
This point, introduced by the episode we have just examined, is
confirmed, a few chapters later, by the incidents immediately
preceding and following the disablement of the *Patna* (pp. 17–27).
As Jim is keeping watch on the quarter-deck in the marvellous
stillness of a tropical night, he falls under the spell of the perfect
beat of the steamer's advance through the water, and once again
gives himself up to those imaginary achievements that are his life's
'secret truth'. And they have their usual intoxicating effects: they
'carried his soul away and made it drunk with the divine philtre of
an unbounded confidence in itself'. This moment of abandonment
is interrupted by one of the squalid grotesques who make up the
ship's set of officers: the wizened second engineer, who, under the
influence of a more literal but scarcely less potent form of
intoxicant, has come up on deck to protest against the conditions of
his work. As if to underline this analogy, the little engineer suddenly launches out into what becomes a drunken parody of the
heroic dream. 'I don't know what fear is,' he boasts. 'I am not afraid
of doing all the bloomin' work in this rotten hooker, b'gosh! And a
jolly good thing for you that there are some of us about the world
that are not afraid of their lives ... Only I am one of them fearless
fellows – ' That very instant, the ship gives a jolt, the engineer is
flung to the deck, and Jim becomes aware of 'a faint noise as of
thunder, of thunder infinitely remote, less than a sound, hardly
more than a vibration.' The *Patna* is slowly dragging her entire
length over some submerged object. The emergency against which
Jim has been so assiduously preparing himself has struck from a
terrifyingly unexpected quarter. And instantly the serenely fault-
less sea and sky become 'formidably insecure in their immobility'.

The timing of this catastrophe is, of course, designed to suggest that the security it interrupts is as much an intoxication as the panic it provokes. This is further emphasized by what follows it (pp. 84–92). Sent down to the hold to inspect the damage, Jim sees the forward bulkhead bend with the weight of the ocean behind it and drop a large piece of rust to the deck in front of him. In a flash he foresees every detail of the coming horror, and at once becomes completely incapacitated. Later, he tells Marlow that at that moment he had decided (correctly, given his belief that the ship was about to founder) to cut the lifeboats. But what does he do in fact? As he returns to the deck, his head filled with images of 700 passengers struggling in the sea, he is interrupted by the father of a sick child, who clings to him 'like a drowning man' inexplicably demanding water. Jim, now utterly out of control, first flings his lamp into the man's face, then dashes into his cabin to fetch his water-flask, then, having parted with it, suddenly discovers how much in need of a drink he is himself: because he sees the passenger as an already drowning man, he himself reacts like a drowning man. When he returns to the deck he has forgotten about the life-boats; and it is only a good while later, when the ship gives its first nod to the swell announcing an approaching squall, that he awakens from his motionless trance and impulsively slashes the ropes. Even when he tries to act decisively, all he can do is betray the extent to which he has lost possession of himself.

Conrad's perception of the latent intoxication in Jim's condition, both before and after the disablement of the ship, gives some idea of what 'duty' is up against in its opposition to 'instinct'. If it is to be effective, confidence in the code has to be – almost literally – as unqualified as a reformed alcoholic's decision to keep off the bottle. Half measures are fatal: either commitment is absolute, or it is nothing. According to Marlow, even the shadow of mistrust in 'the sovereign power enthroned in a fixed standard of conduct ... is the hardest thing to stumble against; it is the thing that breeds yelling panics and good little quiet villainies; it's the true shadow of calamity' (pp. 50–1). That this is scarcely exaggerated is demonstrated by the fate of Brierly, the captain whom we have met as assessor at the Official Inquiry (pp. 56–65). His impeccable record makes him a natural choice for the task; throughout the proceedings he remains aloof and impassive; yet barely a week later, having rejoined his ship, he leaps overboard 'as though in that exact spot in the midst of waters he had suddenly perceived the gates of the other world flung open wide for his reception'. What makes his action even more inexplicable is the orderliness of his arrangements for his successor: even at the moment of supreme irresponsibility, he remains the model of the responsible officer. Is his conduct intelligible?

The clue to this puzzle will be found, here too, in the nature of the commitment the code demands. Brierly has been able to glide smoothly to the top of his profession, and is now serenely convinced of his infallibility. Jim's case, however, completely unnerves him. In the course of a chance conversation, Marlow discovers, to his astonishment, that he is so disturbed by his adjudication that he is ready to bribe Jim to disappear. Brierly's own explanation – that the publicity of the trial is damaging to the good name of 'gentlemen' abroad – is quite inadequate. It is not the crime that he finds intolerable, but the criminal's decision to face the consequences. The other officers of the *Patna* have already absconded; if Jim could be persuaded to join them, he would forgo all claims to the code, and cease to be a threat to those who live by the code. For Marlow, Jim's readiness to submit himself to the Inquiry is the one 'redeeming feature in his abominable case'; for Brierly, however, 'such an affair destroys one's confidence'. To Marlow, who has no illusions about his own nature, Jim's lapse has nothing new to tell. To Brierly, on the other hand, who has lived on an assumption of innate integrity, it becomes one of those 'small things ... by which some of us are totally and completely undone'. Publicly, the man on the bench appears to be, in every essential respect, the opposite of the man in the dock. But secretly he has begun to suspect, for the first time in his life, that he may be harbouring a potential criminal within his bosom. The mere thought of possible failure (which, for the French Lieutenant, is the basis of morality) is intolerable. The very success of his adherence to the code has rendered him incapable of facing his own vulnerability. Whereas Jim is undone by the accomplished fact (his jump), Brierly is destroyed by its mere prospect. Nothing in the novel illustrates with greater irony the code's terrible inflexibility.

IV

Although both men's commitment to the code is similarly flawed (in Jim the code has encouraged the dream of heroism, in Brierly the assumption of rectitude), Jim's weakness demands its own appropriate nemesis. He has imagined himself the hero of an epic romance: the *Patna* emergency will force him to participate in a squalid farce. One of the reasons why Conrad, early in the novel, exchanges omniscient narrative for a system of reports is that this enables him to exploit Jim's retrospective sense of having been the dupe of what he calls 'a joke hatched in hell'. To be sure, the accident itself already has, in its combination of the freakish and the deadly, an element of the bizarre about it. But its full preposterousness is only revealed when Jim discovers that the *Patna*'s passengers have survived, and that the event that has stripped him of his honour was, all along, an opportunity for glory easy beyond his wildest dreams.

Jim's self-esteem is firmly set in a context of black comedy generated largely out of the antics of self-preservation – specifically, the frenzied clownings of his fellow-officers (pp. 101–11). As in the case of the second engineer, their fear is, quite literally, a form of alcoholism. The elephantine bully of a captain, whose speech is like the gush of a sewer, has a capacity for beer that disgusts even the publican whose fortune he is making. The first engineer is a straight alcoholic who tries to obliterate his recent experience in a three-day session of uninterrupted drinking. (Incidentally, Marlow's visit to him in hospital after an attack of D.T.'s provides another hilarious parody of Jim's nightmare vision of the pilgrims swarming all over the sinking ship. Marlow reports the first engineer's gibberings: 'Millions of pink toads ... as big as mastiffs ... the ship was full of them ... You don't believe me, I suppose ... Look under the bed.' Marlow responds.

Of course I stooped instantly ...
  'What can you see?' he asked.
  'Nothing,' I said, feeling awfully ashamed of myself.)

At the first whiff of danger they become intoxicated with terror. Instinct manipulates them like puppets: in their haste to launch the life-boat they dance and gesticulate, they fall over themselves, they get into each other's way, and they jam the mechanism. Jim watches them with an apparently detached immobility; but inwardly he seethes with loathing. 'In this assault upon his fortitude, there was the jeering intention of a spiteful and vile vengeance: there was an element of burlesque in his ordeal – a degradation of funny grimaces in the approach of death or dishonour.' The very intensity of his reaction shows that he is beginning to sense the pull towards his decamping comrades. The heroic ideal is steadily approaching the sordid fact; the shining knight is beginning to dance to the tune of the doss-house. Retrospectively,

Jim will loftily disclaim any kinship with 'these men', despite the fact that he has chosen to work by their side. But kinship is precisely what this disclaimer affirms. Whatever his avowed intentions, by disdaining to fight 'in the ranks' he has elected to associate himself with those who exist outside the ranks.

That Jim is as panic-stricken as the men from whom he insists on being distinguished is revealed by his account of his last moments on board. What he decides to do is instantly contradicted by what he does do. Having taken a firm decision to keep his eyes shut, he sees one of the four men – the so-called donkey-man, 'a white-faced chap with a ragged moustache' – step back, clutch the air, and slide into a sitting posture; at the same moment the life-boat in which the other three have been dementedly struggling suddenly drops heavily into the water. Again, having taken a firm decision to remain motionless, Jim stumbles over the legs of the prostrate man. He has heard the sound of an approaching squall and unconsciously started to move towards the rails. From the life-boat below the three men, 'as if crying up a shaft', call repeatedly after their missing comrade. A sudden gust of rain sweeps over the deck. '"I had jumped ..." He checked himself, averted his gaze ... "It seems," he added.' In the disarray of its tenses (the sudden pluperfect suggests that the event has become historical without having actually taken place) this final admission nicely enacts the discomposure of a man trying to deny the undeniable. 'The infernal joke', Marlow remarks, 'was being crammed devilishly down his throat, but – look you – he was not going to admit of any sort of swallowing motion in his gullet.' And a moment later he adds: 'I listened to a tale of black magic at work upon a corpse.' If instinct has transformed Jim's companions into puppets, it has metamorphosed *him* into – to be exact – a voodoo zombie.

However, the full hellishness of the 'joke' is not yet apparent. The donkey-man, whose name is George, has collapsed and died of a stroke. When, in due course, Jim learns of this he at once claims him as a fellow-victim – a dupe fooled by the villainous trio into killing himself unnecessarily, just as he – Jim – has causelessly been tricked of his honour. What is significant about this reaction is not the fact that it is erroneous – the captain is no more responsible for the collapse of the one than for the disgrace of the other – but that it is naïve. For example, Jim misses what Marlow spots at once – that in shouting for their absent comrade, the three men 'were yelling after the one dead man' (out of the 800 living people on board!) 'to come down and be saved'. Moreover, Jim is blind to at least three real analogies between himself and the dead man. First, by obeying the repeated calls for 'George' as if George were his own name, Jim has taken over, as it were, the identity of a member of the despised gang, and ended up – in every sense of the phrase – 'in the same boat'. Second, by substituting himself for a corpse, he has unwittingly anticipated his future (posthumous) existence as a social outcast. And third, by leaping into what he calls 'an everlasting deep hole', he unwittingly implies that he has performed an action as irreversible as that which has brought George to the resting-place he now occupies. Jim's fate is now plain: the harder he struggles against the ironies into which he has entangled himself, the less he is able to deny their existence. Commenting on his apparent refusal to acknowledge responsibility for what he has done, Marlow says: 'You had to listen to him as you would to a small boy in trouble. He didn't know. It had happened somehow. *It would never happen again.*'[My italics.] This last phrase is in its innocence doubly ironical, for it betrays both the cause and the consequence of Jim's jump. The very glibness of the promise of good conduct tells us why the jump has been possible at all; and at the same time we are made to see that it won't happen twice, not because Jim has decided it won't, but because it can't. In brief, the harder Jim tries to preserve the part of the hero, the more he plays the role of the clown.

V

If the enactment of Jim's disgrace gives rise to a kind of black comedy, it is not only because of surface absurdities, but on account of a radical incongruity. This incongruity, generally diffused over the entire episode, is finally revealed by the jump itself, which is the point of collision between Jim's ideal self, expressed in what he intends, and his real self, embodied in what he does. Up to the point of Jim's disgrace, his self-idealization has been treated as a fatal flaw, first inhibiting him, then preventing him, from doing his duty. But now that he has irremediably fallen from his imaginary height, his refusal to relinquish the dream of honour acquires, *pace* the lieutenant, an altogether more positive force. As in 'Heart of Darkness' there are two incompatible orders of reality in *Lord Jim*. This is the reason why, in the first part of the novel, Conrad feels the need not for one, but two inquiries. The first, or Official Inquiry, is set up to determine the publicly verifiable facts, and can only bear, therefore, on what Jim has actually done. But Conrad,

as I have suggested, is not simply concerned with the betrayal of
the code; he is also concerned with the meaning of that betrayal in
the context of human life at large. This is a consideration quite
outside the competence of an official assessor, whose questions,
necessary in a court of law, are inevitably, in the wider perspective,
'as instructive as the tapping of a hammer on an iron box, were the
object to find out what's inside' (p. 56). Hence Conrad resorts to
another, unofficial, inquiry – that of Marlow's conversation with
Jim during the evening of the second day of the trial. Jim's elaborate confession – for that is what the conversation turns out to be –
exhibits, with a consummate consistency and subtlety, 'the
struggles of an individual trying to save from the fire his idea of
what his moral identity should be' (p. 81). In other words, the
second inquiry is concerned with trying to establish whether anything survives the verdict of the facts. Moreover, this second
inquiry, if it is to produce a reliable result, cannot be without some
standards of verification. Marlow recognizes that a man left to
himself never 'understands quite his own artful dodges to escape
from the grim shadow of self-knowledge' (p. 80). His participation
is therefore more than a device for avoiding the unreality or tedium
of an inner monologue: a competent second person is necessary to
ensure that Jim's debate with himself does not degenerate into
mere self-justification. As Marlow watches Jim oscillate between
the claims of honour and of instinct, and he is made to look 'at the
convention that lurks in all truth and on the essential sincerity of
falsehood' (p. 93), he does indeed find himself repeatedly having to
resist pressure to condone Jim's conduct. For example, Jim tries to
excuse his start of fear with a direct appeal to Marlow: 'Leap! By
heavens! you would take one spring from where you sit and land in
that clump of bushes yonder.' Marlow makes no overt response, for
he feels that he is being 'bullied'. But his private reflection, poin-
tedly literal as it is, neatly disposes of Jim's rhetoric: 'I don't mind
telling you that I did, with a rapid glance, estimate the distance . . .
He exaggerated. I would have landed short by several feet' (p.
107). Part of Marlow's function in the unofficial inquiry is to
reaffirm, when necessary, the claims of moral realism.

But there is a more fundamental reason why Jim's subjectivity
requires Marlow's objectivity. Jim's confession consists of an ultimately hopeless struggle to overcome what is, in the largest
perspective, an opposition between the inner and the outer, or the
private and the public. He can make his problem disappear, of
course, by deciding that the claims of one or the other side are

illusory. To relinquish the rights of his inner self, for example, in favour of the verdict of the court is to accept that he is nothing more than the sum of his actions – that is, a cowardly knave indistinguishable from his fellow-officers on the *Patna*. But his interest for Marlow lies in his refusal to admit defeat – his refusal, in the very teeth of the evidence, to accept that his inner dreams and purposes are merely evasions and lies. Faced with this stand, Marlow has to decide whether to take it seriously or to dismiss it as specious. Throughout the confession he remains in two minds: as a man able to recall the ardours and illusions of his own youth, he is sympathetic; as an experienced master-mariner he remains sceptical. One point, however, remains quite clear. Jim has no choice but to try to persuade Marlow of the validity of his attitude, if he is to continue to believe honestly in it himself. 'It is certain any conviction gains infinitely the moment another soul will believe in it.' Conrad's favourite sentence from Novalis, which he has placed as epigraph at the head of the novel, has the most direct application to Jim's dilemma. He needs the corroboration of another soul because the only evidence of his own worth he has left to offer is his own private conviction of it.

What Marlow thinks of Jim, therefore, is not of merely incidental or contingent importance. Unlike the lieutenant's, his attitude is essentially ambiguous. This ambiguity is defined by the two phrases which he applies to Jim with the regularity of *leitmotifs* throughout his narrative: Jim is 'under a cloud', but he is also 'one of us'. His use of these phrases is demonstrated by his very first sight of Jim. The young man's vigorous physique, clear-cut, dogged look, and immaculate bearing seem to declare him 'one of us' – a member of the community that lives by the code. But Marlow knows what he has done; and from that point of view, he is 'under a cloud' – not only in the primary sense that he is in disgrace, but also with the implication that what he *really* is can no longer be perceived. For twenty-four hours, Marlow is puzzled: can this impressive-looking young officer be a mere fraud? At his second encounter with Jim, the ambiguity is developed a stage further. As an early session of the Official Inquiry closes and the crowd comes out into the forecourt, one of Marlow's acquaintances, noticing a stray mongrel, exclaims: 'Look at that wretched cur.' Jim, who is within earshot, spins round and, assuming that Marlow is the speaker, demands an explanation. He is obviously in a state of extreme anger, but Marlow, who hasn't yet made the connection that Jim's over-sensitivity has taken for granted, is unable to provide the required apology. He gradually gathers that Jim feels his disgrace is being taken advantage of, but he remains utterly baffled until Jim throws out: 'Who's a cur now – hey?'

There may be those who could have laughed at his pertinacity. I didn't. Oh, I didn't! There had never been a man so mercilessly shown up by his own natural impulse. A single word had stripped him of his discretion – of that discretion which is more necessary to the decencies of our inner being than clothing is to the decorum of our body. 'Don't be a fool,' I repeated. 'But the other man said it, you don't deny that?' he pronounced, distinctly, and looking in my face without flinching. 'No, I don't deny,' said I, returning his gaze. At last his eyes followed downwards the direction of my pointing finger. He appeared at first uncomprehending, then confounded, and at last amazed and scared as though a dog had been a monster and he had never seen a dog before. 'Nobody dreamt of insulting you,' I said.

He contemplated the wretched animal, that moved no more than an effigy: it sat with ears pricked and its sharp muzzle pointed into the doorway, and suddenly snapped at a fly like a piece of mechanism.

Lord Jim, p. 74

The whole incident is a brilliantly imagined treatment of the psychology of mortification. Jim is in a state of self-protective tension: he has proved himself a coward, but will not permit the world to insult him with impunity. The passage demonstrates, of course, that to be on the defensive is to confess one's culpability. The most resolute of Jim's attempts to safeguard his pride produces the most abject of his humiliations. In trying to protect his privacy from the indiscretions of the public gaze he produces a self-revealing reflex more odious than the mongrel's snapping at a fly. In fact (to use the terms that the passage suggests) what he does is to transform the very dog with which he could not bear to be identified into a symbol of his own condition.

But this incident produces yet another reversal. Jim has tried to challenge the world, and has only succeeded in delivering himself into its hands. But now he makes the further discovery that in thus capitulating to the enemy he has gained a friend. Without quite knowing why, when Marlow had found himself face to face with the desperately aggressive young man, he had felt induced 'to make all possible allowances for him'. Now that the full enormity of the indiscretion stands revealed, compassion deepens into understanding. He perceives that along with Jim's callowness and immaturity there exists a scalding consciousness of his disgrace – in other words, that if he has betrayed the code it is not because he has not felt its importance. It is no longer the uprightness of his looks that creates the puzzle, but something more serious – the intensity of his suffering. On the strength of what this incident has revealed, Marlow persuades Jim to join him for dinner at his hotel. They spend four or five hours together, in the course of which Marlow finds repeated confirmation that Jim 'did not try to minimize [the] importance' of the appalling discovery that he has made about himself. Jim's capacity for registering the moral consequences of his actions is thrown into sharp relief by the setting in which what I have called the 'unofficial inquiry' takes place. Tony Tanner has pointed out[1] that as Jim relives, detail by detail, the agony of his failure, he is surrounded by all the trivial complacencies of a hotel dinner: the tinkle of the crockery, the deferential movement of waiters, and especially the random chatter of the guests – globe-trotting tourists who have set out to see the world but 'preserve the gummed tickets on their portmanteaus . . . as the only permanent trace of their improving enterprise'. In contrast to these comfortable beings – the 'neutrals' to whom even hell is forbidden by Dante – Jim's suffering is indeed a mark of distinction. His leap, disastrous as it is, has taken him into reality.

His conversation with Jim, therefore, teaches Marlow that there is no easy way out of the dilemma in which the young man has put him. The seven wonderful chapters that Conrad devotes to Jim's 'contradictory indiscretions' (is he concerned with his 'guilt' or with his 'disgrace'? – with what he has lost or with what he has failed to obtain?) sustain a masterly exploration of moral ambiguity. And at the end of it Marlow is persuaded that there is more to a man than the sum of his deeds: that 'we are snared into doing things for which we get called names, and things for which we get hanged, and yet the spirit may well survive – survive the condemnations, survive the halter' (p. 43). The question is, what sense to give to the word 'spirit', and what force to the idea of its 'survival'. The answer, for Marlow at least, takes a negative form: that the realist account (as I have called it) of human action is not mistaken, but inadequate. How the interplay between Marlow and Jim allows this to emerge, almost any episode will illustrate. For example, as his confession draws to an end, Jim describes how his three colleagues and himself wait in an open boat to be picked up

---

[1] Tony Tanner, *Conrad: 'Lord Jim'*, Studies in English Literature 12 (Arnold, 1963), p. 28. Tanner's monograph is steadily illuminating, but particularly in its treatment of the recurring symbols of butterfly and beetle. Two other very useful essays: Dorothy van Ghent, 'On *Lord Jim*' in *The English Novel: Form and Function* (New York, 1961); and, for readers of French, Jean Deurbergue: 'Lord Jim, Roman du Nebuleux?' in *Études Anglaises*, xxv (1972), 147–61.

and, in serene ignorance of the *Patna*'s survival, concoct a story to explain their plight (pp. 133–4). Jim claims to disapprove, but he does not contradict the tale – not even when they brazenly repeat it to their rescuers. Hearing this, Marlow decides that Jim is conclusively damned: how can one credit the good faith of a man who will only stop acquiescing in lies *after* the lies have been exposed? Yet even here Jim manages to turn the tables. For him, failure to speak up is not proof of insincerity. Quite the contrary: he kept silent not because his jump did not matter, but because it mattered too much. 'I had jumped – hadn't I? ... That's what I had to live down. The story didn't matter ... It was like cheating the dead ... Dead or not dead, I could not get clear.' What *is* Marlow to believe? It is hardly surprising that when he is asked pointblank to commit himself he is suddenly overcome by 'a profound and hopeless fatigue'. Is Jim to be taken seriously? No, for he is constantly trying to find excuses for what he has done. But we know that the only lapses that are easy to accept are the unimportant ones. Isn't, therefore, such casting about for excuses proof that the guilt is intolerable? If the spirit survives, it is because such questions obstinately refuse to disappear, despite all the efforts of the moral realists to make them do so.

Although neither Jim nor Marlow is able to settle these ambiguities, their conversation concludes with an incident that crystallizes the issue between them (pp. 152–5). Exhausted by having had for so long to keep balance between sympathy and judgement, Marlow experiences a reflex of revulsion. Suddenly it seems to him that the difficulty has vanished: Jim is the guilty party, he – Marlow – the 'irreproachable man'. For the first time he feels free to indulge in a patronizing gesture. If all there is to Jim is the fact that he is guilty, why return to the court room? Why expose himself to 'the mere detail of a formal execution?' He permits himself, therefore, to do what Brierly had only thought of doing: he offers Jim money. But Jim, instantly recognizing the speciousness of the gesture, checks Marlow with the words: 'But after all, it is *my* trouble.' Marlow replies that better men than he have found it expedient to run. 'Perhaps so', Jim retorts, 'I am not good enough; I can't afford it.' This is unanswerable. Marlow cannot deny that Jim is indeed caught in a diabolical contradiction. The only means left him of proclaiming his honour is to submit himself to the court that will strip him of honour. The only way he can retain his status as 'one of us' is by facing the judgement that will expel him from the ranks. The cloud of uncertainty that has been hanging over him has dissolved, if at all, only into the definiteness of stark paradox. Jim takes his leave: the long evening is over. To Marlow's straining ears, however, his very footsteps, as they recede into the night, are an enactment of his fate. 'He was running. Absolutely running with nowhere to go to.'

VI

Jim's tragedy grows out of the fact that he can only discover the meaning of the code to which he has committed himself by breaking it. Hence he becomes caught in a vicious circle. The more he values lost honour, the more he regrets its loss; the greater his regret, the greater his valuation. This cycle must inevitably accelerate towards a conclusion in which, honour having acquired an absolute importance, its forfeiture becomes absolutely irretrievable. His is clearly a terminal case. This being so, why does Conrad feel the need to prolong his novel by another 200 pages? Once you establish a mechanism, it can only repeat itself. Why then send Jim to Patusan? Conrad himself, in later years, refused to allow *Lord Jim* to be considered his best work on the grounds of 'its great length which the story itself does not justify'.[1] And subsequently critics have written on the book as if the work of the first part had been so well done that there was nothing left for the second part but to become, as it were, parasitic upon it.

Yet, whatever our reservations about the quality of the Patusan episodes – in particular, about the degree to which the characters, and especially Jewel, are made real to us – it remains very difficult to see how Conrad could have truncated the novel at the point of Jim's 'execution' by the Court of Inquiry. Jim's readiness to face his judges makes a claim in favour of the inner life that has scarcely been explored out. The cancellation of his certificate is an execution of his public self, for it deprives him of his role in society. Jim himself recognizes, as he stands in the dock, that the 'facts' to which he can be no other than a truthful witness 'cut him off from the rest of his kind', for (as Marlow reminds us) 'the real significance of a crime is in its being a breach of faith with the community of mankind'. As a man guilty of 'a more than criminal weakness', therefore, Jim is branded with the mark of the original fratricide; he becomes an outcast, a redundant being with nothing to do and nowhere to go to. Yet no sooner is the justice of this sentence established than we are forcibly reminded of its inade-

[1] Baines, *Joseph Conrad*, p. 294.

quacy (pp. 161–9).As Marlow leaves the court-room for the last time, he meets an Australian adventurer called Chester – one of those swashbuckling desperadoes occasionally encountered in Eastern seaports, who 'live in a crazy maze of plans . . . in the dark places of the sea', and whose death is 'the only event of their fantastic existence' that seems to have 'a reasonable certitude of achievement'. This man's current project is a senseless expedition to a remote Pacific island apparently covered in guano. When, in the course of a guarded exchange, Chester learns that Jim has taken the verdict 'very much to heart', he becomes loftily contemptuous: 'What's all the to-do about? You must see things exactly as they are – if you don't you may just as well give in at once.' Chester claims to be a realist on the grounds that he can see through the pretences of morality. In affirming that moral obligation has no real existence, he is, of course, proposing a realism very different from the French lieutenant's. But it does not represent a viable alternative, for it rests on the assumption that ethics and efficiency are wholly unrelated to each other. Marlow is forced to describe this 'realist' as 'a strange idealist', for, by repudiating the code, he repudiates something that exists not only because it is 'good' but because it is 'necessary'. So when we find him endorsing (though for the opposite reason) the official declaration of Jim's uselessness, we begin to wonder whether Jim's case is indeed closed. And this feeling is strengthened when Chester, having identified Jim as 'being no earthly good for anything', finds him fit for the desperately impracticable – that is, 'idealistic' – task he has in hand: taking charge of a shadowless rock in the Walpole Reef, 'up to his knees in guano, with the screams of sea birds in his ears, the incandescent ball of the sun above his head'. If a man is nothing but his deeds, and if his deeds expel him from human society, then this vision of hell is the logical conclusion of Jim's career. But Jim is no Chester; his expulsion from the ranks does not transform him into a gangster. Chester's appearance at this point in the novel illustrates the difference between the outsider who ignores, and the one who acknowledges, the code that condemns them both. As far as Marlow is concerned, his encounter with Chester finally tips the scales in favour of Jim's faith in himself. When Jim eventually makes his way to Marlow's room, he hears Marlow say to him: 'I make myself unreservedly responsible for you.' Not only does this assurance – almost a formal adoption – save Jim from starvation – 'of that peculiar sort that is almost invariably associated with drink'; but, as an unsolicited declaration of faith, it makes it possible for him to retain some shadow of self-respect. Moreover, it marks a small but significant alteration in Marlow's role. Up to this point, Marlow has been sceptical of Jim's dream, hence his interest in him has been governed by the question, 'Is he self-deceived?' Henceforward, he becomes afraid of what threatens this dream, and so his question becomes, 'Can he survive?'

I have argued that the first part of the novel has been concerned with establishing the truth revealed by conduct. This being so, the second part is concerned with exploring, under the sponsorship of the German merchant Stein, the truth inherent in vision. In despair of Jim's ever adapting himself to his notoriety, Marlow decides, in much the same way as he had consulted the lieutenant, to seek Stein's advice (pp. 202–17). This new counsellor is the antithesis of the former one. An original participant in the 1848 German revolution, thereafter soldier and adventurer in the Far East, and finally successful trader and entomologist settled abroad, Stein is a cultivated individualist whose experience of life on land has been both extensive and profound. Yet despite their differences, these men share at least two major common factors in their relationship to Jim. First of all, the lieutenant was qualified to comment on Jim's case not only by virtue of his commitment to the code, but also because of his ability – in contrast to Jim – to bring the *Patna* to safety. Analogously, Stein's competence is established by his commitment to the dream and his capacity to seize his opportunity when it presents itself: he relates to Marlow a youthful adventure in which – again in contrast to Jim's failure to take advantage of the *Patna* emergency – he successfully resisted an ambush and captured a rare butterfly. And, as a second parallel between the two 'counsellors', just as, for all his 'extreme efficiency', the lieutenant's verdict is itself found wanting, so Stein's recommendation, despite his being 'one of the most trustworthy men' Marlow has ever known, does not remain unqualified.

Stein's actual advice to Marlow constitutes the most famous crux of the novel. It has, unfortunately, so often been discussed out of context that it is now difficult to recapture its original effect. Stein rises from his desk, where he has been cataloguing specimens, and takes his finest butterfly back to its case in a shadowy part of the room. Marlow is struck by the fact that he seems to merge into the 'shapeless dusk ... as if these few steps had carried him out of this concrete and perplexed world'. From this vantage ground Stein's voice carries with authority and confidence.

The shadow prowling amongst the graves of butterflies laughed bois-
terously.

'Yes! Very funny this terrible thing is. A man that is born falls into a
dream like a man who falls into the sea. If he tries to climb out into the air
as inexperienced people endeavour to do, he drowns – *nicht wahr?* . . . No! I
tell you! The way is to the destructive element submit yourself, and with
the exertions of your hands and feet in the water make the deep, deep sea
keep you up. So if you ask me – how to be?'

His voice leaped up extraordinarily strong, as though away there in the
dusk he had been inspired by some whisper of knowledge.

Lord Jim, p. 214

The terrible thing that Stein finds so incongruous is, of course, the
irreconcilability of man's aspiration and power. Unlike such flaw-
less creations of Nature as the butterfly, man, though he may be
'amazing', is not 'a masterpiece': in his case perhaps, 'the artist
was a little mad'. And since the complaint from which man suffers
is innate, Stein draws the obvious conclusion: death is the only
cure. To this Marlow replies, not without a touch of malice,
'Strictly speaking, the question is not how to get cured, but how to
live.' Stein approves: '*Ja!ja!* In general, adapting the words of your
great poet: That is the question . . . How to be! Ach! How to be!' For
Stein, as for Hamlet (at least in the nineteenth-century reading),
the problem of life is the problem of consciousness. If man is
flawed, it is because he can think. As a thinking animal, he is
incapable of the indifferent perfection of a butterfly on its 'little
heap of dirt'; he cannot help recoiling from the squalor and yearn-
ing for the beauty. And so, if 'every time he shuts his eyes he sees
himself as a very fine fellow – so fine as he can never be', this
represents an impulse which, being a part of the very conditions of
human existence, man has no hope of evading. Stein concludes,
therefore, that, whatever its falsity, man must boldly entrust himself to his dream.

There are, it seems to me, two main reasons why this recommendation has proved so controversial. The first is that Stein
dislocates our normal sense of the relationship between living and
dreaming. We tend to think of life as 'below' and of the dream as
'above', so that the dreamer, in aspiring towards the stars, seems to
us to rise unnaturally out of his native element. Stein, however,
concerned not so much with the dream as goal as with the dream as
activity, and finding this activity as fundamental as life itself,
assumes a perfect identification between the two: man is born into
a dream by virtue of being born into life. But since to dream is to be

dissatisfied with life, it follows that to be cast into life is to find oneself in an alien, or unnatural, or even destructive element. To suggest, as some have done, that Conrad is thinking of man as some sort of 'flying fish' is to miss the point. We have a *natural* reluctance to commit ourselves to the water. That is to say, we are creatures slightly out of phase with the Nature that has created us. Stein's metaphor defines, with unusual precision, man's fallen or flawed condition. Moreover, it has illuminating implications. Since man is a dreaming animal, any attempt to renounce the dream is as likely to be fatal as an attempt to climb out of the sea. This is borne out in the novel by a whole procession of characters (from the *Patna* captain and Chester to Cornelius and Gentleman Brown) whose entire endeavour is to 'climb out' of ideality altogether. Their very denials of aspiration are an affirmation of it. Far from becoming indifferent to the dream, they become obsessed with it. Beetles made to feel ugly by the existence of butterflies (to refer to the novel's most consistent symbols), they are without exception incensed by Jim's refusal to give up *his* dream. However, their endeavour to live as if their dream could be dispensed with proves self-destructive: the fat captain vanishes into thin air, Chester is swallowed up in a Pacific tornado, Brown is consumed in a furnace of hatred and disease.

The second reason why Stein's declaration has been found puzzling is that it is only partly endorsed by the novel as a whole. As a diagnosis, it is accurate. As a prescription, it is much less reliable. The conviction that man, finding himself afloat in the dream, should not drift or struggle but swim – that is, allow his vision to inspire appropriate practical action – falters as soon as Stein reappears into the circle of lamplight.

The austere exaltation of a certitude seen in the dusk vanished from his face. The hand that had been pointing at my breast fell, and by-and-by, coming a step nearer, he laid it gently on my shoulder. There were things, he said mournfully, that perhaps could never be told, only he had lived so much alone that sometimes he forgot – he forgot. The light had destroyed the assurance which had inspired him in the distant shadows. He sat down and, with both elbows on the desk, rubbed his forehead. 'And yet it is true – it is true. In the destructive element immerse.' . . . He spoke in a subdued tone, without looking at me, one hand on each side of his face. 'That was the way. To follow the dream, and again to follow the dream – and so – *ewig – usque ad finem* . . .' The whisper of his conviction seemed to open before me a vast and uncertain expanse, as of a crepuscular horizon on a plain at dawn – or was it, perchance, at the coming of night? One had not the courage to decide; but it was a charming and deceptive light, throwing the impalpable poesy of its dimness over pitfalls – over graves . . . When at last I broke the silence it was to express the opinion that no one could be more romantic than himself.

Lord Jim, pp. 214–15

In relation to Marlow's response to him, Stein becomes almost as ambiguous as the French lieutenant. The lieutenant's verdict was qualified by the reality of Jim's anguish; Stein's precept – as the imagery of the passage suggests – is unable to survive the light of day intact. I am not trying to suggest that Stein is a naïve optimist. He has it over the lieutenant in that he is conscious of the antithetical truth, and tries to take account of it. But his attempt to reconcile reality and the dream, as he half suspects himself, is doomed to fail. The complaint Jim suffers from is incurable: the remedy offered is itself a dream.

What Stein has been trying to do is to provide a context within which Jim's last hope – his ideal conception of himself – may find some kind of justification. The sanctions of a common code of conduct have left Jim marooned within himself. Perhaps he can be rescued by a different ethic – one warranted not by the authority of external imperatives but by the force of individual vision. This constitutes the second of the two moral premises on which the novel is based. The *saving dream* that Stein urges is a variant of the *positive illusion* encountered at the end of 'Heart of Darkness'. But what can work for a Stein who has withstood the terrors of an emergency, or for a Marlow who has resisted the challenge of the wilderness, can be of little help to a man whose leap into dishonour has once and for all divided him against himself. Illusion is not delusion: living on the assumption that the ideal is not contradicted by the real (as Stein and Marlow still can) is not the same as living on this assumption when the facts (as in Jim's case) declare it to be false. To send Jim to Patusan, as Stein proceeds to do, can only, at best, earn him a limited remission.

VII

Critics like Tony Tanner who have thought of Stein as a new Merlin or a second Prospero[1] have made the further assumption that Patusan is some kind of allegorical province or magic island representing a higher reality than our 'concrete and perplexed

[1] Tanner, *Conrad: 'Lord Jim'*, pp. 43–4.

world'. The miraculous assurance with which Jim seizes his 'second chance' seems at first to confirm the claim that he has moved into an area in which the gap between aspiration and fulfilment has vanished. Protected by nothing but Stein's ring – a credential for the chieftain Doramin, Stein's former comrade-at-arms – Jim assumes Stein's succession and, following in his footsteps, makes a fairy-tale conquest of love ('Jewel', the beautiful step-daughter of the degenerate Cornelius, who parallels Stein's 'Princess'), of friendship (Dain Waris, Doramin's noble-minded son, who duplicates Stein's Mohammed Bonzo), and above all of honour (as a pacifier and justicer of an entire community he overtakes even Stein's chivalrous achievements). Moreover this conquest of his ideal self is accomplished through a step-by-step re-enactment of his original failure (pp. 249–55). It begins with a second leap – this time not over a ship's rail but over a stockade within which the Patusanians have confined him. He lands up to his waist in the mud of the river – as he fell into the defilement of the fugitives' company; he momentarily loses consciousness – as he lost power of action; he drags himself out of the slime – as he forced himself to face the consequences of his deed; he runs through the village disguised in filth – as he endured the odium of his coward's name; he casts himself at the mercy of Doramin, a man like a bull-elephant – as he tried to rely on the captain of the *Patna*, a man like a 'trained baby elephant'. But in the re-enactment, of course, the outcome is systematically reversed. Almost every detail of the Patusan episodes that might have seemed capricious or arbitrary can be justified in terms of its relationship to the events of the novel's first part. Furthermore, Jim is not merely rewriting his past as a success story; he is also reshaping Stein's past into his own present. When – to refer to only one of his exploits – he is attacked one night by four Malays (pp. 295–304), he stage-manages a new version of his dealings with the officers of the *Patna* (where he had felt himself betrayed by three fugitives and a corpse, now he kills one of his assailants and forces the others to jump into the river); but this is also a re-enactment of Stein's daring dispersal of the ambush against him on the morning of his capture of the symbolic butterfly.

Yet it would be a mistake to conclude that by going to Patusan Jim leaves reality behind him. Patusan is not essentially different from the great world: it is merely cut off from it. It is only because the Patusanians have no knowledge of his past that Jim is able to act as if his debt had been miraculously remitted. But Patusan can be visited by members of the outside world: in the past, by Stein; now, by Jim; soon, by Marlow; in due course, by Brown. Hence we know that even in his new refuge Jim will find it impossible to transcend his fate: we cannot be persuaded that his attempt to give substance to his dream will succeed, or that the edifice of his glory will not prove to be a castle in the air. Moreover, our sense of impending catastrophe reflects adversely on the lasting worth of his achievements in Patusan. Marlow, who visits him at the height of his power, feels uneasily that his success has turned into a kind of imprisonment, and that his triumph has bound him in 'the fetters of his strange freedom'. Marlow has discovered, for example, that Jim's love for 'Jewel' has not brought her happiness. He notices that the prolonged agony of her mother's relationship with Cornelius has infected the daughter with the conviction that all men are equally unreliable – that Jim must sooner or later forsake her for the world from which he has come. In his last harrowing conversation with her (pp. 309–19; significantly, it takes place within sight of her mother's moonlit grave – a setting that ominously recalls the vistas evoked by Stein's ambivalent propositions), Marlow tries to persuade her that Jim is to be trusted, but he only succeeds in discrediting himself in her eyes. By resorting to what he takes to be a conclusive argument – that the reason why there can be no life for Jim outside Patusan is that 'he is not good enough' – he convinces her that he – Marlow – is completely disingenuous: how can she believe that the truth of her irreproachable knight is guaranteed by his falsity?

Despite his magnificent fidelity to the natives of Patusan (the converse of his betrayal of the pilgrims of the *Patna*), Jim remains an outsider – a 'romantic' drawing inspiration from himself, not from the community he loves with what Marlow calls 'a sort of fierce egoism'. It is appropriate that he should become known as 'Tuan' Jim, for that title, attached to his personal rather than his family name (we never learn what that is: he remains an essentially private individual to the last), reflects the individualism that inspires his conduct. It is equally appropriate that the dénouement should be initiated by a confrontation between 'Lord' Jim and 'Gentleman' Brown – the rabid aristocrat who crowns the sequence of grotesque individualists from whom Jim has tried to differentiate himself throughout his career. As they face each other on the very spot from which Jim had launched himself into his second chance, they seem to be 'standing on the opposite poles of that conception of life which includes all mankind' (p. 381). They are indeed opposites, in that one stands for honour, the other for instinct; but they are also part of a single conception of life, in that both have chosen to live outside the ranks. The 'butterfly' and the 'beetle' are held in a mutual interdependence of antagonism, the butterfly being driven by fear that he may be a beetle (in what he does), the beetle by fury that he may not be a butterfly (in what he is). Consider Jim's culminating decision, at once Quixotic and fatal, to let Brown go free. For Dain Waris, who is neither 'butterfly' nor 'beetle', the only way of safeguarding the community from gangsters like Brown is to exterminate them. In comparison, Jim's decision to trust Brown may seem the nobler alternative. Yet such nobility is vitiated not once but twice: by its cause, and by its effect. On the one hand, it is a product of weakness. Confronted by a nightmare version of his former self – an intolerable intruder from a world in which only his dishonour is real, and whose appeal contains 'a vein of subtle reference to their common blood' – Jim cannot permit himself the slightest gesture of corroboration: whatever he does must be utterly beyond reproach. On the other hand, it results in the annihilation of his achievement in Patusan. Far from awakening a like generosity, Jim's gesture drives Brown into a positive frenzy of destructiveness. Bent on proving to himself that the values Jim claims have no real existence, he comes upon Dain Waris and his followers, and slaughters the whole party. In an instant, the protector of Patusan finds himself its destroyer. Once again, intention has been horribly contradicted by action; once again, dream and fact have fallen apart. Jim will attempt of course to put them together again. But this time there must be no failure. To atone for contradictions as deep as life, nothing less than life will do. It is no longer sufficient – not that it was ever so – to face the verdict of a court of inquiry; what must now be confronted is the retribution of an outraged people. So Jim presents himself, freely and unarmed, before Doramin, and the old man, in his anger and grief, shoots him down where he stands.

Jim's death has something of the fearful inflexibility of French tragedy, for it demonstrates that, taken to its logical conclusion, honour becomes absolutely incompatible with life. Well may he send, as he falls, a last 'proud and unflinching glance' at the crowd of spectators he has never finally managed to escape, for there is nothing they can do now to deprive him of his dream. Has Jim, then, mastered his fate? It seems to me a measure of Conrad's humanity that he does not close his novel on a note of unqualified heroic absolutism. Its concluding vision – relative, probing, uncer-

tain – is Marlow's, not Jim's. Whatever his death may mean to
Jim, for Marlow it does not resolve, but crowns, the ambiguity of a
tormented career: 'But we can see him, an obscure conqueror of
fame, tearing himself out of the arms of a jealous love at the sign, at
the call of his exalted egoism. He goes away from a living woman to
celebrate his pitiless wedding with a shadowy ideal of conduct'
(p. 416). It takes a Marlow to remind us that by forcibly tearing
himself out of life Jim leaves a gaping wound behind him. Of course
he has no alternative. Jewel urges him to stand and fight: has he not
promised that he will never leave her? But to his reply, 'I should
not be worth having', there can be no answer. Yet at the same time,
his refusal to compromise, even with that which gives his life its
value, has an inhuman coldness: for while it exalts his 'shadowy
bride' above the reach of change or accident, it condemns his living
bride to the immobility of unending grief. Is Jim 'one of us'? That
the answer to this question can no longer be confined to its original
terms is proof of the necessity of the second part. For now, at the
end of this novel of systematic ambiguities, we reply 'Yes', because
Jim has revealed to us, pushed to their limits, the central contradictions of our existence as human beings; but we also reply
'No', because, as ordinary survivors, we cannot but shrink away
from inflexible extremes, whether of victory or defeat.

27
21
48

5

Nostromo

There was something inherent in the necessities of successful action which carried with it the moral degradation of the idea.

Mrs Gould in Nostromo, p. 521

I

With *Nostromo* and *The Secret Agent* we reach the summit of Conrad's achievement as a novelist. I may begin to substantiate this claim by noting that these two novels are at least as closely related as (in one way) *The Nigger of the 'Narcissus'* and 'Heart of Darkness', or (in another) *Lord Jim* and *Under Western Eyes*. It has become standard practice to connect *Nostromo* with its predecessor and *The Secret Agent* with its successor. Thus Robert Penn Warren argues that *Nostromo* is an elaboration of the conflict between the ideal and the real exhibited in *Lord Jim*,[1] and Irving Howe that the sardonic treatment of the anarchists in *The Secret Agent* anticipates Conrad's 'antipathy toward the revolutionary émigrés in *Under Western Eyes*.'[2] I am not suggesting that such correlations are illegitimate; but they have the effect of obscuring how very distinctively these two central masterpieces resemble each other. Notably, both bring to the foreground not a single protagonist doubled by a single narrator but a number of equally prominent individuals, each of whom is repeatedly called upon to comment on his fellows. Furthermore, these foreground characters are not only presented in relation to one another but also in relation to a middle-ground of subordinate figures of great variety, and to the background of an entire population. This means that *Nostromo* and *The Secret Agent* confront much more directly than Conrad's other novels the reality of social interaction. They evoke two complementary communities

---

[1] R. P. Warren, 'Nostromo' in *The Sewanee Review*, LIX (Summer 1951), 363–91, a justly famous essay. See also Juliet McLauchlan, *Conrad: Nostromo*, Studies in English Literature 40 (Arnold, 1969), a finely responsive and balanced reading of the novel.

[2] I. Howe, 'Conrad: Order and Anarchy' in *Politics and the Novel* (New York, 1957, London, 1961), p. 90. E. K. Hay, *The Political Novels of Joseph Conrad* (Chicago, 1963) is a meticulously documented analysis of Conrad's politics.

in all their social range and historical depth. The community represented in *Nostromo* is characteristic of a new or 'under-developed' state; that in *The Secret Agent* of an old or 'over-developed' country. In the Latin-American territory of Cos-taguana, for example, the population is sparse and extraordinarily heterogeneous; nature is felt as a largely untamed presence, often dwarfing the activities of man; laws and institutions exert a weak hold on political life; the local population is exposed to all kinds of foreign pressure and influence; the individual citizen lives on the assumption that his deeds, good or bad, count for the future of his country. The European megapolis of London, on the other hand, offers a complete contrast. There is a monstrous and uniform concentration of population; a constructed environment has almost completely replaced the natural; tradition and precedent exert an almost paralysing pressure; foreign interference can obtain practically no purchase on the density of local life; the individual sees himself as functional and anonymous. Moreover, these paradigmatic societies complement each other politically as well as structurally: the one is as revolutionary as the other is conservative. The story of Costaguana exhibits, as Irving Howe has shown,[1] the typically Latin-American cycle of revolution and counter-revolution, which is not social and utopian, but neo-colonial and militaristic. The exhaustion produced by the struggle for independence (under the romantic leadership of Bolivar) leads to a brutal autocracy (that of the megalomaniac dictator Guzman Bento) which unifies the newly independent state by force. In its turn, this regime crumbles into a phase of rapacious anarchy which largely destroys the wealth of the productive classes. Thereupon foreign capital begins an invasion, first in the extractive industries (led by the investor Holroyd and the mining-engineer Gould), then in such secondary industries as railways and communications. Once established, these new economic forces sponsor a liberal revolt (bringing to the presidency the reformist Ribiera) which in its turn falls before a nationalist–military *coup* (engineered by the Montero brothers). But material interests are not yet defeated: the wealthiest region (the Occidental Province of Sulaco) successfully secedes and opens wide its frontiers to full-scale investment from abroad. Yet even here Conrad's profile of a neo-colonial state is not complete. With ironic prescience he discerns, in the very triumph of material interests, the seeds of their transformation: the emergence of a discontented urban proletariat. In contrast to this

[1] Howe, 'Conrad', pp. 100–7.

cycle, *The Secret Agent* – as I shall show in the next chapter – will present an antithetical pattern in which revolutionary activity will serve only to reinforce an immovable European conservatism: a society in which the sheer inertia of centuries of regulated property accumulation will instantly reduce the radical impulse to merely random anarchic gestures or merely vacant ideological postures.

But this contrast – between what one might call the politics of instability and the politics of stasis – rests, as I have suggested, on a common denominator: the multiplication of protagonists. This fact alone could explain why *Nostromo* shows such an advance over *Lord Jim* in its treatment of what has been considered the earlier novel's special domain: the problems of personal identity. We are now no longer granted unimpeded access to the inner life of a privileged individual; instead we are obliged, even on those occasions when we *are* invited to share the desires and intentions of a particular character, to retain a vigilant sense of his relativity to the desires and intentions of his fellow-citizens. To a far more immediate degree than in *Lord Jim* we are made to see, in the concrete details of the fable unfolding before us, one of the basic conditions of social life: that an individual exists not only in relation to himself but also in relation with others – that each and every member of a group is at once subject and object, observer and observed. What this means in practice is that while the individual will tend to conceive of himself in terms of his own purposes, others will regard him in terms of the part he plays, or the situation he occupies, within the group as a whole. In other words, the problem of identity, so far explored in connection with the code of honour, will now be examined in relation to the idea of a *social role*.

A proper regard for what I have called the 'multiplication of protagonists' provides a vantage-point from which to approach the massive complexities of the two central novels. Take, as a preliminary example, the so-called 'distance' or 'coldness' with which the mature Conrad is supposed to view his men and women. This quality is not due to a failure of imaginative sympathy, as some critics have felt, but to the inevitable consequences of his method. To give as much prominence to a character's objective role as to his subjective purpose is to inhibit facile identification on the part of the reader. It demands an effort of ironic attention, perpetually alert to possible discrepancies between avowals and deeds, between what a man says he does and what others see him doing. This alienating effect is the penalty that we, as readers, have to pay for Conrad's realism – one of his two or three major contributions to the art of fiction: a realism that leads him to present society, not as an 'organic' whole or an abstract aggregate, but as a *community of individuals* – that is to say, a group of which the constituent elements are interlocked in a perpetual permutation of action and reaction.

It seems to me that the very titles of these two novels provide a hint of what it is that relates them. The words 'Nostromo' and 'The Secret Agent' designate individual men not by their personal names (Gian' Battista Fidanza and Alexander Verloc) but by their roles or reputations. Furthermore, these roles are complementary. For whereas 'Nostromo' (literally 'our man') denominates a pre-eminently active individual, a spectacular agent on his own and others' behalf, 'The Secret Agent' refers to a man who, being confidentially engaged by no less than three incompatible agencies, is profoundly, almost pathologically, inactive. A general comparison of these two novels thus provides us with a set of initial bearings. The contrasting ideas of revolution and conservatism, of instability and stasis, and of energy and indolence will act as guide-lines in the discussions that follow.

II

For all its imaginative appeal *Nostromo* has acquired some notoriety as a novel that one cannot read unless one has read it before. As enthusiastic a critic as Albert Guerard has admitted that whenever he tries to 'disentangle the time-scheme' he comes up with a different result, concluding that 'the literal chronology of *Nostromo* ... is presumably irrecoverable'.[1] Given the punctiliousness of Conrad's plotting, this is a difficulty that I am not alone in finding, at best, exaggerated.[2] Guerard's appeal to what he calls 'impressionism' to explain the novel's chronology seems to raise as many problems as it solves. 'Impressionism' in what sense? In *Nostromo* Conrad's elementary purpose is to bring to full actuality the life of an imaginary republic. To organize the novel conventionally – for instance, by providing a preliminary historical survey – would be self-defeating. Instead, he presents Costaguana as if (like the London of *The Secret Agent*) it already possessed an independent historical existence, to be acquired by readers incidentally and piecemeal, rather like the citizens of the country itself. This method of verisimilitude (rather than 'impressionism') is perfectly compatible with consistency of detail. Combined with an

[1] Guerard, *Conrad the Novelist*, p. 211.
[2] McLauchlan, *Conrad: Nostromo*, pp. 9–10.

extraordinary fullness of presentation – Conrad develops not only the historical and geographical, but also the topographical, economic, demographic and cultural aspects of his society – it works so well that many readers have said that their 'residence' in Costaguana has seemed more real to them than their visits to those South American states that can actually be found on the map.

A look at *Nostromo* as a whole reveals that the bulk of the narrative is concerned with a single issue: the impact of foreign commercial interests (specifically the reopening of the San Tomé silver mine by Charles Gould) on the political life of Costaguana. The suspense itself turns on the question whether the province of Sulaco will be able to achieve secession from its parent Republic. The period of crisis lasts exactly seventeen days, and occupies the central portions of the novel.[1] Here, the sequence of events is presented in a relatively straightforward way. For about a year the hinterland of Costaguana has been the scene of an inconclusive civil war between the legal government of Ribiera and the populist party of his military chief, Montero. For Sulaco, the crisis proper begins on 1 May with the dispatch of the crack local regiment in support of the Ribierist forces holding the southern port of Cayta. This departure creates a power vacuum into which arrives: first, on 2 May, a six months' consignment of silver from the San Tomé mine; and then, on 3 May, the broken figure of Ribiera defeated a few days earlier on the landward side of the Cordilleras. Both these events provoke a spontaneous riot of the populace. However, civilian members of the Blanco (or landowning) party, assisted by Italian railway workmen and a team of local dockers under their chief Nostromo, quell the worst of the agitation, and secure the escape of Ribiera and the leading Blanco families. But this respite is only temporary. On the evening of the same day, news of a fresh double threat is received: Montero's brother Pedrito, in close pursuit of Ribiera, has managed to cross the mountains with a small force; and Sotillo, the commanding officer of the small southern port of Esmeralda, has changed sides and is approaching by sea. Considering the position to be hopeless, the Provincial Government decides to capitulate. Left to his own devices, Charles Gould is persuaded by Martin Decoud, a young journalist recently returned to Sulaco with a cargo of rifles, to throw the combined resources of his mine, his American backer, and his own prestige

---

[1] Part I, Chapters 2–4, which plunges the reader *in media res*, thus signalling where the narrative emphasis will fall; Part II, entire (eight chapters); Part III, entire except for the last three chapters (ten chapters).

into a desperate gamble – secession. But the success of this plan seems to depend on two conditions: the preservation of the silver from confiscation and the recall of the Sulaco regiment. Accordingly, during the following night (4 May) Nostromo and Decoud take the silver out into the gulf, the first hoping to intercept a North-bound steamer, the second planning to make his way swiftly down the coast to Cayta. In the darkness, however, their loaded lighter is struck by Sotillo's stealthily approaching transport-ship; and although the silver is saved (it is hidden on a near-by island under the guard of Decoud while Nostromo returns to the mainland) Gould's mine now seems beyond salvation. The morning of 5 May sees Pedrito's triumphant entrance into Sulaco, and Sotillo's occupation of the harbour area. Yet, a second and even more desperate attempt to secure secession is about to be made. While Gould plays for time by threatening to blow up his mine, the San Tomé medical officer, Monygham, delays Sotillo by persuading him that the silver is recoverable; and, meeting Nostromo – the one man capable of the overland ride to Cayta – Monygham induces him to perform the feat. Nostromo sets off on the morning of 6 May, returning with the regiment on 17 May. Sotillo is at once overwhelmed; the mine employees sally forth from their mountain stronghold and rescue Gould from summary execution; Pedrito is driven out of Sulaco; and the secession of the Occidental Province is an accomplished fact.

How are we to take this narrative, which, once cleared of its obliquities of presentation, seems to reveal itself as a tale of high adventure? It is tempting to see it as another, and perhaps more political, version of the characteristic Conradian test. Indeed, the epigraph of the novel – 'So foul a day clears not without a storm' – seems to support the view that the 'storm' of revolution in *Nostromo* works much in the same way as the more literal tempest of the *Narcissus* or the forest of 'Heart of Darkness'. But this does not stand up to examination. The central figures of the novel – Gould, Nostromo, Decoud, Monygham – are not subjected to a merely external ordeal. The Montero revolution is something for which they are, at least in part, responsible, for they have all put themselves directly or otherwise in the service of the 'material interests' that provoke it. Moreover, they become fully engaged in a counter-revolution of their own. If what they experience is a test, it is one of their own making. In *Nostromo* the revolutionary contest is not an impersonal background; it is, as it were, the public reverberation of individual decisions and desires. The political dimension of the novel is an inevitable consequence of Conrad's choice of theme: one cannot explore the nature and limits of human action by confining oneself to the personal and private.

An intentional act, as opposed to an event, presupposes two conditions: a context, and a medium. If what men do is to deserve the name of action, if it is to be raised above the level of mere activity, then it requires the context of an organized community. Without this, individual deeds not only become ineffective but are in principle deprived of all moral significance. In addition, action properly so called also requires what I describe as a medium – some particular focus within the physical world, whether it be a discipline, a convention, or a tradition. A man cannot merely do: he must do *something* – cultivate his garden or dethrone a monarch. In *Nostromo* the most important medium is what Conrad in later life called 'the true hero' of his book – the silver of the mine. Without exception, every character, whether motivated by love, revenge, patriotism, or duty, finds his action affected or shaped by the silver. Two characters in particular stand out for the audacity and directness of their concern with it: Gould who extracts it, and Nostromo who steals it. Hence, as Conrad himself suggests, the structure of the novel must be sought primarily in the counterpointing of the stories of 'the[se] two racially and socially contrasted men' who (he reminds us) are 'both captured by the silver of the San Tomé mine'.

For all its elaborateness, this structure is as regular as that of *Lord Jim*. The opening and closing sections of the novel offer two separate accounts of Nostromo's relationship with the Italian family that has adopted him (*Nostromo*, Part I, Chapters 2–4; Part III, Chapters 12–13). This provides a kind of frame, within which occurs, more discursively, a kind of secondary frame: two accounts, one near the beginning of the novel, the other near the end, of Gould's relationship with his wife (Part I, Chapters 6–8; Part III, Chapters 3, 4, 7). The centre of the picture, as it were, consists of a pair of related events: Gould's transformation of the mine into a system of wealth, and Nostromo's appropriation of the mine's product. Once the centrality of these two men of action is established, the intricate patterning of the novel easily reveals itself. The parallel between Gould and Nostromo as agents is matched by another parallel, that between Decoud and Monygham as critics. This second pairing stands in complete contrast to the first. Although both men are drawn into the current of material interests, they are completely indifferent to the silver as such and sceptical of the progressive claims made in its favour. Hence they make it possible for Conrad to achieve a complex treatment of his primary theme: he is able to set the concept of action against the concept of thought. But Decoud and Monygham also contrast in a different way. Whereas the two agents are cut off from the women they love by their actions on behalf of the silver, the two sceptics, in so far as they engage themselves in the struggle, do so, or claim to, exclusively for reasons of love. This permits Conrad a further elaboration, in terms of a contrast between action and love. It is this structure that steadies the enormous panorama of the novel, and makes possible its range and depth of significance.

III

An analysis of the roles of Charles Gould and Nostromo must begin with a consideration of the folk-tale which Conrad sets in the midst of the descriptive splendours of his opening chapter. According to popular belief, the rocky and waterless promontory which shuts off Sulaco from the Pacific Ocean conceals hoards of priceless but forbidden treasure. All those impious enough to brave the interdiction – including, within living memory, two foreign 'gringos' and an ignorant local peasant – are destroyed, and their ghosts are condemned to stand eternally on guard over the permanently sterile object of their quest.

The question of how this popular tale stands in relation to the narrative that follows has occasioned considerable disagreement. Obviously, as a superstition taken seriously by the local inhabitants, it plays a part within the world of the novel. For example, when Nostromo is asked to take charge of the silver lighter, he becomes obsessed with the tale, for it becomes an image of his danger, and in due course, of his temptation, and of his fate (pp. 255, 258, 264, 460, 462, 496, 501, 526, 531). As a rhetorical device, however, its status is more ambiguous. In some important respects, it seems to act as a predictive moral, determining in advance the outcome of the novel. For example, for both Gould and Nostromo the silver of San Tomé, like the treasures of the Azuera, is a forbidden object. Gould reopens the mine in flagrant contradiction of his dead father's most solemn injunction; and Nostromo decides to secure the escape of the ingots in brutal disregard of his foster-mother's dying request. As a result they are cut off from all personal fulfilment and end in sterility and solitude.[1] Their fate seems to reproduce with an almost mechanical inevitability the fate of the legendary adventurers. Yet as one experiences it there is nothing about the movement of Conrad's narrative to suggest the regularity of an unwinding spring. What, then, is the true status of the legend? It seems to me that it must be taken for what it is – a folk-myth, a tale or belief that embodies the inherited wisdom of the tribe. It is not the key of a mechanism to be traced, but, like such immemorial proverbs as 'radix malorum est cupiditas', the representation of a truth that has to be re-examined and made real in the light of new experience. What the Azuera legend does, as we encounter it at the entrance to Costaguana, is to provide the moral and metaphorical terms, at work in every phase of the novel's imaginative development, of Conrad's exploration of his theme: wealth and enslavement, audacity and impiety, growth and sterility.

In this perspective, therefore, Charles Gould's filial dis-obedience in reopening the San Tomé mine cannot be disregarded. His motives are, of course, the reverse of reprehensible. His father, a wealthy second-generation emigrant to Costaguana, has been morally destroyed by having had the heavily taxed San Tomé concession maliciously wished on him. Charles has qualified in England as a mining-engineer. During a holiday in Italy he meets an orphaned English girl; on the day of his engagement to her, he receives news of his father's death. His decision to reopen the mine is an expression partly of his need, in the midst of his new-found happiness, to redeem his father's failure, and partly of a vigorous impulse to oppose the political corruption which has been the cause of his undoing. Positive as his *motives* are, however, the action he proposes, even at the outset, is placed in a subtly ambiguous light. A year after his marriage, having established his wife in the family residence in Sulaco, he receives a visit from Holroyd, an American capitalist who has agreed to finance his project. On the day of Holroyd's departure, he discovers that his wife has been deeply dismayed by what she calls his 'awful materialism'. He asks her to recall a passage from one of his father's last letters expressing the conviction that 'God looked wrathfully at these countries, or else He would let some ray of hope fall through a rift in the

---

[1] In the case of Nostromo, the legend is almost literally re-enacted. Three men set out with the treasure: two foreigners, who know what they are doing, and a local merchant who has blundered aboard accidentally. By the time the consequences of this adventure have worked themselves out, all three have come to a violent end.

appalling darkness of intrigue, bloodshed, and crime that hung over the Queen of Continents.'

Mrs. Gould had not forgotten. 'You read it to me, Charley,' she murmured. 'It was a striking pronouncement. How deeply your father must have felt its terrible sadness!'

'He did not like to be robbed. It exasperated him,' said Charles Gould. 'But the image will serve well enough. What is wanted here is law, good faith, order, security. Any one can declaim about these things, but I pin my faith to material interests. Only let the material interests once get a firm footing, and they are bound to impose the conditions on which alone they can continue to exist. That's how your money-making is justified here in the face of lawlessness and disorder. It is justified because the security which it demands must be shared with an oppressed people. A better justice will come afterwards. That's your ray of hope.' His arm pressed her slight form closer to his side for a moment. 'And who knows whether in that sense even the San Tomé mine may not become that little rift in the darkness which poor father despaired of ever seeing?'

She glanced up at him with admiration. He was competent; he had given a vast shape to the vagueness of her unselfish ambitions.

'Charley,' she said, 'you are splendidly disobedient.'

Nostromo, p. 84

This conversation reveals two different reactions to the father's despairing outburst: a wondering compassion, and resolute practicality. So much is plain enough. But what may not be so obvious is the precision with which, despite the apparent victory of Charles's point of view, both perspectives are kept alive. Right up to the concluding epigram, which is an acknowledgement of the audacity of a plan to transform the mine that has been the cause of the father's disgrace into an opportunity for his redemption, we are not allowed for a moment to forget that materialist action and moral sensitivity are quite distinct. Indeed, Charles himself is aware that they must not be confused, and if his declaration of faith possesses a real authority, it is because it is not deaf to his wife's moral scrupulousness. He places his programme of action deliberately in the service of an order which he recognizes as higher than the materialistic: 'a *better* justice will come afterwards'. This hope may be mistaken, but it is not the hope of a trifler unable to distinguish between means and ends. Moreover, Charles's programme does not merely take into account his wife's 'unselfish ambitions': it provides them with a shape and purpose without which they would remain vague and unrealizable.

But is materialist, as opposed to political, action Gould's only choice? Rather like Martin Decoud – a native of Costaguana who has spent his adult life in Paris – Gould both is and is not a Costaguanero. As he repeatedly reminds his wife, when she becomes disturbed by the compromises he is forced to make to keep the mine intact: 'You forget that I was born here.' He has inherited a certain commitment to the disorders of Costaguana. His family has been established for three generations in Sulaco, and one of his uncles has held public office and even sacrificed his life for his federalist principles. But as an Englishman – a foreigner capable of detachment – his diagnosis of Costaguanian affairs compels him to reject the political solution. And in this he is surely not wrong, for the entire history of the country confirms that the only political roles open to him are such as to render political activity meaningless. Martin Decoud, who is capable of a like detachment, is convinced that the only alternative available to Sulaco is to opt out of Costaguana altogether. He quotes the great liberator Bolivar: 'America is ungovernable. Those who worked for her independence have ploughed the sea.' And he adds: 'There is a curse of futility upon our character: Don Quixote and Sancho Panza, chivalry and materialism, high-sounding sentiments and a supine morality, violent efforts for an idea and a sullen acquiescence in every form of corruption' (p. 171). This view is vividly confirmed by the endless cortège of political delinquents that Conrad parades with his customary sardonic zest through the pages of his novel: the squat General Montero, straddling the deck of the *Juno* like 'some military idol of Aztec conception and European bedecking'; the gigantic demagogue Gamacho, bellowing in the heat of the Plaza 'like some inferior devil in a furnace' against the landowning 'goths and paralytics'; the insinuating Pedrito cajoling an impassive Charles Gould by promising to make him a count or a marquis; the elegantly booted and spurred Sotillo nursing a colic of terror in his hammock; the solemn parliamentarian Lopez, half his beard burnt off, presenting a profile alternately helpless and dignified. The novel teems with such vignettes, which gradually accumulate to create an overwhelming sense of political futility, as the normal restraints of logic and legality are swept away in a torrent of magniloquence designed only, it seems, to license an abandonment of the self to its more brutal instincts.

Like Decoud's idea of secession, therefore, Gould's choice of materialist action is a necessary opting-out. It represents his refusal to pick up the devalued counters of Costaguanian politics. Instead he will play with his own coinage. He will oppose rhetoric with taciturnity, incompetence with efficiency, instability with economic order. In themselves, 'unselfish ambitions' are impotent: what Costaguana requires is a new practical force, capable of achieving results in the real world of bread and guns, of fear and sloth. Moreover, if his mine is to remain an alternative power for good it must be kept scrupulously insulated, whatever its dependence may be on external dividends and internal bribes, from the pestilence of Costaguanian politics.

The outcome of what one might call the San Tomé experiment cannot be properly assessed unless one is aware of Gould's underlying good faith. Despite his detachment, he returns to Costaguana as a participant, not a profiteer. 'In Costaguana, we Goulds are no adventurers', he tells his wife; and his conception of the public function of his mine, at least initially, bears this out. When he hears the distant 'growling mutter of the mountain pouring its stream of treasure under the stamps' it enters his heart 'with the force of a *proclamation* [my italics] thundered forth over the land' (p. 105). This proclamation affirms a new order, challenging with a new voice the strident tones of those other proclamations under which Costaguana has exhausted itself. And the mine, as such, is a triumphant success. Its wealth provides employment, attracts foreign enterprise, diffuses public order, enriches the province of Sulaco, and, in the end, overcomes the assault of revolution. Yet, in the famous central irony of the novel, this very success guarantees its failure as an instrument of justice. Gould gradually abandons all sense of its humanizing objective. Little by little he loses contact with his wife's redeeming vision, and their relationship is reduced to a sterile formality. This personal disaster, delineated by Conrad with the utmost sureness in the falling graph of the intimacy of their exchanges, is matched by a more general disintegration. Gould registers this public decline through his increasing difficulty in keeping his purposes as a man distinct from the impersonal interests of his role as mining chief. As the mine becomes a force in the land – an 'imperium in imperio' – it inevitably assumes what he most fears: a political function. The Administrator of San Tomé is transformed into the 'King of Sulaco', and the *camino réal* of the old Carlist dispensation sees a new Charles riding down its royal avenues. For all his reticence Gould is forced to acknowledge that his word is law. It is he, not the state, that persuades the landowners to cede their territory to the railway company; it is he, not the law, that guarantees the security of foreign contracts. It is from his reception rooms that the conservative Ribiera is projected into the presidency. The man who originally pinned his faith to material interests as an alternative to politics has himself, through the development of these interests, become a major political force.

Hence, when the Montero revolt breaks out, it precipitates the contradictions that have been inherent in Gould's position. He is confronted with a new choice: either to resist *politically*, or to go under. The extreme reserve, almost amounting to paralysis, which he exhibits during the crisis is a sign of the intensity of his inner conflict. But he is inexorably compelled to adopt whatever means come to hand to safeguard his mine. That he should even be prepared to blow up what he originally considered to be the sole means to 'a better justice' rather than let it fall into the hands of the Monterists shows how far he has allowed himself to drift away from his first hopes. Under the pressure of events, he is driven into a desperate political partnership with the journalist Decoud, and an equivocal military alliance with the bandit Hernandez. It is simply impossible for him to avoid taking his mine, as his uncle once took his sword, into the 'senseless fray'. We have been told that 'his taciturnity, assumed with a purpose, had prevented him from tampering openly with his thoughts'. But now, in the glare of insurrection, he cannot but see that he has joined the ranks of the political opportunists. 'After all ... he perceived that he *was* an adventurer in Costaguana, the descendant ... of men who had sought fortune in a revolutionary war' (p. 365). That the mine should emerge intact, indeed strengthened, from the troubles can therefore bring him little consolation. The triumph of material interests in Sulaco, far from curing the disease, has merely altered or compounded the symptoms; and we are left with Dr Mony-gham's bleak vision of a time when 'all that the Gould Concession stands for shall weigh as heavily on the people as the barbarism, cruelty, and misrule of a few years back' (p. 511).

The reasons for the tragic paradox that material success requires moral failure must not be sought merely in the individual psy-chology of its principal victim – though I am bound to say that the subtlety of Conrad's grasp of the interplay between remorse and resolution in his tracing of the growth of Gould's obsession has seldom earned the notice it deserves. The final explanation will be found in what I have called the 'medium' of Gould's action – the material interests themselves. Given the nature of the passions they arouse, their success can only be achieved at the price of sacrificing every other goal or consideration. The phrase 'material interests' has an admirable precision. Such interests must be distinguished from all others: they possess their own inexorable logic and demand an all-excluding fidelity; having to contend with the most brutal motions of the human heart (the Sulaco crisis – whether as the riot of the populace, the headlong invasion of Pedrito, or the abrupt treachery of Sotillo – has the lust for Gould's silver as its immediate cause), they leave those who serve them with no choice or room for manoeuvre. As Dr Monygham recognizes: 'The Administrator had acted as if . . . the prosperity of the mine had been founded on methods of probity . . . And it was nothing of the kind. *The method followed had been the only one possible*' (p. 370). [My italics.] Hence his final verdict: 'There is no peace and no rest in the development of material interests. They have their law and their justice. But it is founded on expediency, and is inhuman.' Perhaps what Charles Gould may have failed to understand in his justification for his filial disobedience (but what his wife may have instinctively grasped) is that material interests cannot be treated as a means to a moral end, for they cannot be prevented from turning into an end in themselves. It is logically impossible to put Mammon to the service of God.

We have seen that Gould's initial act of faith cannot be dismissed as mere self-deception. But it is not reprehensibly shortsighted? Martin Decoud, who is Gould's antithesis in that he is temperamentally a reporter rather than a participant, has no difficulty in penetrating to the realities of Gould's predicament. To him Gould's public role as Administrator of the San Tomé mine is nothing more than the latest moment in the long tale of what he calls the 'exploitation' of Costaguana. Gould's incorruptible idealism is nothing but a sham designed to protect him from understanding the interests he serves. Decoud's scepticism, however, is far from being confined to calling into question the role of a single individual. It embraces the whole of mankind. In his view, man is but a part of the impersonal system of organic nature, and nature, in its turn, is part of the indifferent mechanism of the material universe. It follows that what we call man's 'humanity' – the hopes, fears, beliefs, ideals, despairs born of his existential consciousness – is ultimately nothing but an irrelevance on the face of nature. Above all, man's so-called 'convictions' – the justifications he gives himself for what he does – are the purest illusion. To idealize one's actions, when the only law of nature is that affirmation of identity known as self-interest, is an almost criminal pose. 'What is a conviction?' he asks his fiancée Antonia Avellanos in the course of a memorable conversation with her on the evening of

entire career provides: the typology of the capitalist–engineer in his heroic phase. To such a man, action means work, and work means conquest. His destiny consists in the creation of a new world, made in the image of man, out of the material of the given world. Secure in the knowledge that he is serving his fellows, his assurance is boundless and his fidelity incorruptible. 'The work would be done: the force would be almost as strong as a faith': Conrad's eulogy seems complete. But the barely perceptible qualification of that 'almost', followed by the more ominous 'Not quite, however', is enough to transform the tone into ironic appraisal. Conrad reminds us, of course, through his engineer, that there are limits to what is practicable. But he does more than that. He unobtrusively summons to our minds the memory of faith of an entirely different order, before which even mountains are obliged to give way. Suddenly the shadow of Promethean revolt falls across the ideal of 'the world's service'. The capitalist–engineer is heroic; but he also conducts himself recklessly as lord and master of creation. The conviction that gives him his energy takes away his foresight. He is afflicted, as Decoud has rightly insinuated, by a form of dementia.

The scepticism of the imaginative materialist allows Conrad to extend his diagnosis of the faith of the active materialist. But the converse is also true. If scepticism allows us to see that faith is an illusion, faith enables us to see that scepticism is a pose. We have noticed that Gould is not the only Costaguanero of ambiguous status. Decoud too, is half a foreigner; but *his* existence abroad has had little meaning. Too much cut off from his homeland to feel the reality of its problems, too wealthy to have to subject himself to the discipline of a profession, too intelligent to sink himself in the intoxication of vice, he has gradually assumed a stance of ironic detachment. But this stance has been acquired much too easily. It has not been tested against the rigours of action. It has cost him nothing. Unlike Gould, therefore, he can afford to 'play his part lightly in [the] tragic farce'. Now, to be convinced that faith is irrelevant is not the same thing as to be convinced that faith is unnecessary. Decoud's fatal lapse is not so much his scepticism as his indifference, his casual assumption that life's absurdity is no special cause for alarm or concern. And this error of superficiality has not been without its consequences. 'He had pushed the habit of universal raillery', Conrad tells us, 'to the point where it blinded him to the genuine impulses of his nature' (p. 153).

It is when Decoud allows himself to be drawn into the affairs of Costaguana that the self-deception on which his flippancy is based begins to be disclosed. Having nonchalantly agreed to bring out a consignment of automatic rifles to Sulaco, he is invited by the Avellanos to participate in the resistance to the Montero revolt. This, to his surprise, he finds impossible to refuse. His theory of human nature does not admit of the possibility of disinterested acts: 'No-one is a patriot for nothing', he tells the high-minded Antonia. What reason, then, can he provide for *his* commitment to the Sulaco party? One compatible with the principles of 'a sane materialism': his love for the daughter of Don José Avellanos, the architect of Ribierism. It is by an appeal to the same reason that he justifies his project of secession. 'She won't leave Sulaco for my sake', he declares in his characteristic tone of cynical conceit, 'therefore Sulaco must leave the rest of the Republic to its fate.' But his feelings are in fact much more complex than this rationalization suggests. For example, he is continually taken aback by the intensity of his concern for the fate of his country. 'I suppose I am more of a Costaguanero than I would have believed possible', he is forced to admit on one such occasion (p. 176).[1] He even begins to allow his scepticism to turn, as it were, upon itself. Writing to his sister about Charles Gould he astonishingly concedes that 'those Englishmen live on illusions which somehow or other help them to get a firm hold of the substance'. But these are only momentary acknowledgements. Fundamentally, he remains dangerously ignorant of the 'genuine impulses' of his nature. His very love for Antonia, which Conrad analyses with the utmost precision, is the emotion of a subjectivity that stands, as it were, beside itself. This curious self-alienation is perhaps most tellingly revealed in his declaration of love to her: in his mouth, the normal phrase 'I love you' becomes: 'I have only the supreme illusion of a lover'. Under such conditions, it is not surprising that the document we are invited to consider as Decoud's last will and testament – his account of the 'three days of Sulaco' written while he waited to take the silver into the gulf – should reveal him to be a man 'with no faith in anything except the truth of his own sensations' (p. 229).

The substance of such a faith is about to be disclosed to him once and for all. By a remorseless irony, his venture on to the unseen waters of the Golfo Placido takes him straight into a world where nothing counts but the evidence of his senses. Foiled of the purpose of his expedition by the collision with Sotillo's transport-ship, abandoned on the Great Isabel to guard a now meaningless treasure, and convinced of the collapse of resistance to Montero on the

[1] Cf. 187. His conversation with Antonia in the Casa Gould is on pp. 173–94.

mainland, he is gradually exposed to an ordeal by matter – by 'the world of cloud and water, of natural forces and forms of nature' (pp. 496–501). In such circumstances, neither memories of Antonia, who appears before him monstrously materialized, 'gigantic and lovely like an allegorical statue', nor fleeting regret for the triviality of his past life, which Conrad calls the 'first moral sentiment of his manhood', are able to save him from the apathetic sadness of a merely physical existence. Unsustained by any moral identity, both 'his intelligence and his passion' are 'swallowed up easily in this great unbroken solitude of waiting without faith'. On the tenth day (the Cayta garrison, alerted by Nostromo, having already re-embarked for Sulaco) he silently rows out into the gulf, weighs himself down with two bars of the metal that has come to represent materiality itself, shoots himself, and sinks without trace into 'the immense indifference of things'.

The irony of Decoud's fate consists in the fact that it is precisely his materialism that renders him incapable of coping with the prospect of a merely material existence. His presence in the novel incomparably extends the tragic reverberations of Gould's predicament. For if in Gould we see a man morally compelled into a form of action that gradually undoes the ideal that inspired it, in Decoud we are enabled to discover the very principle of this tragic process. Decoud's life and death reveal that the faith in the effectiveness or value of human action necessary if an individual act is to be performed at all is totally ambiguous. For while his materialism (by what it enables him to perceive) demonstrates that this faith is illusory, it also shows (in its failure to ensure his survival) that the very same faith is indispensable. It remains, at one and the same time, the indictment and the justification of the deeds of men. This desperate contradiction represents the most uncompromising treatment we have encountered up to now of that doctrine of *positive illusion* propounded by Marlow in 'Heart of Darkness' and more tentatively by Stein in *Lord Jim*.

IV

It is misleading to suggest (like one recent critic) that *Nostromo* is a typical Edwardian double-decker novel. To be sure, the thematic connection between Gould and Decoud is paralleled by that between Nostromo and Monygham; but their stories are far too intertwined to enable us to distinguish two distinct plots. This means that when we move from the first of our pairs of agent and sceptic to the second, we find that the new problems before us are a natural development of those we have just examined. Obviously, the new pair serves a complementary function. Where Gould is a middle-class Anglo-Saxon, Nostromo is racially a Latin and socially a member of what Conrad calls 'the people'; and where Decoud is an irreverent materialistic sceptic, Monygham's scepticism, learnt under the ministrations of Guzman Bento's torturers, is the product of moral despair. Thus by serving as complements, Nostromo and Monygham help to fulfil a single, coherent, evolutionary design.

The parallel between Gould and Nostromo is worked out with considerable care. Decoud rightly calls Nostromo 'the next great man of Sulaco after Don Carlos' (p. 185), for the force and consistency with which these two men sustain their distinctive roles, is unrivalled in Costaguana. Both are formidably masculine, not only in their capacity to inspire and retain the love of women, but in their need for 'action of a conquering kind'. Both combine an unexcitable, even disdainful, reserve of manner with inflexible tenacity of purpose. Both earn themselves, in the midst of the general venality and fickleness, a reputation for complete incorruptibility. Both infallibly accomplish whatever they attempt. And above all, both are engaged in the same public task: although Nostromo is not a member of the San Tomé organization itself, his authority over the labour force of Sulaco makes him an indispensable instrument of the mine, and earns him the title (in Decoud's ironical words) of 'this active usher in of the material implements of our progress' (p. 191).

This elaborate parallel permits Conrad to be exceptionally consistent in his development of the problem of action. We have seen, in the case of Gould, the growth of an apparently insoluble dilemma: the need to reconcile two incompatible elements, action and understanding. And the case of Nostromo will enable us to discover the true basis of this dilemma.

Why has Conrad made Nostromo socially and racially so distinct from Gould? One of the clearest hints is provided by a remark he throws out almost casually in the course of describing Sotillo's occupation of the custom-house. Reflecting on Sotillo's infatuation with Captain Mitchell's gold chronometer, he observes: 'there is always something childish in the rapacity of the passionate, clear-minded, Southern races, wanting in the misty idealism of the Northerners, who at the smallest encouragement dream of nothing less than the conquest of the earth' (p. 333). We have seen what is implied by the phrases 'misty idealism' and 'conquest of the earth'. But what of the other characterization? Southern races, we are told, do not blur the immediacy of their desires. They are 'passionate' and 'clear-minded': like children they know what they want when they see it. Conrad makes Nostromo a Southerner, not because he is interested in social or racial determinants as such, but because he wishes to throw into prominence two basic human traits usually disguised by education or censorship: directness of feeling, and freedom from self-consciousness. The fact that he also makes Nostromo a man of the people serves to highlight these qualities even further. For Conrad, the essence of Nostromo's nature is his uncritical simplicity or spontaneity of being.

When we re-examine the parallel between Nostromo and Gould, we now find that it forms a contrast, from which Nostromo's distinctiveness emerges decisively. For Gould, to act, even in favour of a cause, essentially means to work; for Nostromo, it means to perform an individual exploit. Gould's primary target is not activity itself, but the product of activity, in relation to which he, as a living individual, plays a purely instrumental part, subjecting his immediate desires to the exigencies of past and future. Nostromo, on the other hand, can think of his deeds only in their immediate relation to himself. His individuality is not the means, as it were, but the end, of his activity. From this point of view, he exists in a present that knows neither past nor future, but which offers itself as a perpetually renewed opportunity for self-expression. He is, in the amoral – or, more precisely, the pre-moral – sense of the word, a supreme egoist. This term must not be misunderstood: Nostromo is no ordinary self-seeker. Even his employer, Captain Mitchell, is forced to acknowledge that his usefulness far outweighs his wages. In any case, what he does earn he squanders in splendid disregard of the prudential virtues. The self he serves is a lordly master, incapable of the calculations and compromises of doubt or fear. To be 'Nostromo' is enough: indeed, nothing less will do, for, in Conrad's revealing phrase, his is a profoundly 'subjective nature' – subjective 'almost to insanity' (p. 525)[1] – and hence incapable of conceiving that the world has an existence independent of his own. What he seeks from his fellows is no mere monetary reward (after all, the value of money, being conventional, does not originate with himself), but a reflection of his own splendour; what he requires of them is that complex of responses – gratitude, respect, admiration, awe – which is the

[1] Cf. p. 417.

113

substance of a great reputation. His reckless generosity, whether to the 'pretty Morenita' who cuts off the silver buttons of his coat in the full publicity of a fiesta, or to the aged crone who receives his last dollar in the obscurity of a city-gate corner, is nothing but the expression of his longing, as direct as Sotillo's for Mitchell's watch, for the lustre of a prestigious name.

But there exists another parallel, which in some ways casts a more revealing light on this extraordinary character. That Nostromo should be joined by Decoud in performing the novel's central action is, of course, no accident; nor that both men should share its fatal consequences. Decoud's attitude to Nostromo is the reverse of his attitude to Gould. He does not treat him as an opponent, but as a colleague – even as an accomplice – for Nostromo's conduct is completely free of even the slightest touch of Gould's moral idealism. Referring to Nostromo's qualities in his letter to his sister, Decoud, with his characteristic self-assurance, writes: 'Exceptional individualities always interest me, because they are true to the general formula expressing the moral state of humanity' (p. 246). For Decoud, Nostromo is a striking confirmation of the natural egoism that forms the basic tenet of his materialism. While the Sulaco Europeans take Nostromo's incorruptibility for granted, or, if challenged, interpret it as 'disinterestedness', Decoud discovers, 'not cynically, but with general satisfaction', that it is founded on 'his enormous vanity, that finest form of egoism that can take on the aspect of every virtue' (p. 300). Nostromo's elemental subjectivity seems a brilliant confirmation of the view that every ethical claim is illusory – and not least the claim that humanity has some measure of independence from organic nature. For Decoud, Nostromo is 'natural man'.

Yet here too, for all his acumen, Decoud is subtly mistaken. Carried away by his discovery of Nostromo's vanity, he repeatedly affirms his moral kinship with the man he calls 'that Genoese sailor who, like me, has come casually here to be drawn into the events for which his scepticism as well as mine seems to entertain a sort of passive contempt' (p. 246).[1] But it is a kinship to which he is not entitled. Nostromo is not a sceptic, for – as Conrad says of him – 'the popular mind is incapable of scepticism'. But even on the basis of Decoud's own theory, there is all the difference in the world between 'natural man' and 'artificial man' – between the unquestioning subjectivity of a Nostromo who neither knows nor cares that he illustrates the law of natural life, and the theoretical scep-

[1] Cf. pp. 191, 197.

ticism of a Decoud who, incapable of conceiving of himself as anything other than an object (we recall 'I have only the supreme illusion of a lover'), can only deduce these laws impersonally. The champion of 'audacious action' spontaneously exists; the partisan of 'intellectual audacity' has to assume that he exists.[1] If they rejoin each other at all, it is only as polar opposites. Hence there can be no real solidarity between them. Even at the climax of their collaboration, 'involved in the same imminence of deadly peril', they discover that they are 'merely two adventurers pursuing each his own adventure' (p. 295).

Although Decoud discloses the vanity at the heart of Nostromo's incorruptibility, he cannot provide us with the ironic perspective he was able to offer in relation to Gould. For such a perspective we have to turn to another doubter – Dr Monygham. As we have noted, Monygham's scepticism is not philosophic but experiential in origin. Beginning as an English medical officer, he has been irremediably branded a Costaguanero in the torture chambers of Guzman Bento. This process of naturalization has left him crippled in body and in mind. Although his self-respect has, to some degree, been restored by his work as the doctor of the mine, and by his secret love for the wife of its administrator, the memory of his capitulation to his torturers (he had finally betrayed his associates) has kept him sceptical of all moral presumptions. Yet this scepticism has its limits. He is unable to forgive himself his treachery because, like Jim, he has made 'an ideal conception of his disgrace' – the gesture, in Conrad's view, 'of an eminently loyal nature' (pp. 375, 376) – and thus affirmed the very values breached by his infidelity. For him, unlike Decoud, life does not present itself in the guise of a trivial farce: what he questions is not the ideals men try to uphold, but only their capacity to uphold them. His brief exchange with the Chief Engineer provides an illustration of this. 'He must be extremely sure of himself', the Chief Engineer says of Charles Gould. 'If that's all he's sure of', Monygham grimly replies, 'then he's sure of nothing' (p. 310). However, guided by his sense of personal failure Monygham chooses not Gould but Nostromo – that other specialist in success – as his special antagonist. Nostromo is not only an example of all that Monygham is not; he also presents him with a problem and a puzzle. He agrees with Decoud that vanity is Nostromo's *raison d'être*: 'His prestige is his fortune', he says to the Chief Engineer. But he is not satisfied, for he knows that a human being cannot, by definition, be a mere phenomenon

[1] See p. 501 for this parallel.

of nature, however magnificent, or be impelled by mere self-affirmation, however intoxicating. With Stein, he knows man also to be a creature of consciousness, capable of distinguishing between his own world and that of others, and hence, whether he admits it or not, entangled in the dilemmas of a moral universe. He is aware, almost to the point of obsession, that no sane person can lead his life merely subjectively, on the assumption that the public realm is nothing more than a field in which to exercise his prowess.

It is appropriate that the novel should bear Nostromo's name on its titlepage, for it is Nostromo's career that uncovers the level of the novel's tragic concerns. If we seek to penetrate beyond Gould's dilemma, and Decoud's amplification of it, we come at last to the problem posed by Nostromo's failure, under the impact of the Sulaco revolution, to sustain the innocence of his defiant subjectivity. As for Gould, so for Nostromo: the battle is always simultaneously won and lost: he will perform the most fabulous of his exploits – the saving of Sulaco and its material interests – at the cost of the integrity of the reputation thus achieved. And in so doing, he will demonstrate, with much greater concentration and power than Jim, the truth of Stein's metaphor: that man is an incomplete being, at once alive and utterly out of life – a product of nature compelled to discover himself in terms of values that nature disregards.

The terms of Nostromo's crisis are most clearly exhibited in the famous passage describing his awakening in the ruined fort after his return from hiding the silver on the Great Isabel. Unknown to him, Monygham is approaching the custom-house where their fateful encounter will shortly take place. Meanwhile, the splendours of sunset over the Placid Gulf are augmenting on a celestial scale the images of blood and darkness that have characterized the scenes of revolution on land.

The great mass of clouds filling the head of the gulf had long red smears amongst its convoluted folds of grey and black, as of a floating mantle stained with blood ... The little wavelets seemed to be tossing tiny red sparks upon the sandy beaches ...

Nostromo woke up from a fourteen hours' sleep, and arose full length from his lair in the long grass. He stood knee deep amongst the whispering undulations of the green blades with the lost air of a man just born into the world. Handsome, robust, and supple, he threw back his head, flung his arms open, and stretched himself with a slow twist of the waist and a leisurely growling yawn of white teeth, as natural and free from evil in the moment of waking as a magnificent and unconscious wild beast. Then, in the suddenly steadied glance fixed upon nothing from under a thoughtful frown, appeared the man.

Nostromo, pp. 411–12

This passage has been highly admired for its symbolic power. And rightly so, for it succeeds in integrating to an astonishing degree the literal (a man awakening from a deep bout of slumber) and the metaphoric (a man awakening from a state of amoral innocence). It is not that one level becomes the vehicle for the other; both exist in their own right, both can be regarded as complementary characterizations of the same incident. Every detail of the passage accurately evokes the sensations of a man in the prime of health suddenly recollecting, as he awakens from a long sleep, an unpleasantly problematic reality. But at the same time this description, in its deft evocation of the myth of creation, offers another view – equally valid but inaccessible to the character himself – of what is happening to him. He is undergoing a metamorphosis from what I have called 'natural man' into what could be termed 'conscious man'. Every human being, Conrad suggests, must be born twice: once out of oblivion into subjectivity – into the amoral beauty of a natural paradise; and once again, out of subjectivity into consciousness – into the perplexing responsibilities of a moral existence. Not even Nostromo can escape this second birth. But what, in his case, gives it its momentousness, is the fact that he has tried to live as if it were indefinitely postponable. Partly because of the very perfection of his natural gifts, he has remained arrested in his state of subjective exaltation. But, in the meantime, the demands of an adult existence have not been abolished. Living only for himself, he has been drawn more and more deeply into the activities of others. When the scales finally drop from his eyes, therefore, he discovers that his subjective self and his objective role – what he is to himself and what he is to others – have drifted dangerously apart. This is why Conrad's description of the process (and the passage above represents only a moment of it) strikes so foreboding a note. For most of us, to arise out of sleep is to begin a new day. When Nostromo opens *his* eyes, he beholds the ominous approach of a blood-streaked darkness.

It is this duality – missed by the over-confident Decoud but not by the more discriminating Monygham – that constitutes the secret of Nostromo's personality. The division between 'subjectivity' and 'consciousness' informs his entire career – not only the later and more disturbed parts of it, but also the earlier, and apparently more integrated, phases. However, given the fact that until his crisis he remains in a state of unconsciousness – asleep, as it were, in his thirst for reputation – Conrad is obliged, for the earlier part of his career, to resort to indirect means. Pre-eminent among these is Nostromo's relationship with the Viola family, which, as I have suggested, acts as a kind of frame to the novel as a whole. This relationship is treated in two distinct sections, each of which brings two members of the family to the foreground – the first part, the parents; the second, the daughters. In his handling of these two pairs Conrad deploys his organizing virtuosity to the full, for, without in any way schematizing his characters, he succeeds in making each pair appeal to both poles of Nostromo's duality: to the 'subjectivity' he squanders, and the 'consciousness' he represses. To be specific: Giorgio Viola encourages, and his wife Teresa condemns, his male vanity; just as, in due course, Giselle will stimulate, and Linda inhibit, his masculine instincts.

In some respects, Giorgio Viola, one of the more splendid of Conrad's secondary characters, is a version of Nostromo in old age. He has become blindly fixed in the integrity of his former self – in the adventurous austerities inspired by his hero Garibaldi – to the point of withdrawing into ever-increasing aloofness, isolation, and anachronism. More explicitly even than Nostromo, he is associated with the innocent grandeur of nature, particularly the snowy peak of Higuerota to which he constantly raises his eyes. Monygham's verdict of him is subtly inclusive: 'A rugged and dreamy character', he calls him, 'living in the republicanism of his young days as in a cloud'. And he goes on at once to make the perceptive connection: 'He has encouraged much of the Capataz's confounded nonsense' (pp. 319–20). Bereaved of his own son, old Giorgio takes great pride in the reckless masculinity of the successor he has chosen. 'A man ought not to be tame', he informs his family. But he says this 'in profound ignorance of his wife's fears and hopes' (p. 254). Married to a man twenty years older than herself, and stricken with a fatal heart disease, *she* sees in Nostromo the protector of her growing family, and perhaps even a future son-in-law. Shrewder than her husband, she senses that Nostromo acknowledges loyalty to nothing outside his own reputation; hence she cannot stop herself railing against the virtues her husband celebrates: Nostromo's poverty, his exploits, his fame, and particularly the name he has earned from those she calls 'the English'. '"This is our Nostromo!" ... What a name! What is that? Nostromo? He would take a name that is properly no word from them' (p. 23). ('Nostromo' is a corruption of the Italian *nostro uomo*: 'our man'.) In such outbursts, she succeeds, significantly, in disconcerting Nostromo himself. It is all very well for old Giorgio, in proud contempt of the world in which he lives, to spur Nostromo to achieve his incomparable individuality. But what he cannot see (and not surprisingly, since he is wrapped in contradictions himself – for instance, as a hater of kings, keeping the inn which provides his livelihood only by the 'grace' of the lady who is effectively queen of Sulaco) is that the individualist, however self-sufficient he tries to be, wholly depends on the presence of others, not only for his material existence, but also for his moral identity. By making the name 'Nostromo' her special target, Teresa Viola unerringly strikes at the heart of the contradiction in which her protégé is unwittingly caught: that the name which is the acknowledgement of his personal prestige is also the symptom of his unconscious servitude. Nostromo's relationship with his foster-parents serves to underline the paradox that flaws the entire structure of his identity: that the more one seeks to belong to oneself, the more one becomes the possession of others.

What the Sulaco revolution does to Nostromo is to compel him to recognize this paradox. His appointed task, to safeguard and deliver the cargo of silver, offers him his greatest chance of self-glorifying action, but also represents the most ruthless instance of the Europeans' exploitation of him. Once again, he duplicates Charles Gould's experience: it is the silver that precipitates his crisis, as it is the silver that will resolve it. The ingots become a moral problem to him even before he takes formal charge of them. Although Teresa Viola knows that he is preparing for some desperate venture, she summons him to her sick-bed, to which her disease has finally confined her, and, convinced that she is dying, asks him to fetch her a priest. He refuses to perform this act of futile kindness (even though he is aware that for *her* it may mean the difference between salvation and damnation), leaves the house, and rejoins Decoud at the harbour. But this time the prospect of an exploit cannot quench the stirrings of anxiety. Once out on the gulf, he becomes so uneasy that his companion begins to sense that 'something deeper, something unsuspected by everyone' (p. 282)[1] is coming to the surface. The demands being made of him have apparently gone beyond the limit. Such is the value of the silver, and such the danger it entails, that, for the first time in his life, he is

[1] The episode is on pp. 261–84.

compelled to distinguish between his interests and those of others. 'This thing has been given to me like a deadly disease', he mutters, '. . . but I cannot believe that its loss would have impoverished Don Carlos Gould very much.' The only chance of closing this widening gap, and so preserving him in his solipsism, is to bring the task to a triumphant conclusion. 'I am going to make it the most famous and desperate affair of my life', he vows. But he fails to convince himself. Envisaging the possibility of failure, he decides (like Gould preparing to blow up the mine) to send the entire cargo to the bottom of the sea rather than face the moral consequences of a personal defeat.

In the event, of course, he experiences neither success nor failure, but a mixture of both: he fails to deliver the silver, but he succeeds in saving it. So when he awakens in the dusk of the ruined fort, he enters a period of extreme indetermination: his vanity being only 'half-appeased', he becomes vulnerable to self-doubt without becoming capable of self-knowledge. *Lord Jim* has taught us what Conrad is capable of achieving in the delineation of ambiguous states of mind; his treatment of Nostromo's crisis of identity (which closely resembles Jim's at a number of points) does not disappoint us. Nostromo's suspicion that he has been made use of now hardens into certainty; but he is not prepared to draw from this discovery any conclusion derogatory to himself. Instead – and this is one of Conrad's master-strokes – he is instantly overwhelmed by a feeling of betrayal. To be sure, making use of a man's qualities without taking thought for the man himself is, in a sense, to betray him. But to consider Nostromo as a noble savage undone by capitalist exploitation is to fall short of Conrad's conception. Whether consciously or not, Nostromo has been in collusion with his own exploiters and encouraged them to disregard the man in favour of the reputation. His feeling of betrayal, therefore, is more than the response to a fact; it is a symptom of self-deception. 'The Capataz de Cargadores', writes Conrad, naming a role that no longer quite fits, 'on a revulsion of subjectiveness . . . beheld all this world without faith or courage. He had been betrayed!' (pp. 417–18). This is the instinctive recoil of a damaged personality incapable of questioning its own premises. With the failure of his mission, his passion for public success has received an unwonted check; he has forfeited the praises of the men who have guaranteed his fame. Furthermore, those very men have allowed themselves to fall into the hands of their enemies. Abruptly cut off from the applause that has sustained his identity, he can only conclude, true to his own subjectivity, that this applause has been false, and the applauders traitors. But, in its context, his feeling of betrayal requires a more subtle account still. To make use of a man is, in effect, to treat a human subject *as if he were an object*. For the very first time, Nostromo is forced to consider himself from a point outside himself. His subjectivity has been betrayed in the most radical way possible; and it is scarcely surprising that he should be experiencing a dazed sense 'of having inadvertently gone out of his existence' (pp. 413–22).

This complex experience has two immediate but contradictory effects. On the one hand, it makes him conscious of his poverty; where he once heedlessly squandered his talents, he now begins to measure his deserts and calculate his resentments. On the other hand, it makes him conscious of his solitude; where he had once transformed the whole population of Sulaco into a crowd of dazzled spectators, he is now unable to seek the simple advice and reassurance he needs, even from his immediate employers and protectors. Giorgio Viola, Captain Mitchell, Charles Gould – what are these but undependable and untrustworthy strangers? His sense of betrayal at once provokes his need for help and prevents him from satisfying it.

It is in this dangerously uncertain frame of mind that he comes upon Dr Monygham, who has returned to the deserted harbour with the desperate intention of preventing Sotillo from linking with the Monterists. This unexpected confrontation, developed over two chapters (pp. 425–39 and 452–64), can be regarded as the climax of the novel, for on it hangs the outcome of the Sulaco crisis and the fate of all the major characters. The suspense, which turns on whether Monygham will be able to persuade Nostromo to recall the Cayta regiment, is sustained with all Conrad's narrative skill. But it is also an episode which concentrates, with all Conrad's sceptical insight, the novel's exploration of what could be called the cross-purposes of plurality: the fact that a man's thoughts are his own but his deeds belong to others. It brings to culmination the dichotomies which the novel has gradually built up, and as such becomes the source of an extraordinary multiplication of ironies.

The first and perhaps the most fundamental of these is the fact that a major political and military crisis is actually resolved by two men who have become utterly incapable of understanding each other. At the best of times, Nostromo and Monygham are natural antagonists: the one is an athlete, an egoist, a doer, who half fears his opponent's jeering; the other is a cripple, a self-denier, a doubter, who half envies his adversary's self-assurance. But what now puts them quite out of each other's reach is the fact that they have just undergone a secret inversion of roles. Monygham, blinded by his desire to save Mrs Gould, has no idea that the incorruptible Capataz, feeling that his life has failed him in all its details, is desperately in need of personal recognition and assistance. Similarly, Nostromo is incapable of knowing that the sinister English doctor, far from being identified with the material interests of the treacherous Europeans, is preparing to risk his life for the sake of a disinterested, indeed unrequitable, love.

Out of this mutual incomprehension is spun a web of deadly ironies. It would be a major and perhaps sterile task to disentangle them all; I shall confine myself, here, to bringing out their general function, which is to enact and demonstrate the incompatibility of thought and action. Nostromo feels himself most disregarded precisely at the point when he has become most indispensable. But again, it is precisely because he is so necessary that he is made to feel so unheeded. Monygham, in his excitement at discovering that the one man capable of saving Sulaco (and Mrs Gould) has not been drowned after all, sees before him not 'a fellow-creature escaped from the jaws of death', but a reputation and an instrument. Thus everything he says confirms Nostromo's worst suspicions. In this context, the macabre object that casts its shadow over the entire encounter – the hanging body of Señor Hirsch – assumes its proper significance. For Monygham, it is a clue to Sotillo's nature, which must be unravelled if his purposes are to succeed. For Nostromo, it is a symbol of his own predicament, a 'terrible example of neglect' confirming Monygham's pitiless disregard of men no longer useful to him. (This identification with a man who, as the embodiment of fear, had seemed Nostromo's antithesis barely twenty-four hours before is a measure of the extent of Nostromo's transformation.) The dangling corpse acts as a grim arbiter, defining the two men's differences, but also identifying what is at issue between them. This is, of course, the object from which we are never allowed to stray very far, and to which we always return: the cargo of silver, which has been the cause of Hirsch's death, and which Monygham and Nostromo, each in his own way, are proposing to exploit.

For Monygham, the silver itself is a matter of complete indifference. It is merely a means to an end – the controlling of Sotillo's movements. But – ironically again – this attitude only confirms Nostromo's sense of his exploitation. For him, the silver has acquired an almost moral significance. He has been asked to risk his life to save it: the reasons behind such a request therefore cannot be trivial. But Monygham believes that the whole oper- ation has been frivolous from the start (he considers Decoud's plan to have been merely puerile). Under Monygham's contempt, one of the bases of Nostromo's self-respect – the seriousness of the tasks on which he has been employed – starts to weaken. But as one base dissolves, it is gradually replaced by another – the attraction of the treasure itself, something he has felt almost obsessively from the venture's very inception. This sinister transference takes the form, psychologically, of an overpowering desire to preserve the secret of the silver's survival – to ensure, against his own sense of having been betrayed, that the silver will not share the same fate. This new attitude, in its turn, gives rise to another set of revealing ironies. With everybody except Sotillo, Monygham has assumed that the silver-lighter has been sunk in the middle of the gulf. It occurs to him, however, that if he can persuade Sotillo that it is recoverable, he will be able to retain a measure of ascendancy over him. So he begins to elaborate a scenario. Yet the more he invents, the closer he gets to the truth; and the closer he gets to the truth, the more Nostromo is driven into active deceit. Finally, he decides to inform Sotillo that the silver is hidden on the Great Isabel (fiction and truth now coincide). The horrified Nostromo at once makes a counter-proposal: that Sotillo should be told that the silver is concealed in the harbour, on the grounds (valid both for Mony- gham and for himself, though for opposite reasons) that the island can be searched out too easily. Monygham welcomes this sugges- tion as yet another example of the Capataz's formidable resource- fulness; but he cannot guess how *really* resourceful he has been. Nostromo, however, knows it only too well, and in a sudden revulsion of feeling at what is happening to him he tries to break free from the fateful doctor, rushing away from him as from the arch-tempter himself. But to no avail: as Monygham catches up with him again, he is already half resigned to his fate. When the opportunity presents itself, he will let himself trade the truth of public glory for the reality of furtive greed; and his ride to Cayta, the act which will crown his incorruptible reputation, will seal his enslavement to the incorruptible metal.

Inevitably, the outcome of this encounter produces paradoxical consequences for both participants. In stepping into the public arena, Monygham, the arch-opponent of material interests, has helped to guarantee their survival, and in saving the life of the woman he loves, he has ensured the conditions of her lasting misery. But this unwonted venture into action is only temporary, and, once Sulaco is safe, he quickly reassumes his stance of ironic observer. Nostromo, on the other hand, remains an agent to the end, and thereby retains all his representative significance. The career of Charles Gould tragically illustrated the impossibility of keeping thought and action in significant relation to each other. In Nostromo's career, this tragic incompatibility takes a slightly different form. For him, the difficulty consists in rising to thought at all – in achieving an understanding of his moral predicament. Having reached a point at which he is squarely brought up against the relativity of his own existence, he proves incapable of adjusting himself to the fact. But once a man has experienced the challenge of consciousness, he can no longer retain his innocence: by trying to remain the same person, Nostromo alters himself drastically; the hero becomes a thief.

I have no intention of denying, of course, that Nostromo takes the silver because he wants it for himself. But there is much more to this than vulgar greed. It is a direct consequence of the way he has lived his life: a demonstration of the fragility of an integrity founded on vanity. He is perfectly aware that he is committing a crime, not only against those who have entrusted the silver to him, but also – and chiefly – against the one to whom it has been entrusted. But he turns his back on this knowledge because he has built his career on the assumption that his is a special case. He does not pretend that what he is doing is right; rather, he takes it for granted that its wrongness does not matter to a man like him. Referring to his part in the deaths of Teresa Viola and Martin Decoud, he tries to justify his decision to keep the silver: 'First a woman, then a man, abandoned each in their last extremity, for the sake of the accursed treasure. It was paid for by a soul lost and by a vanished life' (p. 502). He may seem at first to be acknowledging the logic of crime and punishment; what he is in fact doing is using his own moral sense (his feeling of guilt at the death of two human beings) as an object of barter. His is the classical bargain, the exchange of a soul for a certain number of pieces of silver, and it exacts the classical consequences.

His damnation – for that is how Conrad encourages us to think of his fate – consists in his being compelled to *become the silver*. 'His courage, his magnificence, his leisure, his work, everything was as before', Conrad writes, 'only everything was a sham. But the treasure was real' (pp. 523–4). Nostromo's public image has remained unchanged, but he is no longer the same man. His reputation, once the shop-window of his personality, has become an impenetrable blind, cutting him off completely from the gaze of others. It guarantees his secret, but at the price of absolute solitude. This deprivation of human contact produces, as a sort of compensation, an increasing obsession with the silver; this in turn sharpens his isolation, and thus accentuates yet further 'the concentration of his thought on the treasure' (pp. 523–4). Reflecting on this vicious circle, Conrad writes: 'A transgression, a crime, entering a man's existence, eats it up like a malignant growth' (pp. 523–4). In Nostromo's case, this is no over-statement, for what he has transgressed, finally, is the source of spontaneity within himself. By identifying himself with what the novel has taught us to regard as the quintessence of materiality, he gradually acquires a new and perverted kind of objectivity. In this too, he resembles Gould, though he has obviously gone much further, and exposed the underlying issues more nakedly.

In becoming the slave of the silver, Nostromo has not escaped the related claims of 'subjectivity' (or individual fulfilment) and 'consciousness' (or moral responsibility); he has merely placed them beyond his reach. This, the final insight of the novel, brings Conrad's massive design to a logical (but perhaps slightly overwrought) conclusion. Nostromo's relationship with the other half of the Viola family, the daughters Linda and Giselle (pp. 529–54), performs much the same general function in the novel's last two chapters as his relationship with their parents earlier. Both girls are passionately in love with him. Linda loves him with a concentrated, uncompromising fidelity that will defy all time and chance. Giselle, indolent and demure, like 'a young panther', abandons herself to the variable intensities of immediate sensation. But Nostromo's responses are now contaminated at their source. The moral austerities of Linda fill him with dismay: he is no longer free to reject her, for fear that her father (who, at Nostromo's own request, has become the keeper of the newly built lighthouse on the Great Isabel) will forbid him the island and cut him off from the treasure. The amoral seductiveness of Giselle profoundly appeals to his instinctual self: but he cannot unreservedly give himself to her without betraying the secret of the treasure's hiding-place. His loves and his silver are located in the same spot. Unable to forgo either, he sets up a situation of such ambiguity that it has to conclude in disaster. Mistaken for an undesirable suitor of Giselle's (which in fact he is), he is shot down like a thief (which indeed he is also) by her father and his patron. But even this is not the end of his sufferings. Mortally wounded, he makes a last attempt to liberate himself from the curse of the silver. He summons Mrs Gould to his bedside – much as Teresa Viola, years ago, had summoned him to hers – and tries to tell her where the treasure is concealed. But, in accordance with the laws of poetic justice, he is, in his turn, left to his fate. The lady whose compassion in Sulaco has earned her the title of the Madonna herself has, at this supreme moment, her single lapse. Her only intervention in the affairs of Costaguana (keeping the news of the impending invasion from her husband in order to allow the transport train to come down from the mine) has made her hate the very mention of that fatal consignment. So with the words, 'No-one remembers it now. Let it be lost for ever' (p. 560), she stops Nostromo from speaking, and thus prolongs his silence into eternity.

V

The degree to which the fate of the individual characters of the novel is integrated into the fate of their country poses a fundamental problem. The kind of tragedy with which we are all familiar, whether in Sophocles or Ibsen, which confronts a heroic, or at least defiant, individual with the consequences of his actions, does not compromise the whole of existence. Something usually survives the fall of the tragic hero. The gored state is able to recover at least a measure of its original integrity, the scattered universe to reassemble itself into at least some degree of order. By enlarging individual into national tragedy, however, Conrad seems to offer a historical perspective from which all hope has been removed. The cynical insights of Decoud, amplified by Monygham's more committed and therefore more embittered scepticism, seem irrefutable. Their grasp of the nature of the historical forces at work in Costaguana seems to lead to a despairing prospect, in which every victory promises to be a defeat, and every conquest an enslavement. This hopelessness has had the effect of undermining the confidence of a number of readers in the reality of the novel's values, and therefore – since traditional tragedy comes of a thwarting rather than a nullification of values – of diluting its tragic impact. F. R. Leavis, who greatly admires the novel, has said, 'For all the rich variety of the interest and the tightness of the pattern, the reverberation of *Nostromo* has something hollow about it.' This he explains by suggesting that it lacks any 'intimate sense ... of the day-to-day continuities of social living' to counter-balance 'the futilities of a public drama'.[1] Yet Conrad does not leave the vision of a Decoud, or even of a Monygham, wholly unqualified. Over and against their historical scepticism he sets an investigation of what could be called historical faith. Such a faith must not be confused with the confidence in material progress of the engineers and the financiers. Rather, it involves a commitment to the country for its own sake – inspired by personal emotion and sustained by individual assumptions about the nature of public events.

The most limited representation of this view can be found in Captain Mitchell, the chief officer of the small merchant fleet servicing Costaguana's coast. He is infatuated with Sulaco, but it is the infatuation of a man with his hobby. Conditioned by the self-sufficient tradition of the Merchant Service, he remains perpetually 'astonished at the importance of the transactions (other than relating to shipping) which take place on dry land' (p. 112). But this is the magnification of foreignness – the response of the tourist sundered from the standard familiarities of his life. The great affairs of Sulaco seem to him exactly like adventures out of a popular history book – with the single difference that, since the story is happening all around him, he can really play a part in it ('I am a public character, sir!'). This conception of history, of course, prohibits any real understanding of history: the more he feels himself to be in the thick of 'epoch-making' events, the more completely he is outside them. Like many people protected from the darker realities by lack of imagination coupled with a sense of customary well-being, what he really values is moral respectability. For him, progress means the propagation of respectability. It is for the sake of respectability that he supports material interests; and when, in a splendid late chapter (Part III, Chapter 10), he celebrates their triumph, he does so by showing off a Sulaco purged of Latin incompetence and native disreputability. In other words, material interests receive their homage from the man least capable of grasping their true significance.

Yet the contribution of this naïve, pompous, and affectionate man is not wholly negative. His attitude to Sulaco (like his attitude to Nostromo) may be obtuse, but it is not ungenerous. As the last, and perhaps the most severe, of Conrad's studies of uncritical

[1] Leavis, *Great Tradition*, p. 221.

service, he has not lost all traces of the original ideal. Consider his encounter with the irrationally ferocious Sotillo (pp. 328–42). To be sure, it merely confirms his prejudices as a conservative British master-mariner. (The experience will not cure him, for example, of the habit of referring to every political disaster as 'a mistake'.) But at the same time it brings out a not-unimpressive indestructibility. In the matter of his confiscated watch, his outraged indignation even defeats Sotillo's hysterical greed. In the context of Costaguana's desperate history, Mitchell's unimaginative probity may be a small thing, but what it offers is neither inhumane nor contemptible.

The feelings of Don José Avellanos for Costaguana are altogether more serious. His is the love of a disinterested patriot – of a man who has represented his country as ambassador, and who profoundly desires to bring it under the rule of law and see it assume 'an honourable place in ... the comity of civilized nations' (p. 140). It is as a sponsor of legality and a guarantor of treaties that he welcomes the prospect of material progress. Under its impetus, he is able to mobilize the party of educated landowners and bring the constitutionalist Ribiera to power. His hopes for the country are grounded on the old liberal assumption that men are fundamentally rational. Knowing that Costaguana has inherited a tradition of anarchy and violence (he has himself been one of its victims), he believes that if his compatriots can be made to understand it honestly, they will be able to liberate themselves from its influence. Accordingly, he becomes its historian, calling his book *Fifty Years of Misrule*. Yet his concept of 'misrule' is not finally much more adequate than Mitchell's notion of a 'mistake'. Under what is virtually the first gust of the revolutionary tempest, the entire structure of his life's work collapses. The historian is overtaken by history: the pages of his book become wads for muzzle-loaders; and the last enactment of this life-long constitutionalist is to sanction an illegal project of secession. Yet his contribution to the meaning of the novel, like Mitchell's, cannot be dismissed as merely irrelevant. Subjected, for example, to the worst cruelties of Guzman Bento's torturers, he retains all his scrupulous fairness of mind. The truth and justice that make him describe his former persecutor as a victim of ignorance (p. 142) are qualities that shine out with great purity in the surrounding darkness of obsessions and fanaticisms. They may be defeated, but they are not invalidated, by events.

However, it is in Emilia Gould that the subtlest and richest vision of Costaguana is to be found. Avellanos tells her she is 'as true a patriot as though you had been born in our midst' (p. 86): but she is not a patriot as he understands it. She could never make a study of the horrors of the recent past, for she refuses to take on its own terms the 'puerile and bloodthirsty game ... of saving the country'. During her travels over campo and mountain, however, she responds with an extraordinary vividness to the enduring life of landscape and people. Her old Spanish house in Sulaco, which she keeps open to all comers, evokes all that is noble and spacious in the traditions of her adopted land. Capable of the most 'delicate shades of self-forgetfulness' in her relations with others, she dispenses a kind of redemptive grace. If she decides to associate herself with the impersonal forces of material progress that her husband brings to Sulaco, it is largely because of her compassion for the ordinary people of the land, whom she sees 'suffering and mute, waiting for the future in a pathetic immobility of patience' (p. 88). But unlike Mitchell, or even Avellanos, she mistrusts these forces from the start. She welcomes them as a means of amelioration, but she fears their transforming power. 'The future means change – an utter change', she tells the visiting Railway President, when she asks him to preserve Giorgio Viola's old tavern from the destructive zeal of his survey engineers. And her words are prophetic, for she lives to see them fulfilled beyond even her worst fears. She witnesses Sulaco overtaken, with all the fiestas, traditions, and customs of former days, by 'the material apparatus of perfected civilization which obliterates the individuality of old towns under the stereotyped conveniences of modern life' (p. 96); she observes her social work in the mining community reduced to 'mere insignificant vestiges of the initial inspiration' (p. 222); she experiences, as a person of generous affections, all the anguish of a solitary and childless existence. What she has tried to uphold, with her simplicity and charm, is not a principle, or a system, or an ideology, but the life of the moral imagination. 'The wisdom of the heart', Conrad writes, glancing at the rhetorical vices of Costaguana, 'having no concern with the erection or demolition of theories any more than with the defence of prejudices, has no random words at its command. The words it pronounces have the value of acts of integrity' (p. 67). Such an appraisal of Emilia Gould comes very close to associating her special gift with the art of the novelist himself. That this gift is not merely ideal is demonstrated by the part it plays in the saving of Sulaco. What finally persuades Nostromo to recall the Cayta regiment is not

Monygham's machinations (themselves, we remember, inspired by love for Mrs Gould), but old Giorgio Viola's request, out of gratitude for Mrs Gould's original kindness in keeping a roof over *his* head, that a roof be kept over hers. The centrality of her imaginative faith is even more clearly demonstrated by the fact that it is exposed to the full force of the scepticism, first of Decoud, who confirms her suspicions that her husband has sacrificed her for his mine, then of Monygham, who endorses her fears of the futility of this sacrifice. Meeting the doctor again after a long absence, and talking over past times with him, she feels suddenly, with a greater pang than ever before, all the sterility of the work on which she has staked and lost her happiness. But her moment of despair, as she sits in the sunlit stillness of her garden, is also a moment of illumination. 'It had come into her mind that for life to be large and full, it must contain the care of the past and of the future in every passing moment of the present. Our daily work must be done to the glory of the dead, and for the good of those who come after' (pp. 520–1). In its simplicity and precision, this thought seems to me to light up every detail of the elaborate action we have just witnessed. That her faith can coexist, though it cannot be reconciled, with the terrible knowledge she has been obliged to acquire is itself a triumph – not least in that she makes it possible for Monygham's scepticism to resist the corrosions of indifference or unconcern. That their friendship, which endures all the vicissitudes of Sulaco's tumultuous history, should continue to flourish in the desolation of material success is not irrelevant to a final assessment of the novel's quality. However unsparing Conrad's exposure of the tragic contradiction of faith and scepticism may be, there is nothing nihilistic about *this* 'Tale of the Seaboard'.

6

The Secret Agent

I had no idea to consider Anarchism politically, or to treat it seriously in its philosophical aspects.

(from a letter of 12 September 1906 to John Galsworthy)

I

Conrad himself acknowledges that *The Secret Agent* was conceived as a contrast to *Nostromo*. 'One fell to musing before the phenomenon – even of the past', he writes in the 'Author's Note' to the new novel:

of South America, a continent of crude sunshine and brutal revolutions, of the sea, the vast expanse of salt waters, the mirror of heaven's frowns and smiles, the reflector of the world's light. Then the vision of an enormous town presented itself, of a monstrous town more populous than some continents and in its man-made might as if indifferent to heaven's frowns and smiles; a cruel devourer of the world's light.

The Secret Agent, p, xii

And Conrad does not confine himself to stating this contrast in a preface; he actually builds it into the novel itself. Among his major characters, he includes one whose function is partly to highlight the differences between life at home and life abroad. The Assistant Commissioner who takes charge of the inquiry into the Greenwich explosion can be regarded as a diminished Charles Gould. Like Gould, he is a man whose 'real abilities, which were mainly of an administrative order, were combined with an adventurous disposition' (p. 113).[1] But because of a socially advantageous marriage, he has been obliged to exchange the freedom and initiative of a police career in the colonies for a high departmental post in Scotland Yard. Despite the advantages of the new rank, he continues to feel 'a square peg forced into a round hole'. He can adapt himself neither to the climate of England, which obliges him to remain indoors, nor to its institutions, which seem to have a repressive life of their own. Being subjected to a task defined not by

[1] Cf. pp. 99–100, 114.

himself but by the department to which he belongs and conducted on the basis of instructions from above and reports from below, he becomes susceptible to periodic fits of depression. This maladjustment, which the novel emphasizes in a variety of ways, has one major function: to highlight the degree of organization, integration, institutionalization, *socialization* even, reached by the society that stifles him. And at no point does this society's tendency to cramp and frustrate emerge more sharply than when the individual momentarily escapes its clutches – when the Assistant Commissioner, slipping his official bonds with a pleasurable sense of 'evil freedom', reverts to the style of his former occupation, and plunges into the rainy darkness after Verloc like a hunter into the jungle after his prey.

Failure to take into account the *kind* of society represented in *The Secret Agent* is largely responsible for what has become virtually the standard charge against the novel: that, for all its extraordinary virtuosity, it lacks (as Jocelyn Baines puts it) 'a unifying theme',[1] and fails to be (in Albert Guerard's words) 'a work of exploration and discovery'.[2] As long as we assume that its main concern is the exposure of anarchism, we shall continue to regard it as a work in which execution completely outstrips content: for it is quite plain that Conrad has nothing new to tell us about anarchism as such. The society which is the target of this anarchism, however, is quite a different matter. Inasmuch as *The Secret Agent* is concerned with a so-called 'advanced', or 'evolved', or 'developed' nation, it is concerned with an essentially conservative one. The novel's central purpose is the exploration of this conservatism. Such a subject, of course, is quite sufficient to engage Conrad's most creative attention. But in the form it assumes in *The Secret Agent*, it acquires an additional interest. The conservatism it exhibits is not that of any long-established society, but specifically of what Conrad calls 'the very centre of the Empire on which the sun never sets' – that is, of the land of his choice and adoption.

However, as soon as Conrad's special interest in the nature of English conservatism is granted, a qualification becomes necessary. The novel is not concerned with conservatism in any strictly *political* sense – in the principles of English Toryism, for example –

[1] Baines, *Joseph Conrad*, p. 408.
[2] Guerard, *Conrad the Novelist*, p. 224. Critical essays on *The Secret Agent* have been collected by I. Watt (ed.), *Conrad: 'The Secret Agent'* (Macmillan 'Casebook', 1973). In particular, Watt reprints Thomas Mann's short essay, an introduction to the 1926 German translation of the novel, which contains much the most intelligent discussion of Conrad's attitude to England that I have come across.

but in a more general and diffused *social* sense – in an identifiable pattern of conduct and feeling more fundamental than commitment to this or that political party. For instance, the political complexion of the England Conrad describes is, strictly speaking, Liberal, not Conservative. The Home Secretary, Sir Ethelred, to whom the Assistant Commissioner is ultimately responsible (and who is modelled, as it happens, on the Liberal leader Sir William Harcourt), is engaged, against the frantic opposition of his Tory rival, in the 'revolutionary measure' of nationalizing the fisheries. Yet much of the comedy of the two scenes in which he features (pp. 135–46 and 214–22) derives from the fact that the man wildly accused of initiating nothing less than a 'social revolution' is, in every possible respect – in the antiquity of his name, the monumentality of his person, the augustness of his office, the absurdity of his prejudices, and even the nature of his infirmities – a veritable incarnation of the late Victorian establishment. What we remember about him is not his specific political stance, but the symbolic weakness of his eyes under their green shade, or his lofty aversion to details, or his bafflement at the proposition that the world is less than perfect.

So far as conservatism in *The Secret Agent* finds political expression at all, it is in the form of a national policy of moderation. Such a policy must not be taken as a symptom of the weakness of the body politic; on the contrary, it is a mark of its stability, its cohesiveness, and its confidence in itself. The British government's toleration of revolutionary refugees from abroad smothers them in a demoralizing embrace, reducing their principles to vacant clichés and their programmes to private posturings. The only positive action against the *status quo* in this story of stasis – the Greenwich explosion – is not a revolutionary, but a reactionary, deed which provokes greater alarm and despondency in the ranks of the anarchists (Ossipon's reaction is representative) than in those of the police. The state remains wholly unendangered by the existence of expatriate revolutionaries within its borders. To Verloc, the best-informed character in the novel, the very 'notion of a menaced social order' seems derisory. What, then, is the function of the anarchists in *The Secret Agent*? It is to provoke questions not about themselves, but about what they nominally oppose; to promote an inquiry not into the politics of revolutionary anarchism, but into the prevailing climate of English public life.

Since the main effect of such moderation is to neutralize revolutionary activity, it follows that its antithesis is not anarchism but *extremism*, whether of the left or of the right. Accordingly, *The Secret Agent* offers two brilliantly contrasted extremists: on the far right, the Russian *agent provocateur* Vladimir, and on the far left, the American terrorist known as 'the Professor'. It is they, not the sorry collection of plotters who haunt Verloc's shop, who represent the novel's real principle of opposition. Although these two men are nominal antagonists in almost every respect, they join each other in the virulence of their hatred of English *laissez faire*, for they recognize how fatal it is to the fanaticism on which political violence feeds. Thus they collaborate, in fact if not in intention, in the Greenwich explosion, the one providing the motive, the other the means. And – to seal this appropriately ironic alliance – they dismiss the ideology of moderation in identical terms. 'There is a proverb in this country which says prevention is better than cure', Vladimir tells Verloc. 'It is stupid in a general way. There is no end to prevention. But it is characteristic. They dislike finality in this country ... Don't you be too English', he adds; 'this country is absurd with its sentimental regard for individual liberty' (pp. 25, 29). The Professor endorses these sentiments to the letter. 'It is this country that is dangerous with her idealistic conception of legality', he tells Ossipon. 'The social spirit of the people is wrapped up in scrupulous prejudices, and that is fatal to our work ... Nothing would please me more than to see Inspector Heat and his like take to shooting us down in broad daylight with the approval of the public' (p. 73). The Professor's target is no more the autocratic viciousness of a Russia than Vladimir's is the collective 'lawlessness' of an America. The purpose that unites them is the attempt to provoke the British establishment into passing what Vladimir calls 'universal repressive legislation'.

For all this, however, the conservatism represented in the novel remains more social than political. What this distinction implies can be brought out by a further analysis of Conrad's pair of extremists. Their hostility is not confined to English political moderation; they are also at odds with something more fundamental – with the very idea of the social life. They themselves are socially dislocated outsiders. Vladimir has never been attached to society – or at least to the kind of society we call civilized. The urbanity which he parades in various upper-class salons is only a performance – a piece of sustained mimicry; he has no understanding of the real thing. His conversation with Verloc is full of random tacks and reversals; the 'unprincipled' nimbleness with which he switches from menace to frivolity and from contempt to jocularity suggests a man spinning in the void of his own conceit, unable to find any purchase on the surfaces of the social edifice. Underneath all his glitter, he remains the irredeemably 'hyperborean' savage he has been from birth. As for the Professor, he has, as we say now, 'dropped out' of society altogether. By temperament and upbringing an otherworldly puritan, he has caught a violent dose of the disease endemic in the country of his birth – the compulsion to return to first principles at the least social or political provocation. He has aimed at achieving worldly success 'without the medium of arts, graces, tact, wealth – by sheer weight of merit alone' (p. 80): that is to say, in abysmal ignorance of the realities of life, he has pursued the rewards of compromise through the practice of inflexibility. His inevitable failure leaves him fanatically persuaded of the injustice of cultural institutions and turns him violently against the 'very framework of an established social order'. Both men (but especially the Professor, who is intelligent where Vladimir is merely glib) declare war against the very idea of organized life.

The precise objective of the Professor's attack is admirably defined by a man who, in a number of important respects, is his antithesis: Chief Inspector Heat. A chance encounter in a side street at dusk brings them up briefly against each other (pp. 80–4, 91–6). Healthy (to the point of self-satisfaction), conventional (with a mind 'inaccessible to ideas of revolt'), and successful (aware, unlike the Professor, that 'a reputation is built as much on manner as on achievement'), the Chief Inspector mentally compares 'the unwholesome little agent of destruction' before him with the ordinary burglars he has known – 'sane, without morbid ideas, working by routine, respectful of constituted authorities, free from all taint of hate and despair'. The instinctive kinship he feels with the professional thief is an acknowledgement of the fact that, despite their apparent antagonism, they belong to the same world, recognizing the same conventions, and sharing the same values – whether in their regard for property or in their regard for the rules that define success and failure. Heat's moment of nostalgia for the simple housebreaker is described as 'a tribute to what is normal in the constitution of society'. The idea of the 'normal' forms one of the fundamental concepts of the novel. In attacking everything that goes under its name, the Professor opposes one of man's most basic instincts – the essentially conservative tendency to avoid the exceptional and the aberrant in favour of the received and the familiar. If, as I have argued, political conservatism in *The Secret*

Agent presupposes the idea of *moderation*, social conservatism rests on the idea of *normality*.

Conservatism in the social sense can be described as a kind of cement binding individuals together and preventing communities from losing cohesion and continuity, and disintegrating into their constituent atoms. It follows that, however deeply rooted the individual's need for change may be, it remains under the censorship of an even deeper necessity. The pervasiveness of this deeper instinct can be demonstrated by a moment's examination of the Professor's relationship with the ordinary anarchists, and particularly with the failed medical student Ossipon, the only member of the group to whom he deigns to speak. The first of their two conversations in the Silenus restaurant is, in essence, a demonstration of how drastic anarchism must be if it is to escape the sway of conservative normality (pp. 61–79).

The Professor's contempt for the ordinary anarchists stems from what he calls their lack of 'character'. 'What you say means nothing', he tells Ossipon brutally. 'You are the worthy delegates for revolutionary propaganda, but the trouble is not only that you are as unable to think independently as any respectable grocer or journalist of them all, but that you have no character whatever.' The Professor justifies *his* possession of this commodity on the grounds that the police really believe that if they try to arrest him he will blow himself up. To have character, then, is to be capable of really meaning what you say – of bringing your words and actions into line with each other. This is precisely what the other anarchists are unable to do. The violence and extravagance of their views, which Conrad caricatures with his typical sardonic zest, are flatly contradicted by the passivity and conventionality of their lives. The lurid terrorist Karl Yundt is in fact helplessly dependent on the care of an old woman; the utopian marxist Michaelis owes his security to the patronage of a great lady; the scientific materialist Ossipon keeps himself in pocket by exploiting a clientele of girl-friends. All three are too compromised by their participation in ordinary life to impart any real meaning to their attacks on society. In this respect they even become indistinguishable from the forces of law and order. 'You revolutionists', mocks the Professor, 'are the slaves of the social convention, which is afraid of you; slaves of it as much as the very police that stands up in defence of that convention.' And how right he is a telling little parable immediately demonstrates. Ossipon is appalled by the danger to which the unscheduled Greenwich explosion exposes the anarchist exiles. 'Under the present circumstances it's nothing short of criminal', he declares. But to call a revolutionary explosion 'criminal' is to use the language of the police – that is, to espouse the cause of legality. The Professor spots this at once. 'Criminal! What is that? What *is* crime? What can be the meaning of such an assertion?' Ossipon's reply is conclusive: 'How am I to express myself? One must use the current words.' One must indeed. But the point is that if one does so one has *already* presupposed the fact of social convention. By using language at all, one automatically submits to an infinitely subtle system of inherited codes. To speak intelligibly is to perform a conservative act.

The reason for the Professor's moral authority is that he sees this point perfectly clearly. He understands with an undeviating logic that the only way for an anarchist to avoid self-contradiction is total renunciation. This is the justification of his perverted martyrdom – of his isolation, his poverty, his silence, his asceticism, his unremitting industry. 'But what do you want from us?' asks the exasperated Ossipon. 'A perfect detonator', is the peremptory reply. Anything beyond single-minded concentration on physical violence, irrespective of who uses it or even why it is used, infallibly absorbs the anarchist into the very thing he is trying to destroy. There must be no explanations, no definitions, no hope – for hope (as a more orthodox mystic has it[1]) would be hope for the wrong thing. And therefore, alone of the anarchists, the Professor can boast: 'It is I who am the true propagandist.' No one else is prepared or able to pay the full price of consistency. And indeed the price is high. The Professor's systematic rejection of normality costs him his sanity.

II

One of the main functions of the anarchists in *The Secret Agent*, then, is to establish the meaning of conservatism of a certain kind: to show, especially through the Professor, that such a conservatism is a necessary, if not a sufficient, condition for the mutual stability of individual and society. To conclude from this, however, that the purpose of the novel is to affirm the need for the more conventional virtues would be grossly mistaken. On the contrary: one truth having been established, Conrad's entire project becomes the establishment of a counter-truth – to persuade us, in this case, that life is not only ordinary, but also terrible, and that the difference

[1] T. S. Eliot in 'East Coker', Section III.

between the 'normality' that keeps us sane and what the novel refers to as 'madness and despair' may be no more than a function of the direction and depth of our gaze.

The idea of the simultaneous existence of the commonplace and the catastrophic is implicit in the very structure of the novel's narrative. Consider, for example, the way in which Conrad exploits the conventions of the ordinary crime story, which work on the principle that an apparently superficial event (the crime) requires a profound interpreter (the detective). Early in *The Secret Agent* we are offered through Ossipon an unremarkable newspaper report of an apparently pointless explosion; at the same time, the novel takes us downwards, as it were, into the more devious practices of a foreign embassy, and the less official activities of the metropolitan police, and the domestic affairs of an insalubrious shopkeeper, until the essential horror of the event stands fully revealed. These ever-deepening disclosures do not falsify the superficial facts. The two realities – the one open, through newspapers, reports, gossip, to the curiosity of an indifferent public, the other available, through first-hand experience, to the appalled imagination of the participants – exist side by side. Or again, consider the same narrative back to front. Here too, and again through Ossipon, the novel's concluding pages offer us a newspaper report – the very voice of misinformed humanity – recording the 'impenetrable mystery' of Mrs Verloc's disappearance. And the effect of this inverted perspective is much the same. A terrible private catastrophe passes almost unnoticed. An entire family – husband, wife, brother – is obliterated, and the stream of life flows on unperturbed. Society, it would seem, survives on the strength of its members' capacity to disregard the madness and despair that infects them. 'It's extraordinary how we go through life with eyes half shut, with dull ears, with dormant thoughts. Perhaps it's just as well; and it may be that it is this very dullness that makes life to the incalculable majority so supportable and so welcome.'[1] Conrad has not forgotten Marlow's words in *Lord Jim*. In *The Secret Agent* 'normality' is the habit, acquired early and well, of looking without seeing. The conservatism that keeps men stable does so by making them blind.

The force of this paradox is stressed by the fact that the novel's only character whose sight is wholly unclouded is a congenital simpleton. Mrs Verloc's brother, Stevie, is as significant as the Professor to the novel's exploratory pattern. We have seen that

[1] *Lord Jim*, p. 143.

Vladimir is the Professor's natural analogue; Stevie, in a different and more fundamental way than Heat, is his natural opposite. Both the Professor and Stevie are mentally abnormal, though in contradictory directions: the Professor through sheer logical consistency (a kind of madness in reason), Stevie through sheer simple-minded innocence (a kind of reason in madness). Together they serve to fix the two poles of the novel's central antithesis. The Professor's case has demonstrated that that normality is indispensable; Stevie's is about to demonstrate that it is indefensible. An examination of the part he plays in one of Conrad's great scenes – Winnie's mother's last cab-ride (pp. 152–74) – shows why the conservative habit of taking suffering for granted is radically inadequate.

Accompanying his mother and sister on their brief but harrowing journey to the almshouse which the mother has decided to make her last abode, Stevie becomes acutely distressed by the infirmity of the cab-horse. The cabman, who is himself maimed, eventually explains to him, in a hoarse alcoholic's whisper, that he has no choice: 'I've got to take out what they will blooming well give me at the yard. I've got my missus and four kids at 'ome.' A little later, as Stevie and Winnie, their task accomplished, are passing in front of a public house on their way home, they recognize their conveyance standing by the kerbstone.

Its aspect was so profoundly lamentable, with such a perfection of grotesque misery and weirdness of macabre detail, as if it were the Cab of Death itself, that Mrs Verloc, with that ready compassion of a woman for a horse (when she is not sitting behind him), exclaimed vaguely!

'Poor brute.'

Hanging back suddenly, Stevie inflicted an arresting jerk upon his sister.

'Poor! Poor!' he ejaculated, appreciatively. 'Cabman poor, too. He told me himself.'

The contemplation of the infirm and lonely steed overcame him. Jostled, but obstinate, he would remain there, trying to express the view newly opened to his sympathies of the human and equine misery in close association. But it was very difficult. 'Poor brute, poor people!' was all he could repeat. It did not seem forcible enough, and he came to a stop with an angry splutter: 'Shame!' Stevie was no master of phrases, and perhaps for that very reason his thoughts lacked clearness and precision. But he felt with greater completeness and some profundity. That little word contained all his sense of indignation and horror at one sort of wretchedness having to feed upon the anguish of the other – at the poor cabman beating the poor horse in the name, as it were, of his poor kids at home. And Stevie knew what it was to be beaten. He knew it from experience. It was a bad world. Bad! Bad!

Mrs Verloc, his only sister, guardian, and protector, could not pretend to such depths of insight. Moreover, she had not experienced the magic of the cabman's eloquence. She was in the dark as to the inwardness of the word 'Shame'. And she said placidly:

'Come along, Stevie. You can't help that.'

The Secret Agent, pp. 170–1

This passage dramatizes the contrast between two ways of seeing: the normal or practical mode, and the naïve or visionary mode. Mrs Verloc is struck by the misery of the horse but, preoccupied as she is with the problem of being left her brother's sole 'guardian and protector', her response is necessarily cursory. Stevie, on the other hand, being wholly free from adult responsibility, reacts with unqualified directness to the marks of woe around him. We recall the intensity with which he has watched the limping cabman lead his horse away: 'There was an air of austerity in this departure, the scrunched gravel of the drive crying out under the slowly turning wheels, the horse's lean thighs moving with ascetic deliberation away from the light into the obscurity of the open space.' Hence, when Stevie inarticulately exclaims 'Poor! Poor!', what the words refer to is present to his mind in all its reality. Furthermore, the difference between himself and his sister isn't simply in how they see, but in what they see. Where Winnie notices a merely isolated case of deprivation, Stevie manages to conceive of the poor as part of a veritable system of suffering, in which the relief of misery requires the infliction of misery. This momentary but appalling vision of society as some kind of pain generator is clearly not one in terms of which a normal life can be led. Mrs Verloc's placid dismissal of her brother's excitement ('Come along, Stevie. You can't help that.') is scarcely reprehensible. Yet Stevie's momentary lifting of the veil has revealed something that is really there. In fact, the concluding aphorism – 'Bad world for poor people' – in which he concentrates all the force of his inarticulate compassion proves that the Professor is after all mistaken in laying exclusive claim to the title of 'true propagandist'. Faithful to their antithetical roles in the novel, the Professor and Stevie are also complementary revolutionists. If the Professor contemptuously rejects the anarchists' blood-curdling slogans, Stevie takes them fervently and literally. If the Professor attacks society out of excessive regard for himself (from vindictiveness at what society has done to him), Stevie rebels out of excessive regard for others (from indignation at what society is doing to them). The Professor's abnormal self-sufficiency insulates what he does from any redeeming vision of the plight of his fellow-men. Stevie's equally abnormal dependence prevents what he sees from ever bearing fruit in effective action.

But at least Stevie gives some reality to the doctrine of compassion, which so far has been merely bandied about by assorted connoisseurs of injustice. He has been able to discover for himself – that is, directly and at first hand – why it is that the world we live in is a bad one for poor people. It would be misleading, however, to assess the discovery independently of the discoverer. As Conrad conceives him, Stevie is a variant of the traditional 'holy idiot': a figure defined by the fact that its holiness and its idiocy are interdependent. In Conrad's version, Stevie's helplessness is both what gives him his capacity for perception and what makes him an embodiment of what he perceives. He is, of course, the degenerate son of an alcoholic father; he is shortly to fall victim to an ignorant and pitiless plot; he illustrates in a general way the social deprivation he laments. But in his helplessness he is also the immediate cause of what becomes the novel's central demonstration of the truth he has seen: that poverty gives rise to a 'system' of suffering.

The principals in this demonstration are Stevie's sister and mother. It is scarcely surprising that Stevie should have earned their unreserved devotion. The appeal of his trusting dependence is made vivid to us in a few deft and poignant touches: he dusts and sweeps his sister's parlour 'intent and conscientious, as though he were playing at it'; or he flings up his hand at her request and, 'tremulous and important', stops an approaching bus 'with complete success'. But because the two women, along with millions of other Londoners, live under the shadow of destitution, their love exacts self-sacrifice. Winnie turns down her chance of happiness because the young man of her choice cannot provide for her brother as well as herself. Instead, she marries the unromantic Verloc because he can. On her side, her mother condemns herself to what we are invited to regard as a premature coffin in the hope that this will strengthen her son's claims on his sister and her husband. Conrad's treatment of Winnie's mother ('She *is* the heroine', he wrote to Edward Garnett[1]) deserves special attention. He discreetly compares her experience of old age with that of another old woman, also engaged in protecting a vulnerable dependent: Michaelis's aristocratic patroness (pp. 104–6). For all

[1] E. Garnett (ed.), *Letters from Joseph Conrad, 1825–1924* (Indianapolis, 1962), p. 204.

the latter's extraordinary prestige, Winnie's mother possesses a delicacy and tact that outstrips the great lady's 'serene and cordial' superiority; yet this sensibility is lodged in a body repulsively swollen, coarsened, and maimed by the 'fires of adversity'. Without any of the 'serene fearlessness' of those whose advancing years have 'escaped the blight of indifference', Winnie's mother finds applying for a place in a 'charity' an intolerable effort. She is obliged to solicit the attention of patronizing strangers, to plead, to humiliate herself, even to deceive. And in so doing, she experiences all the contradictory paradoxes of poverty. First, her act of maternal devotion takes the form of an act of abandonment: in order to be able to help her children she must be seen to reject them. Second, the welfare of the son requires the sacrifice of the daughter: in order to secure her place she has to convince the trustees that Winnie has driven her out. Third, her heroic sacrifice exposes her to the charge of selfish ingratitude: Winnie, who is as ignorant of her mother's motives as her mother is of hers, assumes that she is leaving out of dissatisfaction.

When Conrad comes to describe the fulfilment of these preparations, he produces a scene of extraordinary depth and power. I will confine myself to noting a single element: the last cab-ride itself. In his indignation and pity, Conrad, without any loss of specificity, transforms this journey into one of his most suggestive symbols. It presents, through the particular case, the experience of unremitting hardship as a passage through life in which the travellers are isolated from one another in an endlessly distorting succession of shocks, strains, jolts, buffets, and dislocations:

In the narrow streets the progress of the journey was made sensible to those within by the near fronts of the houses gliding past slowly and shakily, with a great rattle and jingling of glass, as if about to collapse behind the cab; and the infirm horse, with the harness hung over his sharp backbone flapping very loose about his thighs, appeared to be dancing mincingly on his toes with infinite patience. Later on, in the wider spaces of Whitehall, all visual evidences of motion became imperceptible. The rattle and jingle of glass went on indefinitely in front of the long Treasury building – and time itself seemed to stand still.

The Secret Agent, pp. 156–7

It is appropriate that the suffering the two women undergo on behalf of a mentally deficient dependent should acquire representative resonance, for it forms a link in a pattern of pain that includes the whole community. How pitiless this pattern can be is revealed in the irony that shadows the entire sequence: that the mother's very efforts to safeguard her son seal his fate. For in her inevitable ignorance of the true thoughts of others, she initiates a causal chain the outcome of which she can neither foresee nor control. Her stratagem *does* succeed: her daughter is made to feel solely responsible for Stevie's welfare; in turn, Winnie's efforts on his behalf *do* bear fruit: her husband is induced to take Stevie under his care. But, unbeknown to them, that last step fatally brings together Verloc's panic and Stevie's exaltation; and in so doing, it cocks the mechanism that will blow Stevie out of existence.

III

A general examination of *The Secret Agent* suggests that the fact of suffering is as fundamental to organized society as the fact of inertia. It reveals, moreover, that the first of these facts makes the second necessary: that if society is to survive at all it is because of the individual's almost incurable propensity for evading painful truths. There is more, however, to the connection between conservatism (in the general sense in which I have been using the term) and impercipience than the impulse to keep the social system *lacking in perception* going. The urge to keep one's eyes tightly closed is rooted in an area of the self even more fundamental than the gregarious. I have already referred in passing to the episode in which the Assistant Commissioner, having shrugged off administrative constraints, descends into Soho in pursuit of Verloc. As he approaches the entrance to Brett Street, he rediscovers an almost forgotten thrill of naked excitement. 'This joyousness and dispersion of thought before a task of some importance', writes Conrad, 'seems to prove that this world of ours is not such a serious affair after all' (p. 150). Although the Assistant Commissioner can have no idea that he is about to precipitate a tragedy, he is aware that he is involved in 'a task of some importance'. Yet his irresistible sensation of personal release renders him incapable of taking anything seriously. He is not to blame for this spontaneous feeling: it may be inappropriate, it may even be irresponsible, but it is also joyful – a rebounding of high spirits. If impercipience is, for Conrad, a condition of normally healthy existence, it is because it originates in the instinctive egoism of every positive assertion of individual life.

In emphasizing the naturalness of egoism, *The Secret Agent* takes up, of course, an idea which we have already explored in connection with the figure of Nostromo. But whereas in the earlier novel egoism was associated with the energy of positive action, in *The Secret Agent* it is associated with passivity. Every character in the novel, the Assistant Commissioner included (the sensation we have just examined is not a deed, but a reflex of liberation), tends automatically to pursue the line of least resistance. The story as a whole more than adequately supports the view that 'the majority of revolutionists are the enemies of discipline and fatigue mostly' (p. 53). But anarchist sloth is not the only form this passivity takes; the police themselves are affected by a similar complaint, and the Professor is scarcely exaggerating when he describes both professions as 'forms of idleness at bottom identical'.

Let us consider, in this respect, the richly comic interview between the Assistant Commissioner and Chief Inspector Heat, in the course of which the Assistant Commissioner catches out his subordinate in the act of concealing a vital piece of evidence (pp. 96–103, 112–34). Paradoxically, Heat's attempted deception is a direct consequence of the indolent egoism that makes him the perfect 'old departmental hand'. The conventionality that has encouraged too easy an adaptation to the routines of police work has also tempted him to become too dependent on a private informant. Now that this secret source of intelligence is threatened (examination of Stevie's fragmented remains has produced a tab with Verloc's address on it), he has no compunction whatever in trying to protect it; and he calmly prepares to divert suspicion on to a man whose life has already been largely destroyed by an irresponsible judicial sentence – the blamelessly vulnerable Michaelis. Heat even manages to persuade himself that he is cheating his own department for its own good. It has not often been noticed that the quandary into which the Assistant Commissioner puts him is analogous to Verloc's predicament when Vladimir calls *his* bluff as an informer. The earlier interview – treated with sardonic rather than genial humour – anticipates the later one in at least two important respects. Both Heat and Verloc share a sense that their familiar world has been unfairly shaken by an ignorant newcomer; and both are unscrupulously determined to retain all the privileges of a well-established groove. This parallel serves to bring out the fact that, for all his show of activity, Heat's response to the challenge of his superior officer is, in its pompous deviousness, no more positive than Verloc's recoil of indignant dismay. Incapable of self-criticism, both men remain steeped in all the inertness of a conventional existence.

In contrast to Heat, the Assistant Commissioner is not allowed the luxury of total self-deception, partly because he finds the departmental post he occupies too irksome for complacency. And yet he receives Heat in a positive torpor of depression; he scarcely listens to his report; and it takes a threat to his domestic arrangements to shock him back into alertness. To allow Heat to arrest Michaelis would offend Michaelis's great lady; and the great lady (being, as it happens, a close friend of the Assistant Commissioner's discontented wife) would not let him get away with a second outrage against her protégé. The Assistant Commissioner is brought into the fray not out of concern for Michaelis's innocence, but out of a craving for domestic peace. That this immediate motive is left behind as the case develops (it is replaced by a desire to unmask Vladimir) should not obscure how far interest and duty have to coincide before even a man of the Assistant Commissioner's calibre is provoked into action.

As one examines the interview between the two police officers, one discovers that they share another common factor. Both men have illustrated the passivity of self-interest; both now also demonstrate a further characteristic: its secrecy. In the course of the narrative, the Assistant Commissioner is challenged at least twice on the subject of Michaelis. To Heat's highly improper inquiry whether there might be some special reason why Michaelis should not be interfered with, he unhesitatingly replies: 'No reason whatever that I know of.' Officially, of course, this answer is true. But *unofficially*? Similarly, at the end of his successful interview with the Home Secretary (whom he handles not with less cynicism but with greater finesse than Heat has handled him), he is asked pointblank about his 'immediate motive' for wanting to take personal charge of the Greenwich investigation, and he is obliged to prevaricate. Compared with Heat's indignant furtiveness, his reticence may seem innocent enough: after all, the existence of an unacknowledged private motive does not invalidate, let us say, his arguments against police employment of informers in the pay of foreign powers. Yet an organization that depends on collaboration for its proper functioning cannot afford too much internal secrecy. Although the police succeed, with a swiftness that owes a good deal to luck, in tracing the identity of the person ultimately behind the Greenwich affair, they hopelessly bungle their attempt to protect the one witness capable of exposing him and the government he represents. In so far as the police department is run by men who, in their dealings with one another, have acquired the habit of keeping their own counsel, it develops an idea that has already received extensive treatment in *Nostromo*: that of society as a system of interdependent egoisms.

IV

On both the occasions on which the Assistant Commissioner is granted audience with the Home Secretary, he lets fall a remark which helps us to approach the pivotal relationship of the novel – that between Mr and Mrs Verloc. The first is a reference to the address tab found on Stevie's clothing after the explosion: 'It is an incredible little fact', he says, 'so incredible that the explanation which will account for it is bound to touch the bottom of this affair' (p. 141). It does indeed – though the bottom of the affair is considerably deeper than the Assistant Commissioner, who is professionally confined to verifiable facts, is able to imagine. His second remark is a kind of epigram on what he has found at No 32 Brett Street: 'From a certain point of view', he says with a little laugh, 'we are here in the presence of a domestic drama' (p. 222). And again he is right – except that this 'drama' is not an amusing little sketch, but an implacable revelation of 'madness and despair'. The ironic style of the novel, which is an expressive instrument of much greater range than it is generally credited to be, has so far extended from satirical caricature (the anarchists) and comic characterization (the police) to indignant compassion (the last cab-ride). But now, as it probes darker areas of experience, it begins to acquire a tragic resonance. The story of the Verlocs constitutes the centre of the novel. It is the element by which the novel as a whole stands or falls, for it claims to make good the promises inherent in Conrad's chosen subject. Not only does it concentrate all the ambiguities that have so far been discerned in the idea of 'normality', but – and this is the crucial point – it establishes the appalling fact that 'normality', far from shielding us from 'disaster', may in fact drive us straight into it.

The Verlocs' relationship is marked by two catastrophic reversals. The first, in which Vladimir abruptly checks the established momentum of Verloc's life, results in the blowing-up of Stevie. The second, in which Stevie's death quite abruptly overturns the settled pattern of Winnie's existence, results in Verloc's murder and her suicide. That Conrad's treatment of these two dénouements should so successfully escape the vacuities of melodrama is in large measure due to the degree to which the Verlocs' relationship is able to reflect the concerns of the novel as a whole.

Mr Verloc is the representative figure of *The Secret Agent*. As one example of how he acquires this function, we may consider the way in which his interview with Vladimir transforms his attitude to London. Making his way through the morning sunshine to his West End appointment, he surveys 'with an approving eye' all the evidence of the security, power, stability and wealth of the imperial capital. Replete with wellbeing, he relaxes into his usual views.

All these people had to be protected ... their horses, carriages, houses, servants had to be protected; and the source of their wealth had to be protected in the heart of the city and the heart of the country; the whole social order favourable to their hygienic idleness had to be protected against the shallow enviousness of unhygienic labour.

The Secret Agent, p. 12

Not that he believes that society is really in need of protection: it is enough for him that it should *think* it is. Verloc's conservatism is not of the embattled or aggressive kind; it takes the form of satisfaction with the existing order of things – an order that generates illusory fears which, in their turn, generate sinecures for men like himself. But conservatism it emphatically remains: for all his anarchist's pose, his indolence (to which he is 'devoted ... with a sort of inert fanaticism') shows him to be as parasitic on the labour of others as the most socially exalted *rentier*.

When an hour later, he is dismissed from the embassy, this vision of London has ceased to exist. All the certainties of his life have been shattered: his self-esteem, his laziness, his security, and his common sense have been routed by the contemptuous and arbitrary ferocity of Vladimir's ultimatum. Accordingly, the great metropolis vanishes from his gaze, and for a while he remains incapable of consciously registering anything at all. When later that evening, as he stands gloomily looking through his bedroom window, he again glimpses the rain-soaked city, all evidence of that morning's solidity, weight and permanence seems to have disappeared. In its place, only 'a fragile film of glass stretched between him and the enormity of cold, black, wet, muddy, inhospitable accumulation of bricks, slates, and stones, things in themselves unlovely and unfriendly to man' (p. 56). Scenes of opulent ease have given place to an alien and ominous landscape; the city that seemed sprinkled with 'powdered old gold' has become the grim setting for a struggle for survival. Which of these two visions is the true one? The fact is, of course, that they both are. Splendour and misery are but two aspects of a single reality. Verloc's predicament rests on an ambiguity that Conrad continues to expand throughout the novel. For example, what are the metropolitan police? Are they, as Stevie in his simplicity imagines them to be, 'a sort of benevolent institution for the suppression of evil' (p. 172)? Or do they exist, as Winnie, mindlessly echoing her husband's clichés, tells him, 'so that them as have nothing shouldn't take anything away from them who have' (p. 173)? Verloc's double vision of London epitomizes all the subsequent antinomies of the novel: soporific complacency against waking horror, the commonplace world of 'normality' versus the catastrophic world of 'madness and despair'.

Verloc's representative function is confirmed, of course, by the title of the book. His complex role as multiple agent – as a clandestine purveyor of illegal goods, as an underground organizer of anarchism, as a top-secret spy of a foreign embassy, as a confidential informer of the police – suggests the significance for the novel of his career in secrecy. His avocation must be taken, not (as in a conventional thriller) as a means of discovering or disclosing hidden facts, but as a mode of withholding facts, of not revealing oneself. In other words, the point about his secrecy is not what it enables him to do (compare Nostromo's secret missions), but how it defines his standing in relation to others. What this implies can be brought out in a brief examination of the two main ways in which Conrad exploits Verloc's – and the novel's – title.

First, there are the standard connotations of the phrase 'secret agent'. The aura of stereotyped glamour that adheres to the spy's *métier* provokes expectations that, in this novel, are repeatedly disappointed. Vladimir is stunned to discover that 'the famous and trusty secret agent ... so secret that he was never designated otherwise than by the symbol Δ' (p. 27) should turn out to be fat, vulgar and lazy, and should own not only a shop but a wife. ('Married! And you a professed anarchist, too!' (p. 36) etc. And it is not only Vladimir who finds this last piece of intelligence surprising:

'You say that this man has got a wife?'
'Yes, Sir Ethelred ... A genuine wife and a genuinely, respectably marital relation.'

The Secret Agent, p. 221)

The purpose of such responses is to underline the fact that Conrad's secret agent is no James Bond, but a typical, commonplace, conventional, domesticated *petit bourgeois*. Do we conclude, then, that Vladimir has seen right through him? He certainly thinks so. Yet his domination of Verloc is not quite complete. There remains a small item of information that he knows nothing about, but which will eventually undo him utterly: the fact that the man he patronizes so contemptuously is an unofficial employee of the police. We should note that this is an irony which we are made to experience directly for ourselves. No sooner have we uncovered one layer of Verloc's identity than we begin to suspect the presence of another one beneath it; having learnt, as we enter into the story, that the seedy shopkeeper is an embassy spy, we are at once made to wonder whether he is not in fact playing a yet more devious role.

We have seen that Conrad's treatment of English political moderation involves a double-take: the perception that domestic tolerance is preferable to foreign extremism yields to the further perception that this tolerance may be complacent, shallow, and shortsighted. Conrad's presentation of Verloc re-enacts the same procedure at a different level. Just as we begin to relax into the belief that the 'celebrated agent Δ' is nothing more than an unexceptional citizen, we begin to wonder how trustworthy this harmlessness really is. Is Verloc quite as commonplace as he seems? Or is ordinariness itself quite what we think it is? Consider one of his major characteristics – his good nature. To his wife this seems a trait to which she owes the welfare of her brother; hence she interprets it as a mark of his unostentatious generosity and reliability. As for her mother, her very words 'fail her' when she thinks of her son-in-law's 'excellence'; and she does not hesitate to join her daughter in persuading Stevie that his protector and provider is 'good' in the most dependable sense of the word. Verloc's good nature, however, can also wear a very different face. 'There was about him', Conrad writes, 'an indescribable air which no mechanic could have acquired in the practice of his handicraft however dishonestly exercised: the air common to men who live on the vices, the follies, or the baser fears of mankind: an air of moral nihilism' (p. 13). Here, Verloc's easy-going tolerance is not a mark of virtue, but a sign of depravity – of the cynical indifference of someone too comfortable to care for anything at all. 'What I want to affirm', Conrad adds, 'is that Mr Verloc's expression was by no means diabolic.' This carries the sinister implication that, contrary to common belief, ordinariness is by no means incompatible with wickedness. Under the effect of Vladimir's demands, Verloc becomes dangerous not despite but *because of* his 'ordinariness'; for the very conventionality that makes him erect domestic comfort

perdition. Every stage of the process bristles with Conrad's characteristic ironies, but none more powerfully than the concluding
stage (pp. 229–65). Just as Winnie's effort to secure Stevie's future
guarantees his destruction, so Verloc's attempt, in his last fatal
conversation, to safeguard his marriage transforms his wife into his
killer. The evening after the accident he returns home in a state of
prostration. He receives Heat's unscheduled visit, and, having
seen him off the premises, re-enters the house. Now that the
immediate shocks and tensions seem over, he suddenly feels an
overpowering urge to confide in his wife. For the first time in the
history of their relationship he is ready to tell her the truth. The
release of confession makes him positively garrulous; but the more
he talks, the less she takes in. The fact of Stevie's death has finally
put the Verlocs permanently out of earshot of each other. As far as
Winnie is concerned, the news of her brother's fate, picked up from
a brutally casual Heat, has subjected her 'moral nature ... to a
shock of which, in the physical order, the most violent earthquake
of history could only be a faint and languid rendering'. Having
committed herself to marriage as to a bargain – her loyalty to
Verloc in exchange for his protection of Stevie – she can only
conclude that the dishonoured contract is now null and void.
Indeed, she feels so monstrously betrayed that she cannot recognize the man before her as her husband, only as her brother's
murderer. As for Verloc, he has conceived of their marriage conventionally, as an exchange of affections in which he loves his wife
'maritally' – that is, as his most valued possession – in return for
being loved 'for himself'. Thus Stevie's death can only affect him in
so far as it affects Winnie. 'It was his marital affection', Conrad
notes sardonically, 'that had received the greatest shock from the
premature explosion.' He is therefore almost organically incapable
of sharing his wife's anguish: 'in this he was excusable, since it was
impossible for him to understand it without ceasing to be himself'.
Excusable perhaps – but not exempted from the consequences.
Any outburst of candour on his part can do no more than show her
at last the man he actually is – that is to say, a being who grows
steadily more insufferable as he becomes more distinct. His
attempt to communicate his loathing for Vladimir strikes her as
incomprehensibly irrelevant; his concern for his own future (he
expects a short prison sentence) seems to betray an intolerable
assurance of impunity; his gesture of comfort ('Can't be helped',
'Come! This won't bring him back', etc.) exacerbates her sense of
isolation; his assumption of marital affection ('What would it have

that kills her husband. But it seems to me to imply much more than merely the idea that we are all so-called 'savages' under our 'civilized' skins. What it really indicates is that the crust separating the normal and the extreme is exceedingly thin, and that to tread too boldly – that is, to take the normality in which we move too much for granted – is to invite disaster. Certainly, the case of the Verlocs suggests that conservatism is only able to impart stability and order to society by keeping society in a condition of criminality. ('Le crime est une condition nécessaire de l'existence organisée', Conrad wrote to Cunninghame Graham.)[1] The instinct to accept the given at its face value is the reason for the Verlocs' destruction of each other; but it is also the reason why the whole of society, from a cabman to an assistant commissioner, and from a paroled convict to a minister of the Crown, is implicated in this destruction.

But however satisfactory such an account of the novel might perhaps be in establishing the existence of a 'central theme', as it stands it does not do justice to the narrative's tragic force. It suggests a work at once too detached and too negative to achieve the necessary intensity. Above all, it does not adequately reflect the significance of Winnie Verloc's suffering, nor, indeed, the quality of a life which Conrad describes as being 'without grace or charm, and almost without decency, but of an exalted fidelity of purpose, even unto murder' (p. 298).

The missing dimension is brought fully into play in the final movement of the novel, which concerns itself with the last hours of Winnie's existence – a period stretching from her murder of Verloc to her suicide on the cross-Channel packet – presented in relation to Ossipon, who now moves into the forefront of the action. This is not to suggest that the conclusion of *The Secret Agent* marks an entirely new departure. The undeviating march of ironies, for example, is not interrupted: the woman who has made use of a man who believed himself loved for his own sake now suffers an identical fate, becoming herself the gullible victim of an unscrupulous philanderer. Nor is the procession of cross-purposes interrupted: Ossipon's assumption that it is Verloc who has been blown up gives rise to a sequence of irreversible misunderstandings on one side and the other. But the novel's closing phase permits a new aspect of its general theme, largely implicit hitherto, to emerge clearly. The reason why Conrad presents his heroine's anguish in

---

[1] C. T. Watts (ed.), *Joseph Conrad's Letters to R. B. Cunninghame Graham* (Cambridge, 1969), p. 117.

incongruous juxtaposition with the medical student's pre-
datoriness is that it enables him to treat the contrast between the
terrible and the commonplace in terms of the 'subjectivity' of
suffering and the 'objectivity' of scientism.

The way in which this new distinction enters the narrative is
shown by Conrad's description of the exact moment at which
Winnie steps over the line separating the uninquiring spouse from
the terrified murderess. Mr Verloc speaks:

'I wish to goodness,' he growled, huskily, 'I had never seen Greenwich
Park or anything belonging to it.'
The veiled sound filled the small room with its moderate volume, well
adapted to the modest nature of the wish. The waves of air of the proper
length, propagated in accordance with correct mathematical formulas,
flowed around all the inanimate things in the room, lapped against Mrs
Verloc's head as if it had been a head of stone. And incredible as it may
appear, the eyes of Mrs Verloc seemed to grow still larger. The audible
wish of Mr Verloc's overflowing heart flowed into an empty place in his
wife's memory. Greenwich Park. A park! That's where the boy was killed.
A park – smashed branches, torn leaves, gravel, bits of brotherly flesh and
bone, all spouting up together in the manner of a firework. She remembered now what she had heard, and she remembered it pictorially. They
had to gather him up with the shovel. Trembling all over with irrepressible
shudders, she saw before her the very implement with its ghastly load
scraped up from the ground. Mrs Verloc closed her eyes desperately,
throwing upon that vision the night of her eyelids, where after a rainlike
fall of mangled limbs the decapitated head of Stevie lingered suspended
alone, and fading out slowly like the last star of a pyrotechnic display. Mrs
Verloc opened her eyes.
Her face was no longer stony. Anybody could have noted the subtle
change on her features, in the stare of her eyes, giving her a new and
startling expression; an expression seldom observed by competent persons
under the conditions of leisure and security demanded for thorough analysis, but whose meaning could not be mistaken at a glance.

The Secret Agent, pp. 260–1

This decisive moment has been very carefully prepared. Winnie
has overheard, but without taking it in properly, a few phrases of
Heat's account of the physical effects of the explosion; and she has
had within her reach the detailed report of a newspaper thrown
aside after a single distracted glance. But it is only now that she
registers with full consciousness the actuality of Stevie's annihilation. His death is indeed particularly dreadful, and it is understandable that his sister should take it hard. But why, now that he
has ceased to exist, should the manner of his death be so impor-

tant? However strong our belief in an afterlife, death must always fill us with a unique horror, for it involves the instant reduction of individual identity into inert matter. On the one hand, we recoil from the unnatural objectivity of the corpse; on the other, the body poignantly evokes the subjectivity of the vanished self. Stevie's violent disintegration intolerably sharpens this disjunction. Even Chief Inspector Heat, who does not know the identity of the victim and is aware that death has been instantaneous, is overcome by the impression that the dead man must have suffered 'the pangs of an inconceivable agony'. How intolerable, therefore, the reaction of the woman from whom Stevie's abnormal susceptibility to pain has drawn all the fierce devotion of a protective love.

This passage is remarkable for dramatizing the flash-point of contact between the subjectivity of Winnie's love and the objectivity of Stevie's dismemberment. That these are the terms in which we are meant to understand Winnie's experience is demonstrated by the number of questions concerning the object–subject relationship that the passage brings to our attention. Why, for example, should a human utterance, demonstrably reducible to a set of acoustic properties, carry an almost explosive charge of significance? Why, at another level, should a dry little fact, locatable as a small patch of green beside a river on a map, suddenly flood the mind with hallucinatory images? And why, at yet another level, should the vision of a man's organic disintegration be all the more appalling for hovering, as it does here, on the edge of the comic? To these questions, Conrad does not propose any answers; but the fact that they are asked at all demonstrates that the subjective–objective duality, so important in *Nostromo*, has reappeared in *The Secret Agent*. With one significant difference, however: whereas the earlier novel explored this duality in relation to the problem of identity, the present work examines it in relation to the problem of suffering.

As a man is simultaneously a product of impersonal forces and a conscious being in his own right, his suffering can be approached in two distinct ways: 'scientifically' and 'imaginatively'. Stevie's disability, for instance, makes him both a pathological case and an appealing innocent. Thus Ossipon, who has scientific pretensions, regards him as a phenomenon for analysis. The observable data that Stevie provides – an obsession with geometrical circles, the droop of a lower lip, the shape of the ear-lobes – are symptoms of a general disorder, or proofs of a general theory. When he learns the true identity of the Greenwich Park victim, Ossipon instinctively exclaims: 'The degenerate – by heavens!' (p. 290). However, only a few moments before this 'scientific' reaction, Winnie has described the very same Stevie as 'the loving, innocent, harmless lad' (p. 289). What counts to *her* is the world he inhabits – the felt perceptions of his individual life. Hence his physical attributes – the 'thin neck and the peaked shoulders raised slightly under the large semi-transparent ears' (p. 186) that she notices with such poignant affection – are simply aspects of a unique identity.

If the scientific attitude must, logically, short-circuit the subjective experience of suffering (both of the observed and of the observer), the imaginative response, equally logically, presupposes it. To respond imaginatively to the suffering of others is to expose *oneself* to the possibility of suffering. So Winnie suffers on behalf of Stevie, who suffers on behalf of the cabman. The difference between their suffering and Verloc's or Ossipon's is that the latter's is merely passive. All the energy of Winnie's love for Stevie goes into her outbreak of violence. She kills, certainly, and so declares herself a murderess; but she does so (in Conrad's deliberate phrase) out of 'an exalted fidelity of purpose'. Positive and negative are locked together in a tragic embrace. The source of her moral stature and the source of her destructiveness are one and the same. The significance of this contradiction is shown in the fact that it inspires the last example, and the most dramatic, of the novel's uses of the subject–object distinction. A final glance at the passage reveals that as Winnie reaches the pinnacle of subjective intensity she is turned into an objective medical case – a problem for scientific investigation 'by competent persons under the conditions of leisure and security demanded for thorough analysis'. And if this lapse of subjectivity seems arresting, its return, once the deed is done, acquires an almost Shakespearean power. Her gradual realization that the small regularly repeated sounds she hears are not the ticking of the clock but the dripping of her husband's blood – that the impersonal medium of time in which her deed now objectively exists is, as it were, dyed red with all the horror of her subjective guilt – makes her stand, if only for a moment, among the heroines of traditional high tragedy.

The tragic *impasse*, then, takes the form of a paradox: Winnie's moment of supreme vision (her appalled sense of Stevie's obliterated life) produces her act of supreme imperception (her blank disregard of Verloc's independent life), and thus puts her objective self (her scientifically diagnosable condition) at fatal variance with her subjective self (her imaginative horror at her deed). Is a life that produces such results defensible? Whatever the answer, one thing is certain: her commitment finds no satisfactory alternative in Ossipon's detachment. The medical student's re-entry into the narrative permits Conrad to present scientism as a form of dishonesty. As Ossipon prepares to abandon Winnie on the Southampton train, his attention is caught by the expression on her face: 'Comrade Ossipon gazed at it as no lover had ever gazed at his mistress's face ... He was scientific, and he gazed scientifically at that woman, the sister of a degenerate, a degenerate herself – of a murdering type' (pp. 296–7). The particular inhumanity of this gaze (underlined by the contrasting mention of the 'lover') is partly accounted for by its ruthless disregard of subjectivity. Indeed, what Ossipon takes as a symptom of Winnie's organic depravity is in fact a gesture of response to him: Winnie, mistaking his rapt attention for 'devotion', has, for the first time, allowed her features to relax. Conrad makes it quite clear that he has no quarrel with the true scientific spirit: the word 'science' he describes as 'a term in itself inoffensive and of indefinite meaning' (p. 47). But he makes it equally clear that it is open to the most cynical abuse. Because objectivity and detachment are necessary conditions of the scientific method, even when its concern is to alleviate human suffering, it can easily turn into a technique for disowning all moral liability. By disregarding, as it must do, the obligations of imagination, it abandons all principle of self-correction, once it separates itself from the checks and standards of its proper tasks. In other words, it ceases to be science and becomes superstition. Vladimir's proposal to plant a bomb in 'astronomy' is obviously absurd – but not his claim that science is the 'sacrosanct fetish' of modern life. When Ossipon looks at Winnie, he invokes Lombroso 'as an Italian peasant recommends himself to his favourite saint'. The phrenology in which he believes is, of course, a spurious discipline; yet it remains true that he is filled with the 'insufferable, hopeless, dense, sufficiency which nothing but the frequentation of science can give to the dullness of common mortals' (p. 46). Science has become an excuse for an invulnerable egoism.

Yet even this fails to account completely for the almost obscene effect of his scrutiny of Winnie's face. Up to this latest adventure, the scientific attitude has made it possible for Ossipon to treat women as objects – to play with their feelings indifferently, and to fleece them with a clear conscience. But with his encounter with Winnie, what starts as standard procedure ends in absolute nightmare. The scientism which begins as an excuse for selfishness concludes as a rationalization of cowardice. If he invokes his saint, it is out of fear; the detached gaze he rivets on her, as Conrad's tone suggests, is not really 'scientific', but a glare of terror, a panic attempt to keep her at a safe distance. And the news of her eventual suicide, far from bringing him any relief, only redoubles his obsession: to his existing burden of fear he adds a further burden of guilt. It is almost as if he has become forced by his own horror to acknowledge hers. But – as so often in Conrad – the lesson is learnt too late; and the man whose whole life has been an implicit denial of the suffering of others receives an appropriate reward. The appalling knowledge he alone possesses, and which the risk of implication in Verloc's murder makes it impossible for him to divulge, cuts him off from all serious communication with his fellow-men.

Ossipon's fate could be described as the result of the collision between his mean, unostentatious 'normality' and Winnie's 'madness and despair'. He is, after all, but a mediocre representative of the 'objective' attitude, and if he uses the 'subjectivity' of his victims it is only in order to serve his own uninspired private ends. In any case, he lacks the courage – and the consistency – of his scientific convictions. This is certainly the view of the Professor, in whose company, seven days later, he keeps imagining the last moments of Winnie Verloc's existence on earth (pp. 302–11). For the Professor (as for Vladimir, of whom he reminds us again as the novel draws to its close) any scientific attempt, serious or otherwise, to ameliorate the human condition must be self-deceived, for it starts from premises that only reinstate what it endeavours to remove. For example, in his view, Michaelis's vision of the welfare state as 'an immense ... hospital ... in which the strong are to devote themselves to the nursing of the weak' is nothing but a systematization of society on the basis of its deficiencies. For him, in fact, the scientist is merely the old arch-enemy – the conservative weakling – in his latest disguise.

Only the strong can stand alone. The weak are obliged to depend on each other. Weakness therefore constitutes the basis of social life. On the strength of these propositions, the Professor deduces that any radical attack on society implies the destruction of the weak ('the source of all evil on this earth'). The duty of the strong is inflexible objectivity; their task the pitiless exploitation of suffering. At the beginning of the novel Vladimir had stated: 'Madness alone is truly terrifying, inasmuch as you cannot placate it.' At the end of the novel the Professor completes the thought:

'Madness and despair! Give me that for a lever and I'll move the world!' In terms of method, this is a realistic proposal: since he cannot take on the world single-handed he must use the momentum of its own anguish against itself. But in terms of purpose, it is hopelessly deranged: a programme of destruction in the service of regeneration has all the nightmare self-cancellation of Karl Yundt's 'death enlisted for good and all in the service of humanity'.

I have tried to argue that *The Secret Agent* is concerned with the conservatism of vast anonymous populations. Winnie's love for the vulnerable Stevie, involving her in mankind, exposes her to all the contradictions inherent in this conservatism. Thus her fall from normality into the 'fiery depths' becomes a searing enactment of them. In his abhorrence of the compromises of collectivity, the Professor tries to rise above mankind. But to try to rise above mankind is to contract into one's sole self, as the following exchange wryly brings out:

'First the great multitude of the weak must go, then the only relatively strong ... Every taint, every vice, every prejudice, every convention must meet its doom.'

'And what remains?' asked Ossipon in a stifled voice.

'I remain – if I am strong enough.'

The Secret Agent, pp. 303–4

But the Professor can never be strong enough. He has not escaped contradiction, but merely encountered it at a different level. By making himself into a minority of one, he has ensured that the despised multitude stays indestructible. And even he cannot wholly insulate himself from knowledge of this fact. Although the thought of men's indifference cannot shake his confidence in his *idée fixe*, the spectacle of their sheer multiplicity makes him falter in his assumption of omnipotence. But such intimations of powerlessness serve only to fuel his abstract ferocity. This is why his crimes – like those of his European successors in the decades that followed the publication of this prophetic novel – lack any redeeming trace of tragic dignity.

7

Under Western Eyes

I know I am but a reed. But I beg you to allow me the superiority of the thinking reed over the unthinking forces that are about to crush him out of existence. ·

Razumov in Under Western Eyes, p. 89

I

At a first glance the resemblances between *Lord Jim* and *Under Western Eyes* are more striking than between any two other works by Conrad. The two novels have a similar theme: the exploration of the consequences of an act of betrayal; they have a similar form: an elderly narrator's examination of the motives of a young protagonist over two periods and two locations. These parallels, however, must be treated with caution, for they are so immediately convincing that they tend to blur the essential originality of the later work. Indeed, nowhere is *Under Western Eyes* more distinctive than at the points of its alleged resemblances with *Lord Jim*: the nature of the act of betrayal, and the nature of the relationship between narrator and protagonist. In any case, the later novel's affinities with *The Secret Agent*, though less obvious, are most profound. Far from marking a clean break with its immediate predecessor (as some critics have alleged),[1] *Under Western Eyes* can be described as taking up its essential concerns (including, of course, the motif of the secret agent), and carrying them into unexpectedly challenging new areas.

Consider, in this respect, Conrad's controversial use of a narrator. The teacher of languages and literature who presents Razumov's diary is quite unlike the Marlow of *Lord Jim*, both in the kind of man he is himself, and in the sort of relationship he establishes with the protagonist. Whereas Marlow is at once intensely interested in the world about him and unshakeably faithful to the tradition of active service, the language teacher, protected as he is by an adequate independence of means and a

---

[1] Most recently: C. B. Cox, *Joseph Conrad: the Modern Imagination.* (London, 1974), p. 102.

self-confessed conventionality of outlook, leads a peaceful existence in unadventurous Geneva; whereas Marlow, who has made
Jim his protégé, is deeply concerned in the ambiguities and contradictions of his career, the language teacher, who dislikes
Razumov, claims to be incapable of understanding his conduct
and attitudes. The language teacher's function in the novel is not
so much to interpret a predicament as to represent a point of view.
And this point of view can be quickly identified: as a reasonable
liberal Englishman, he stands for the tolerant conservatism that
has played so central a part in *The Secret Agent*.

This said, however, an immediate qualification must be made.
The narrator of *Under Western Eyes* raises this tradition of conservatism to an altogether more intellectual level than in *The Secret
Agent*. The theme of conservative normality *does* enter the new
novel in its original form, but not through the narrator. It is
represented by the city in which he lives – by what he calls 'the
respectable and passionless abode of democratic liberty ... ten-
dering the same indifferent hospitality to tourists of all nations and
to international conspirators of every shade' (*Under Western Eyes*, p.
357). The narrator may indeed be a liberal democrat, but he must
be distinguished from liberal democracy in its more mechanical
aspects. By profession, he is a transmitter of Western culture, and
he is sufficiently intelligent and critical to deplore the 'perfection of
mediocrity' (p. 203) towards which it is always tending. There is
no reason to assume that the disdain he repeatedly expresses for
the average Swiss citizen, who is 'made secure from the cradle to
the grave by the perfected mechanism of democratic institutions'
(p. 175), is not really his, but Conrad's. Conrad's conception of
'western' values is complex enough to allow him to discriminate
between their various forms.

What the narrator stands for is defined with considerable precision by his conversations with Natalia Haldin in Part II of the
novel. Natalia and her mother, who have progressive views, have
been more or less forced out of Russia; and, in the expectation that
their son and brother Victor, a student at the university of St
Petersburg, will shortly join them, they have taken up residence in
Geneva. In her rather vague, cultivated way, Mrs Haldin complains about the corruption of education and religion in her native
land; but Natalia is much more passionate and decided. 'I knew
her well enough', writes the narrator, 'to have discovered her scorn
for all the practical forms of political liberty known to the Western
world.' And, reflecting on this discovery, he makes a general

comment on the Russian character which, although he qualifies it with his usual self-effacement as 'a digression', announces the central point of view of the novel.

> I suppose one must be a Russian to understand Russian simplicity, a terrible corroding simplicity in which mystic phrases clothe a naïve and hopeless cynicism. I think sometimes that the psychological secret of the profound difference of that people consists in this, that they detest life, the irremediable life of the earth as it is, whereas we westerners cherish it with perhaps an equal exaggeration of its sentimental value.
>
> *Under Western Eyes*, p. 104

The general implications of this diagnosis will be brought out by the narrative as a whole; but its immediate significance is established by the narrator's discussions with the Haldins and their fellow-exiles in Geneva.

Despite her rejection of Western political practice and her awareness of the violence of the coming conflict within Russia, Natalia foresees the early establishment of general 'concord' in her native land. The narrator feels obliged to demur:

> 'You say it is not a conflict of classes and not a conflict of interests. Suppose I admitted that. Are antagonistic ideas then to be reconciled more easily – can they be cemented with blood and violence into that concord which you proclaim to be so near?'
>
> She looked at me searchingly with her clear grey eyes, without answering my reasonable question – my obvious, my unanswerable question.
>
> 'It is inconceivable,' I added, with something like annoyance.
>
> 'Everything is inconceivable,' she said. 'The whole world is inconceivable to the strict logic of ideas. And yet the world exists to our senses, and we exist in it. There must be a necessity superior to our conceptions. It is a very miserable and a very false thing to belong to the majority. We Russians shall find some better form of national freedom than an artificial conflict of parties – which is wrong because it is a conflict and contemptible because it is artificial. It is left for us Russians to discover a better way.'
>
> Mrs. Haldin had been looking out of the window. She turned upon me the almost lifeless beauty of her face, and the living benign glance of her big dark eyes.
>
> 'That's what my children think,' she declared.
>
> 'I suppose,' I addressed Miss Haldin, 'that you will be shocked if I tell you that I haven't understood – I won't say a single word; I've understood all the words . . . But what can be this era of disembodied concord you are looking forward to. Life is a thing of form. It has its plastic shape and a definite intellectual aspect. The most idealistic conceptions of love and forbearance must be clothed in flesh as it were before they can be made understandable.'
>
> *Under Western Eyes*, pp. 105–6

The gist of the narrator's objections is not that Natalia's propositions are wrong but that they are unintelligible. They are too 'disembodied' to make any sense. She claims that they transcend not only the historical reality of 'parties' and 'interests', but also the limits of the 'conceivable'. The narrator replies that unless ideas can be related to life as we know it historically, that is, concretely and specifically, they can have no meaning. He cannot understand how 'antagonistic ideas' – for instance, contradictory moral or political principles – can be 'reconciled', or shown not to be contradictory, by any act of physical violence. In other words, he cannot see any *logical* reason why opposites should, by the mere fact of their opposition, cancel each other out into a synthesis. Natalia, who is no Hegelian, recognizes the difficulty; but she boldly confounds it by asserting that the world present to the senses transcends human reason. She defends her vision of Utopian concord not on the grounds of its possibility but of its necessity; the Western alternative is too compromised to warrant consideration.

It becomes clear from the narrator's arguments that what he represents in the novel is the power of rationality. His reiterated confessions of incompetence or bafflement when confronted by the effusions of the Russian mind are not without some overtone of Socratic irony. If he does not understand the Russians, it is because he is sharp enough to see that they are not understandable. Their mystical outbursts – what Natalia calls their *'mouvements d'âme'* – seem to him gestures of pure self-deception. He is, as it were, a descendant of David Hume – of the Hume who said of Rousseau (who gets something of a drubbing in this novel): 'His enthusiasm clouds his wit.' He is on his guard against metaphysics. The rationality he represents, as part of the pragmatic–scientific tradition examined in *The Secret Agent*, is essentially commonsense raised to the level of intellect. This explains, of course, his reliability and trustworthiness – qualities to which Natalia gratefully responds – for it makes him a man who keeps a clear head and a sober heart. But it also makes him, as his professional concerns indicate, more critical than creative. Conrad, however, betrays no desire to devalue the critical faculty; on the contrary, the novel as a whole can be considered a warning against the public and private effects of the proscription of criticism. Whatever its limitations, the critical faculty in this novel never loses its status as a touchstone of the real. The professional critic of *Under Western Eyes* is certainly not the most interesting example of the characteristic Conradian sceptic; but he is perhaps the most central.

In his function as defender of rationality, the narrator cannot be brushed aside as a merely fussy and cautious old man. The penetration of his mind compels respect. In his diagnosis of Natalia's irrationalism it is not finally her mysticism that he objects to, but something subtler: 'a terrible corroding simplicity in which mystic phrases clothe a naïve and hopeless cynicism'. To identify cynicism as the antithesis of rationality may seem, at first sight, eccentric, even precious. In common speech, a cynic is a person who is contemptuous of the claims of virtue. But this usage can be legitimately enlarged to include the dismissal of any form of non-coercive obligation. In *Under Western Eyes*, Conrad can speak of the Russian official's cynical disregard for truth, or the Russian intellectual's cynical disbelief in the existence of paradise (pp. 306, 339). Nor is explicit or audible railing a necessary property of cynicism; indeed, cynicism does not even have to be fully conscious. Natalia's lack of concern for intelligibility is not calculated, but instinctive; but it is not the less cynical for that. But even so, why should the narrator associate cynicism with simplicity? What is the justification of Razumov's startling deductive sequence: 'We are Russians, that is – children; that is – sincere; that is – cynical' (p. 207)?

The cynical clear-sightedness of the child who cuts through adult pretences to point out the emperor's nakedness is more ambiguous than the received interpretation of the story suggests. The reason why it takes a child to proclaim the obvious is not simply that the child is more honest than the adult; it is also that, in his 'simplicity', he has not yet become fully responsive to the claims of a convention. In the case of the emperor's clothes, we approve of his cynicism, because it is directed against an absurd adult conspiracy. But what is a convention if not an unspoken conspiracy? A child may be termed cynical because he is still in the process of learning to respect the 'invisible' norms and rules that govern every aspect of our activity as cultured beings. He may have learnt to recognize them; but he has not yet internalized them. Hence, the devastating impudence or frankness (as the case may be) that he is capable of has its origin in the fact that he has not yet been properly located and fitted into the culture within which he is being brought up.

The narrator's sensitivity to Natalia's latent cynicism demonstrates how thoroughly he understands the rationality he represents. He sees that reason does not necessarily presuppose what Natalia calls 'the strict logic of ideas' – that is to say, some

a-historical absolute system of demonstration – but rather a coherent social and cultural context. Henri Bergson has called common sense, which bears on our intercourse with people, a kind of
'social sense', and points out that 'a man may be a first-rate
mathematician or an expert physicist ... and yet completely mis-
understand the actions of other men, miscalculate his own and
perpetually fail to adapt himself to his surroundings'.[1] That the
narrator should be a language teacher is no accident. Intelligible
speech tells us something about rational thought; a man has not
mastered a language merely when he has memorized the words; he
has to be able to use them for himself so as to make sense to others.
Similarly, a man is not yet rational if all he has learnt to do is to
identify facts. Kierkegaard's 'intelligent' madman who, having
escaped from the asylum, tries to prove his sanity by assuring every
passerby that the earth is round demonstrates that the mark of
sanity is the perception of relevance or significance.[2] For the narrator of *Under Western Eyes*, rationality is a function of the interdependence of the individual and the community.

II

The narrator insists throughout his tale that cynicism is a
specifically Russian ailment. Scanning Razumov's diary for the
word which 'if not truth itself, may perchance hold truth enough to
help the moral discovery which should be the object of every tale',
he finds he cannot escape the term 'cynicism': 'For that is the mark
of Russian autocracy and of Russian revolt. In its pride of numbers, in its strange pretensions of sanctity, and in the secret readiness to abase itself in suffering, the spirit of Russia is the spirit of
cynicism' (p. 67). For the narrator, this means that the individual
Russian has not been able to obtain proper possession of the values
and ideas that should be his birthright as a social being. In choos-
ing to write about Russia, Conrad has chosen to explore the path
signposted by the figure of Vladimir in *The Secret Agent*. Civilized
values and ideas seem always to remain a little unreal to the
Russian; so that even his most fervent professions of principle
manage to transform themselves into a parody of the real thing.

This endemic cynicism is explained by the fact that the Russian

[1] H. Bergson, *Two Sources of Morality and Religion*, trans. R. A. Audra and C.
Brereton (originally published 1935, reprinted Doubleday Anchor Books, n.d.),
p. 106.
[2] S. Kierkegaard, *Concluding Unscientific Postscript*, trans. D. F. Swenson (Princeton,
1968), pp. 174–5.

cannot escape what the narrator calls 'the shadow of autocracy'. The interdependence of the individual and the community on which rationality depends presupposes one essential condition: that the individual should be free to commit himself to his community in the expectation that the community will respect the freedom without which obligation cannot exist. Human society is an association of relatively free members, not an automatically regulated organism, like the swarm or the anthill. Under Czarist autocracy, however, obligation is replaced by coercion, and the integrity of the community is destroyed. The state and the people draw violently apart: the state is deprived of the service of the great majority of its citizens, who become either slaves or rebels; the citizens, for their part, either orphaned or disinherited by the state, are inhibited from developing into normally responsible adults. 'Whenever two Russians come together', says the narrator of the Russian colony in Geneva, 'the shadow of autocracy is with them, tinging their thoughts, their views, their most intimate feelings, their private life, their public utterances – haunting the secret of their silences' (p. 107). Part of his function in the narrative is to make it clear that this shadow arrests the normal growth of whatever it covers. The brand of despotism is neurosis.

The so-called 'Russian Mazzini', Peter Ivanovitch, whom the narrator selects for his special aversion, is a test-case of this national malaise. With his shapeless hairy face, his dark glasses, his bull neck, and his *basso profundo* voice, he is in the tradition of Conrad's comic grotesques. But, like his predecessors, he is carefully dovetailed into the intellectual structure of the novel. He has an 'Egeria', or secret female counsellor, in the form of a certain Madame de S—, a heavily made-up long-waisted, glassy-eyed lady of indeterminate age who considers herself a sacred fount of modern ideas. On occasions, they drive through the streets in a big landau:

Thus, facing each other, with no one else in the roomy carriage, their airings suggested a conscious public manifestation. Or it may have been unconscious. Russian simplicity often marches innocently on the edge of cynicism for some lofty purpose. But it is a vain enterprise for sophisticated Europe to try and understand these doings. Considering the air of gravity extending even to the physiognomy of the coachman and the action of the showy horses, this quaint display might have possessed a mystic significance, but to the corrupt frivolity of a Western mind, like my own, it seemed hardly decent.

Under Western Eyes, pp. 125–6

What is most striking about this vignette is its ambiguity. Is it a public demonstration of *avant-garde* ideals, or is it the shameless exposure of a perverted liaison? What makes the intellectual pose – if that is what it is – so disturbing and absurd is the incongruity of the suspected alternative. It is possible that this solemn pair is attempting to match such former leaders of fashionable thought as Voltaire and Madame de Staël, both of whom 'sheltered ... on the republican territory of Geneva'. But if so, they are nothing but extravagant parodies. Even their fashionable garments look like disguises: Peter Ivanovitch's top hat, which always seems in the way, serves almost every purpose (from that of a fan to that of a basket) except the conferring of respectability; and in due course his Egeria will strike Razumov as being 'a witch in Parisian clothes'.

The case of Peter Ivanovitch demonstrates that the first thing a man uneasy in the world of ideas will try to do is to 'spiritualize' them. In a relatively open and civilized society, judgements and thoughts are given reality through acts of individual judging and thinking. Under an autocracy, however, they tend to cease to be part of daily life, harden into separate entities, and get erected into 'ideals' – that is, become increasingly remote from material realities. Thus the ideal becomes emptier, the physical more brutal. Russian neurosis is in fact a kind of schizophrenia in which the 'spiritual' and the 'material', collapsing apart, spin off into separate orbits. The 'burly spiritualist' (the very phrase is symptomatic of this split) owes his fame to his escape from a Siberian penal colony. Fettered by a chain that is 'in the number of pounds and the thickness of links an appalling assertion of the divine right of autocracy' (p. 120) he manages to carry it with him into the woods, but he loses his file before he is able to free himself. In the months that follow, he is obliged to continue carrying this iron load around with him, and he quickly sees his freedom turn into a living nightmare. He has escaped the grasp of tyranny, but not its effects. Yet his massive physical strength sees him through. The humanitarian within him, in 'fearful anxious dependence' on the emergence of his savage cunning, watches with awe the development of the 'wild beast'; and the chasm between the spiritual and the physical – between 'the cloud of mosquitoes and flies hovering about his shaggy head', and the visions of 'spiritual love' which that head contains – continues to deepen (p. 122). Finally, a young woman whom he comes upon by chance takes pity on him and gets the chain struck off. He immediately allegorizes this incident into a doctrine of national redemption through 'feminism' – the cult of spiritual values as mediated by woman. But in this he remains as divided as ever. His feminist idealism barely masks a copious virility, and his general worship of woman (as his brutal exploitation of his pathetically devoted secretary Tekla indicates) conceals a ruthlessly uncompromising will to power. Every one of his aspirations is cancelled out by a contradictory reality: the Château Borel, whence flows his stream of revolutionary utopianism, reveals itself to be an appropriately squalid rented villa; and its priestess, Madame de S—, turns out to be a vulgar occultist whom he cultivates solely for the money she supplies.

Peter Ivanovitch's cynical idealism is in every respect the antithesis of the narrator's practical humanism. The two men are natural opponents, and in the narrative their opposition takes the form of a contest for the possession of Natalia Haldin's soul. At once sensitive and vigorous, Natalia has great beauty of form; but the secret of her seductiveness is the expressiveness of her glance. Her clear grey eyes, fringed with dark lashes, reveal (in contrast with the unfathomable 'impudence' detectable behind Peter Ivanovitch's black glasses) 'a naïve yet thoughtful assurance'. The narrator, himself half in love with her look, which he finds 'as direct and trustful as that of a young man unspoiled by the world's wise lessons' (p. 102), is determined to keep her from the sway of the unseemly feminist sultan. Natalia, however, has received news that her brother has been arrested and executed by the Russian authorities for assassinating a particularly vicious minister of state. Under the effect of this terrible bereavement, she begins to take a more serious interest in revolutionary activity. Hence the narrator finds himself having to combat the appeal not only of the idealism of revolt, but of its practice. To him, cynicism of thought is but a prelude to cynicism of action: both seem equally pernicious. Natalia senses his disapproval. 'I believe that you hate revolution', she tells him; 'you fancy it is not quite honest' (p. 134). And she is, of course, quite right. The existing laws and institutions of a country are as necessary to rational action as the norms and conventions of its language to intelligible thought. They can be reformed, but if they are destroyed or abolished intentional deeds will become merely random events. 'Hopes grotesquely betrayed, ideals caricatured – that is the definition of revolutionary success', the narrator tells her. 'Reform is impossible', she replies. 'There is nothing to reform. There is no legality, there are no institutions. There are only arbitrary decrees. There is only a handful of cruel – perhaps blind – officials against a nation' (p. 133). Autocracy has deprived the citizen not only of the possibility of serious political thought, but also of rational public action: either he sinks into hopeless submission, or he flings himself into desperate revolt. Even if we limit ourselves to the case-histories provided by the members of 'la petite Russie' in Geneva, we will find overwhelming evidence that a Russian revolution is necessary. Peter Ivanovitch's grotesque pilgrimage across the Siberian wilderness, Natalia's experience of the ostracism meted out to police suspects, Tekla's identification with the misery of the down-and-outs, Sophia Antonovna's perception of the causes behind the destruction of her father's life – all these and more serve to build up a formidable case against the Russian state. But there is very little in the novel to suggest that revolution will be productive. Sophia Antonovna, the most efficient of the revolutionaries, has enough integrity to know that revolt is justified not by its goals (Utopian blueprints) but by its causes (unjust suffering). In a later conversation with Razumov, she describes the 'subservient, submissive life' as 'vegetation on the filthy heap of iniquity which the world is'. And she adds: 'Life, Razumov, not to be vile must be a revolt – a pitiless protest – all the time' (p. 260). This declaration justifies the narrator's suspicion that Russians are distinguishable on the basis of their hatred of life, 'the irremediable life of the earth as it is'. Yet if Sophia Antonovna's case confirms this diagnosis, Natalia's shows up its inadequacy. Her cry, 'I would take liberty from any hand as a hungry man would snatch at a piece of bread' (p. 135), is a passionate call for life, and it rings out with such conviction that it finds its way into the epigraph of the novel. But what if the bread turns out to be a stone? That she proposes to seek the liberty she craves from the hand of Razumov, the man responsible for betraying her brother to the Russian authorities, seems an unqualified vindication of the narrator's scepticism. Yet, in a characteristic Conradian paradox, the choice that seals Natalia's defeat is also that which marks her greatest triumph; and the moment that reveals the futility of her faith in liberty is also the moment which demonstrates most clearly its reality and force. To discover the meaning of this paradox, however, we have to turn to the protagonist of the novel.

III

In order to emphasize the outrageous foreignness of Russian life, the language teacher asserts more than once that 'it is unthinkable that any young Englishman should find himself of Razumov's situation' (p. 25). But Razumov's situation consists precisely in the fact that in many essential respects he is a young Englishman abruptly transported into the middle of Czarist Russia. In the first few pages of the novel he is called an Englishman twice: 'I cannot expect you with your frigid English manner to embrace me' (p. 16), he is told by the emotional Haldin; and a few moments later: 'Collected – cool as a cucumber. A regular Englishman' (p. 22). In fact – and is this perhaps a hint that an ordinary Russian is not as different as all that from an ordinary Englishman? – Razumov is to all intents and purposes a portrait of the narrator as a young man. Like the elderly teacher of languages in Geneva, the philosophy student at St Petersburg is 'one of those men who, living in a period of mental and political unrest, keep an instinctive hold on normal, practical, everyday life' (p. 10). He has the same kind of mind: he is liberal in his openness to different points of view, sceptical in his instinctive suspicion of dogmatic abstractions. And he has the corresponding virtues: he is sober, industrious, and considerate (always ready to 'oblige his comrades even at the cost of personal inconvenience' (p. 67)), and inspires confidence in all who meet him. His political creed, spelt out into five basic principles ('History not Theory. Patriotism not Internationalism. Evolution not Revolution. Direction not Destruction. Unity not Disruption.' (p. 66)), could stand virtually unchanged as a paradigm of the narrator's convictions. But it is above all in his function as representative of the rational, as against the mystico–cynical, alternative that he duplicates the narrator's role. Razumov's very name (*razumov* is the genitive plural of *razum*, meaning 'mind, intellect, reason', and is typical of family name forms meaning 'men of mind, intellect, etc.'[1]) defines his representative quality; his solitude underlines it. As an illegitimate son, acknowledged only by an anonymous remittance, he has nothing but his reason which he can call his own. 'You are a son, a brother, a nephew, a cousin – I don't know what – to no end of people', he tells Haldin. 'I am just a man. Here I stand before you. A man with a mind' (p. 61).

A man whose survival depends on his sense of normal reality is by definition committed to the defence of a viable public realm. Deprived of all family relationships, Razumov has no alternative but to look to the state for recognition and advancement. No subordinate obligations intervene between himself and his coun-

---

[1] I am indebted to David Jones for this information, and indeed for several improvements to this chapter as a whole.

try: in that connection he is wholly a Russian and nothing but a Russian. His legitimate loyalties to, and expectations from, what is in an almost literal sense his fatherland, are reflected in his life as a student – which is serious and regular – and particularly, as the novel opens, in his decision to compete for the Ministry of Education essay prize. 'There was nothing strange in the student Razumov's wish for distinction', the narrator comments. 'A man's real life is that accorded to him in the thoughts of other men by reason of respect or natural love' (p. 14). However, if Russia has so far seemed to him to offer the prospect of an orderly ascent of a professional ladder, it is because he has deliberately kept the condition of Russian public life unreal to himself. 'This immense parentage suffered from the throes of internal dissensions, and he shrank from the fray as a good-natured man may shrink from taking definite sides in a family quarrel' (p. 11). To take sides would compel him to face the fact that his inheritance has no integrity. He has up to now been able to retain his normality – 'he was accessible, and there was nothing secret or reserved about his life' – but only at the price of self-deception. In the context of Russia, even the most soberly rational existence acquires a paradoxical character.

How deep the paradox goes is shown by the fact that this rational existence, far from acting as an 'armour to the soul', actually summons its own opposite. The lithe, martial figure of Haldin, whom Razumov finds waiting for him in his room, has not got there by accident: Haldin has been drawn to Razumov by his extraordinary reputation for trustworthiness, which is of course a product of his sanity and sobriety. These two young Russians have the interdependence of complementaries: where Razumov represents the spirit of criticism, Haldin, generous, ardent, and brave, stands for the spirit of idealism. He too is undone by his own nature: his nobility of mind makes him seek the help of a man who has no family to implicate, but who, for that very reason, is excessively dependent on the institutions of the state.

If Razumov takes his stand on common sense, Haldin is inspired by the ideal of common feeling. He passionately espouses the causes of the brotherhood of man, and is instantly brought into headlong collision with the Russian state. In a country governed by consent, morality and legality are more or less in accord: political institutions are justified by ethical principles and ethical principles substantiated by political institutions. Russian autocracy, however, puts obligation and compulsion, fraternity and force, into implacable opposition. The minister of state whom Haldin assassinates has turned the full weight of the apparatus of repression against the rising generation, and thus aimed at 'the destruction of the very hope of liberty itself'. This has had the effect of condemning Russian youth to self-contradiction: the only way left to them of serving virtue is to perform a criminal act. Haldin is conscious of this, but he is not fully aware of its consequences on himself.

> I respect your philosophical scepticism, [he tells Razumov] ... but don't touch the soul. The Russian soul that lives in all of us. It has a future. It has a mission, I tell you, or else why should I have been moved to do this – reckless – like a butcher – in the middle of all these innocent people – scattering death – I! I! ... I wouldn't hurt a fly!
>
> *Under Western Eyes*, p. 22

At this point he breaks down and weeps. This collapse is more than a delayed reaction to the physical shock of the explosion; it is a result of the strain of moral conflict – of being obliged to act in defiance of his deepest feelings. If Razumov's position is defined by the word 'sanity', Haldin's is epitomized by the word 'trust'. His appeal to Razumov is in the name of 'confidence', and he reinforces it by calling him 'brother'. He describes his sister as having, in a phrase that Razumov will have cause to remember, 'the most trustful eyes' in the world. And he seems constitutionally incapable of suspecting anyone whom he has chosen as an ally. That this man should be forced to advance the cause of a trust-inspired concord by means of random disruptive violence is an intolerable paradox, and he takes the only way out: he begins to talk mysticism. His vague invocation of 'the Russian soul that lives in all of us' obviously has very little substance. Nor does it have much external reality, as Razumov discovers almost at once. Haldin has asked him to contact a peasant named Ziemianitch who has promised to smuggle him out of St Petersburg. He describes this man as a 'bright Russian soul', adding: 'it is extraordinary what a sense of the necessity of freedom there is in that man' (p. 56)[1] Beside himself with dismay and rage, Razumov struggles through the snow to a remote slum, where he finds that the peasant is so drunk that even a savage beating fails to rouse him. Razumov has tried – admittedly in his own interests – to secure Haldin's escape; but he has succeeded only in getting trapped between 'the drunkenness of the peasant incapable of action and the dream-intoxication of the

[1] Cf. pp. 18, 30.

idealist incapable of perceiving the reason of things, and the true character of men' (p. 31).

Razumov's recoil from Haldin is not cowardice; it is not even moral abhorrence; it is chiefly a despairing resentment that the prospect of a sane, normal future is being taken away from him. Confronted by the 'spectral ideas' and 'disembodied aspirations' of the revolutionary terrorist, he is overcome by the need to reassert the reality of the fabric of his own society. He too, however, understands only in part what is happening to him. He fails to perceive, for example, that the invasion of his rooms by 'the irrational' (as he calls Haldin's visit) is no accident, but the emergence of the contradiction on which his legitimate aspirations have been raised: that the community on which he relies for the fulfilment of these aspirations is, in its denial of the inner loyalties, quite incapable of sustaining rational life. Much as Haldin seeks refuge in the doctine of the Russian soul, so Razumov, 'like other Russians before him ... in conflict with himself', feels 'the touch of grace on his forehead' (p. 34). As he walks the snowbound streets after his failure with Ziemianitch, he is suddenly overwhelmed by a vision of the truth of Messianic Czarism.

Razumov's conversion to the ideology of 'Holy Russia' vindicates the narrator's view of the fate that awaits even the least extravagant of Russian lives. In his dependence on the public realm, Razumov has no alternative but to choose Russia as it is rather than as it might be – the Russia of historical fact rather than of the Utopian dream. But what is this Russia? As he wanders under the night, he receives, between the snow beneath him and the stars above him, 'an almost physical impression of endless space and countless millions'.

He responded to it with the readiness of a Russian who is born to an inheritance of space and numbers. Under the sumptuous immensity of the sky, the snow covered the endless forests, the frozen rivers, the plains of an immense country, obliterating the landmarks, the accidents of the ground, levelling everything under its uniform whiteness, like a monstrous blank page awaiting the record of an inconceivable history.

Under Western Eyes, p. 33

In the words of Bismarck (which Conrad quoted to Edward Garnett in defence of this novel): 'La Russie – c'est le néant.'[1] Russia is a gigantic emptiness. The page of its history is blank because the Russian citizen has not been left free to inscribe his actions upon it; the history itself is inconceivable because history cannot

[1] Garnett (ed.), *Letters from Conrad*, p. 233.

spontaneously come into being out of nothing. We are reminded of Natalia Haldin's 'There is no legality, there are no institutions'. Russia seems to have no tradition of compromise, tolerance, participation, reciprocity; there seems to be no legacy of public dialogue, argument, criticism. But if Russia is a void, it is also vast – vast enough to induce a sense of mystic vertigo, infinite enough to require the mystery of an incarnation. Searching, like his compatriots, for some Messianic mediator, who will be at once the emblem and the saviour of Russian identity, Razumov inevitably settles on 'the one great historical fact of the land': Czarist absolutism. In his exaltation, he commits himself to the reactionary dogma that 'absolute power should be preserved ... for the great autocrat of the future'. His attempt to retain the basis of an intelligible existence has led him straight into an obscurantism scarcely distinguishable from Haldin's mysticism.

Having concluded that Haldin is, in the organicist terms of his new faith, 'the withered branch that must be cut off', Razumov suddenly overhears an isolated shout: 'Oh, thou vile wretch!' It comes from a sledge-driver reprimanding one of his fellows, and Razumov shakes his head and walks on. But he has unconsciously applied the phrase to himself, and he suddenly sees the figure of Haldin stretched on his back across the pavement in front of him.

This hallucination had such a solidity of aspect that the first movement of Razumov was to reach for his pocket to assure himself that the key of his rooms was there. But he checked the impulse with a disdainful curve of his lips. He understood. His thought, concentrated intensely on the figure left lying on his bed, had culminated in this extraordinary illusion of the sight. Razumov tackled the phenomenon calmly. With a stern face, without a check and gazing far beyond the vision, he walked on, experiencing nothing but a slight tightening of the chest. After passing he turned his head for a glance, and saw only the unbroken track of his footsteps over the place where the breast of the phantom had been lying.

Under Western Eyes, p. 37

It is in Razumov's mind here, rather than in the study of his father, Prince K—, a few minutes later, that Haldin is betrayed. Razumov's reaction to the hallucination dramatizes with extraordinary force the full ambiguity of his predicament. On the one hand, he demonstrates the reality of reason and power. In terms of reason, the phantom has a rational explanation: it is a product of his obsessive concentration on his uninvited guest. In terms of power, to walk across the figure of a man is, in contrast to the concrete facts of guns, whips, chains and fortresses, even less consequential than the bursting of a cobweb. On the other hand, it is an indirect affirmation of the reality of trust and conscience. Although, looking back, he can see nothing but his footprints in the snow, he has performed an act of ritualistic sacrilege, the consequences of which are not the less serious for being invisible. We have just seen that his horror at the deed he is envisaging is such that he cannot come to a decision to do it until he has given himself a justification for it. And even then, as we see here, he has to force himself to trample, quite literally, over his own conscience before he can actually bring himself to pronounce the words (as he does immediately afterwards) 'I shall give him up.' After he has arranged for Haldin to be picked up, he says to himself:

Extraordinary things do happen. But when they have happened they are done with. Thus too, when the mind is made up. That question is done with. And the daily concerns, the familiarities of our thought swallow it up – and the life goes on as before with its mysterious and secret sides quite out of sight, as they should be. Life is a public thing.

Under Western Eyes, p. 54

But is it? The rest of Razumov's career provides a searching inquiry into the truth of that proposition.

IV

The critical intelligence which the narrator is able to defend perhaps too easily, and which Razumov upholds, if at all, at the cost of his own integrity, flourishes only under conditions guaranteeing the individual a certain degree of independence. A man's reliance on cultural conventions does not imply that he is determined by them, or in any serious sense programmed by his own society. Rules and conventions exist to be used – that is to say, to be used by individuals on their own behalf. However, up to the moment of Haldin's entrance into his life, Razumov's independence – rather like the narrator's – has been independence *from* rather than *in* the world. But even in that phase of withdrawal (illusory, of course, for even the most private existence is sustained by the public realm) Razumov has shown evidence of instinctive independence, particularly in his reluctance to confine himself to a single side of a question. And now that he is plunged into the schizophrenia of Russian political life, he reveals the same tendency. He withholds assent from the revolutionary Haldin in the name of sanity: 'I did not hate him because he had committed the

crime of murder', he tells the official in charge of his case, Councillor Mikulin, when he learns that Haldin has been executed. 'I
hated him simply because I am sane' (p. 95). But at the same time
his attempt to seal in blood his commitment to his autocratic
opponents is equally unsuccessful, for it destroys his independence
of mind. 'I take the liberty to call myself a thinker', he tells Mikulin
on the same occasion.

'It is not a forbidden word, as far as I know.'
  'Why should it be forbidden?' [Mikulin replies]. ' ... The principal
condition is to think correctly.'

Under Western Eyes, p. 90

Even for the most intelligent of the servants of the Czar, thought is
not unconditional.

If, as we have seen, Jim can only discover the true meaning of
honour by losing it, Razumov only finds out the real significance of
independence by giving it up. 'Practical thinking in the last
instance is but criticism', he tells the official into whose hands he
has delivered his future. And indeed, it is impossible for him – try
as he might – to make a sincere surrender to the ideology of
absolutism. He cannot, like Haldin, obliterate his doubts in a
theory of resignation. This he discovers almost immediately after
his experience of conversion, when he encounters, first General
T—, chief of the secret police, then Councillor Mikulin, head of
counter-espionage (pp. 43–53, 86–99). (These two representatives
of autocracy balance in the St Petersburg part of the novel the
revolutionary Sophia Antonovna and Peter Ivanovitch in the
Genevan sections.) Razumov's first glance at General T— fills him
with instant loathing, not so much because of his cold perspicacity
as an investigator, but because he seems totally 'unable to understand a reasonable adherence to the doctrine of absolutism'. But if
he is incapable of understanding such an adherence, it is because it
is impossible. As Razumov comes to realize, 'General T—
embodied the whole power of autocracy because he was its guardian ... and his omnipotence made him inaccessible to reasonable
argument.' General T—'s defence of autocracy is entirely unthinking because entirely unqualified. 'My existence has been built on
fidelity!' This terrifying declaration (a perversion of one of Conrad's key moral concepts) betrays a will, as undeflectable as a force
of nature, to obliterate every vestige of independent life within the
orbit of its influence.

Fortunately for him, Razumov – who has, after all, just delivered another victim into the maw of this Moloch – experiences this force only indirectly; but the effect on his self-respect could scarcely be more destructive. He is treated as a suspect. As soon as he feels the breath of the 'merciless suspicion of despotism' on him, he is plunged into complete disarray. To be sure, with an instinctive awareness that even a moment's deviation could be fatal, he has kept his visit to Ziemianitch from the authorities; but that is not the true source of his anguish. Rather, it is the discovery that under an autocracy every citizen becomes an automatic suspect – including the servants of the autocracy itself. (Mikulin's eventual fate is a case in point.) And this discovery destroys the justification of his crime against Haldin.

As we have seen, the point at issue between Razumov and Haldin is the principle of trust. Haldin's confidence in Razumov may have been misplaced, but the fact remains that Razumov has not undeceived him. On the contrary, he has acted as if to justify this confidence. Unlike coercion, which makes its power felt at once and without argument, trust is vulnerable to appearances, for it creates a bond confirmable only on the basis of an inner act of free choice. But its very vulnerability is the source of its power, for in making its appeal to an independent decision, it engages the self much more profoundly than, paradoxically, any self-interested resolution. Thus Razumov's desecration of Haldin's helpless image is really an act of self-mutilation. His violation of the bond of obligation, like Jim's breach of the code of honour, is a self-betrayal.

However hard Razumov tries to persuade himself that he is not guilty of Haldin's death, he cannot suppress the knowledge that the responsibility is his alone. General T— makes it perfectly clear that had Haldin 'not come with his tale to such a staunch and loyal Russian as you, he would have disappeared like a stone in the water'. He cannot even share the blame with Haldin himself. When he returns to his rooms he discovers that the fugitive is perfectly ready to remove himself (indeed, he does so) as soon as he senses that Razumov does not approve of what he has done. Razumov has never been under any external pressure to betray him to the authorities. His decision is wholly his own. He is entirely guilty. In defining Razumov's predicament, Conrad brings his skill in creating paradoxical situations to an unprecedented level. If Razumov loses his independence before the state, it is not mainly for outward reasons – because he is afraid of what the state will do to him – but from an inner compulsion – out of fear of what a full knowledge of his deed may do to him. Therefore, the more vehemently he embraces the ideology of coercion, the more plainly he reveals his adherence to the principle of trust.

It is completely appropriate that Razumov should become a counter-revolutionary secret agent. For what is a spy if not a man whose task it is to exploit or abuse the confidence of others? And one, moreover, who has to do so with unremitting vigilance? By spurning Haldin's confidence, Razumov does not gain peace; on the contrary, he condemns himself, like Sysiphus, to a never-ending cycle of repetitive effort, obliged to walk across the shadow again and again in a vain endeavour to prove that the bond he has denied has no real existence.[1] In a vigorous essay on the narrator, Terry Eagleton argues that Razumov's transformation into a 'cruel, arrogant, malicious egoist' is unconvincing because it is inconsistent.[2] But there is nothing arbitrary about a cynicism which represents his ever more desperate attempts to repress a conscience that simply will not lie down. Consider his treatment of the 'Madcap Kostia', a fellow-student who, convinced that he is Haldin's associate, offers to help him escape (pp. 312–15). In his innocent eagerness, this Kostia is threatening to take the part that Razumov himself should have played in relation to Haldin. Razumov cannot allow him to perform this role seriously. Accordingly, he persuades him to rob his own father; he accepts the money and then, once on his way, flings it out of the train window. Of course, a man convinced of the speciousness of Kostia's devotion would not have felt the need for this vicious gesture. And this Razumov himself comes to recognize. In his confession to Natalia Haldin, he writes: 'I had to confirm in myself my contempt and hate for what I betrayed' (p. 359). It is therefore fitting that he should be cast as an anti-revolutionary agent – a role that gives him every opportunity to discredit its dupes. It is specially fitting that he should be playing the part of Haldin's accomplice, for it is Haldin whom, as the ghost who haunts his life, he most needs to degrade and exorcise.

V

The more Razumov tries to give up his independence, the less he succeeds. His convulsive efforts to do so, however, transform him from a man who declared that 'life is a public thing' to one who

[1] See Guerard, *Conrad the Novelist*, p. 240.
[2] T. Eagleton, *Exiles and Emigrés* (Chatto, 1970), p. 26.

reflects, on Rousseau's little island, that 'perhaps life is just like that, ... a dream and a fear'. In one of the best essays on *Under Western Eyes* Tony Tanner has traced the evolution of Razumov's inner experience from 'well-regulated normality' into 'a grotesque pantomime, a hideous farce, a monstrous puppet show, a nightmare'. He also demonstrates how the presentation of Razumov's descent into abnormality is enhanced by the use of a double perspective: within Razumov himself, through the narrator's interpretation of his diary, which shows what the world looks like to him; and outside him, through the narrator's own observation of him, which shows us what he looks like to the world.[1] Of all the consequences of suppressed guilt, however, I would like to single out one: the sense of overpowering moral solitude. Razumov's betrayal of Haldin is not only a self-defeating endeavour to retain independence of mind; it also represents an attempt at integration into the life of the aristocratic group from which the accident of his birth has shut him out. And this attempt, too, is self-defeating, for it instantly excommunicates him from the community of mankind.

Moral isolation consists in this: that what really counts in a man's life cannot be communicated to anybody else. As we have seen from Conrad's treatment of the latter part of Nostromo's career, to commit a secret crime is to be cut off from one's fellows. To be sure, Razumov is in complicity with at least three men – his father, General T— and Councillor Mikulin – who do not consider his crime to be one at all. Moreover, these men erase, even from the most secret state archives, all record of his role in the Haldin affair. If life is a public thing, then the fact that no one knows about a crime is almost as if the crime had not been committed at all. But Razumov's private knowledge persists, and it isolates him utterly – both from the autocrats, whom he unconsciously despises, and from the revolutionaries, whom he unconsciously envies. Here too the secret agent's role is a perfect expression of his inner state. A spy is isolated by the mask he presents to society: in addressing themselves to him, men can only speak to his face. As Haldin's 'heroic' comrade, Razumov earns the esteem of Russian exiles in Geneva. This gives him every opportunity for reductive cynicism. But at the same time, since 'a man's real life is that accorded to him in the thoughts of other men by reason of respect or natural love' (p. 14), it condemns him to a kind of non-being. From the moment of taking his decision to betray Haldin, he has been in a state of

---

[1] Tony Tanner, 'Nightmare and Complacency; Razumov and the Western Eye', *The Critical Quarterly* IV (1962), 197–214. The quotation is on p. 207.

posthumous existence. Tanner notes that after he has arranged for Haldin's arrest his watch stops. For Tanner, this symbolizes the end of the reassuring routine of a student's existence. But the stopping of the watch, which is given considerable emphasis (Razumov notes that the clock in General T—'s reception rooms is silent, etc.) has even greater significance. While waiting for midnight to strike, he and Haldin talk about their conceptions of eternity. According to Razumov: 'I imagine it ... as something quiet and dull. There would be nothing unexpected – don't you see? The element of time would be wanting' (p. 59). But in this he is expressing what has *already* happened to him. After Haldin has disappeared down the stairs and into the street, never to be seen again, Razumov sinks into a state of aimless passivity in which he acquires the dull feeling that life without happiness is impossible. And 'what was happiness? ... Looking forward was happiness – that's all – nothing more.' And as external hours, days, and weeks pass by, it becomes ever clearer that his internal clock has stopped. The insulated self has ceased to be capable of change. Natalia Haldin has said to the narrator: 'Time they say can soften every sort of bitterness. But I cannot believe that it has any power over remorse' (p. 117). Razumov's arrested life is a dreadful demonstration of the truth of this belief.

A single illustration of the complexity with which Razumov's role as secret agent expresses his individual predicament will have to suffice here. His various exchanges with the Genevan exiles are brought to a climax by his conversation with Sophia Antonovna (pp. 237–82). Particularly noteworthy is the moment at which his credentials as a *bona fide* revolutionary are finally established beyond dispute. She tells him that the peasant Ziemianitch has hanged himself. Since she takes this to be proof of the peasant's remorse at betraying Haldin, the last remaining flaw in Razumov's disguise – how Haldin fell into the hands of the police – is removed. He is now wholly free from all external pressure. But far from assuring his happiness, this has the effect of driving him yet further into cynicism and isolation. He takes a savage pleasure in the sight of his enemies' discrediting themselves out of their own mouths: at the fact that the closer Sophia Antonovna, in her reconstruction of what happened to Ziemianitch, gets to the truth, the further she is from identifying the real culprit. But at the same time, unable to endure his knowledge of what has really driven Ziemianitch to suicide – guilt at failing to meet Haldin's rendezvous on the fatal night – he tries to persuade himself that his self-destruction is the result of the disorderly excesses of his life. The crowning detail of Sophia Antonovna's story – that Ziemianitch has attributed his frenzied thrashing to 'the devil' – is almost perfectly ambiguous: what seals Razumov's safety as a spy is exactly what defines his guilt as a man. Now locked up in his posthumous solitude far more securely than in any material jail, he suffers the effects of imprisonment more deeply than any ordinary convict:

He made a gesture of despair. It was not his courage that failed him. The choking fumes of falsehood had taken him by the throat – the thought of being condemned to struggle on and on in that tainted atmosphere without the hope of ever renewing his strength by a breath of fresh air.

Under Western Eyes, p. 269

VI

'Who knows what true loneliness is – not the conventional word, but the naked terror? . . . No human being could bear a steady view of moral solitude without going mad' (p. 39). It is in order to escape this fate that Razumov, in some of the most powerful pages Conrad ever wrote, confesses his crime and reinstates himself in society. He is punished, of course, but by his confession he is able to collaborate in the judgement against him, and so becomes – to borrow Bergson's phrase – 'the author of his own condemnation'.[1]

The dénouement of the novel, however, is complicated by the device of a double confession. Razumov's main confession to the revolutionaries assembled in Laspara's apartment is preceded by a private confession to Natalia Haldin in her mother's drawing-room, prompted, of course, by his hopeless love for her. This device is much more than a decorative flourish; its origins go right back to the initial trespass. In betraying Haldin, Razumov has not merely broken an unwritten human law; he has also resisted the appeal of an act of exemplary virtue. He has not only felt the glamour of Haldin's presence (he mentally compares him to the 'exquisite' statue of a fleeing youth glimpsed in General T—'s reception rooms); he has also responded to the power of his independence (he knows of his refusal, even at the point of death, to implicate the man who has given him away). It could be said, therefore, that he has betrayed a double obligation: the *pressure* of his social–moral conscience, and the *attraction* of Haldin's personal–moral example. Haldin's own vision of eternity – 'they can kill my body, but

[1] Bergson, *Two Sources*, p. 18.

they cannot exile my soul from the world' – proves prophetic: he survives with such vividness in Razumov's tormented memory that he brings his victim to the point of actual identification with him.[1]

But to Razumov the most disturbing of Haldin's reincarnations is his sister. Ever since her brother's recommendation of him as one of the 'unstained, lofty, and solitary existences', she has devoted all the limpidity and trustfulness of her attention to him. She seems a living personification of her brother's faith in freedom – almost an incarnation of the liberty Razumov has betrayed. Her extraordinary attraction makes her the most dangerous of temptations. On the one hand, her faith in him intensifies his guilt to an intolerable level; on the other, it offers him a chance of reaching a new height in cynicism: he knows that if he proposes to her he will be accepted. For a man like himself – a Czarist agent responsible for her brother's death – to make her his wife would be the 'unpardonable sin of stealing a soul' (p. 360). But this marks the limit of the villainies he is prepared to perform. She is as helplessly in his power as her brother had been: but he cannot bring himself to repeat his crime. As her love for him makes his possession of her a possibility, so his love for her places her finally out of his reach. In their last confrontation, witnessed by the helpless narrator, the only form Razumov's declaration of love can take is to point the finger of accusation against his own breast.

By this gesture, Razumov loses her for ever, but he has flung open the window of his cell and can at last breathe freely. Yet even this triumph does not escape the shadow of autocracy. The rush of air that saves his soul extinguishes her. Like her compatriots suddenly exposed to the contradictions of their inheritance, she relinquishes all claims to a mind of her own. Her brother justified his crime in terms of resignation ('When the necessity of this heavy work came to me ... I thought "God's will be done", etc.'); now, under the defeated gaze of the narrator, she renounces her identity, and is swallowed up by 'the corrupted dark immensity claiming her for its own'. In the narrator's reflections: 'There was no longer any Natalia Haldin, because she had completely ceased to think of herself. It was a great victory, a characteristically Russian exploit in self-suppression' (p. 375).

But Razumov cannot escape *his* fate either. He has indeed broken the shell of his solipsism. For the first time his diary, which he has kept for himself 'as a threatened man may look fearfully at

[1] E.g. pp. 256–8.

his own face in the glass' (p. 214), becomes a means of communication. His last entry is addressed to Natalia: 'After all it is they' – the revolutionaries – 'and not I who have the right on their side! – theirs is the strength of invisible powers' (p. 361). Yet this admission is not a second conversion, antithetical to the first. Having refused to commit the same crime twice, he will not relinquish his intellectual independence for a second time. But now he recognizes the consequences: 'I am independent – and therefore perdition is my lot' (p. 362). It is because he cannot join the revolutionaries that he has to confront them with the man he really is.

Conrad's famous description of this confrontation brings the book to a fitting climax. The novel began with a murderous explosion muffled under the snows of a Russian winter; it ends with an act of concussive violence – the bursting of Razumov's ear-drums – which instantly transforms the roar of a Swiss summer thunderstorm into a soundless tumult of rain and lightning. Razumov's career opened with a crime that morally sundered him from his kind; it closes with a penalty that cuts him off physically from his fellows. No English writer can match Conrad in his understanding of physical violence. Neither sentimental nor sensational, his presentation is always overpoweringly in focus. In this case, its obscene horror is brought out by the creature that administers it: the huge-bellied, squeaky-voiced Nikita Necator, who mutilates Razumov under the bare electric light of an apartment landing, squatting beside his head as he is forcibly held pinned to the floor. Not many characters in Conrad's work equal this executioner in viciousness. But the immediacy of the effect he creates should not be allowed to obscure his further significance. In one of the novel's concluding ironies, we discover that he is a double agent, that is, an agent acting on behalf of both sides. And in nothing is his double function more appropriate than in the retribution he visits on Razumov, sending him out into the night to wander the streets until he is struck down by a tram he cannot hear. In reassuming his independence – that is, in relinquishing his role as a spy – Razumov has simultaneously antagonized those who have employed him, and those against whom he has been employed. Perdition is indeed his lot.

It has become almost conventional in discussion of *Under Western Eyes* to assume that the novel's main contrast is between the smug lucidity of the narrator and the incoherent profundity of the Russians. Whether the teacher of languages be seen as a vehicle for Conrad's self-deceiving conservatism (and his Polish Russophobia), or as a consistently defective commentator incapable of grasping the significance of the material before him, he has generally been taken to represent views and attitudes that are the opposite of Razumov's. Against this tendency, I have tried to argue that the narrator is a serious representative of rationality: that is to say, that what he stands for is not qualified out of existence by the ironies of his narrative, but that it constitutes the dilemma on which that narrative is based: the problem of how far rationality is dependent on the existence of a viable public realm. I do not wish to imply, of course, that the narrator's point of view is unreservedly endorsed. As a man whose conscience is at rest, he can see that revolutionary hopes are futile, but he cannot see why they cannot be given up. He is quite capable of perceiving Russian irrationality; what he cannot do is understand its significance. Hence his outlook is not only limited; it may even be pernicious. By encouraging Razumov's attentions to Natalia, in the hope of frustrating Peter Ivanovitch's designs on her, he unwittingly tempts him to perform the unpardonable sin. And Razumov reacts accordingly: 'Could he have been the devil himself in the shape of an old Englishman?' he asks in his diary. And although the narrator's presence at Razumov's confession helps to define the outrage it constitutes against Natalia, Razumov's description of his conduct – 'He raged at me like a disappointed devil' (pp. 360, 361) – appears much more inappropriate than it really is.

Yet, for all this, it seems to me a mistake to look for the novel's tragic point in the antagonism between the narrator and the protagonist. I have tried to show that, contrary to received opinion, *Under Western Eyes* does not offer two kinds of rationality, one pragmatic and Western, the other mystical and Russian. Whether they recognize it or not, Razumov and the language teacher in fact share an identical conception of reason. If there is a difference between them, it is not so much in what they are as in where they live. Yet the strength of the novel is in part its recognition that such a difference is not merely incidental or contingent. Conrad understands, as so many of his contemporaries failed to, that the life of reason is not some sort of self-sufficient absolute, impassively transcending all historical or cultural particulars. As the product of a tradition that protects individual thought, the narrator may assume that reason owes nothing to time and place. But liberal societies can only retain their liberalism at the cost of what Natalia Haldin has called 'a bargain with fate' – that is, accommodation with all the imperfections of actuality. Hence the illusion of self-sufficiency has to be paid for: as the narrator's career demonstrates, disengagement gradually produces a kind of intellectual impotence. In contrast, absolutist societies (and it is in this representative sense that Conrad's historical Russia must be finally assessed) cut off all possibility of retreat into detachment. Whatever their merits, Razumov's claims to rationality do not remain untested. Yet the seriousness thus released also has to be paid for. The price, as Razumov's career demonstrates, is nothing less than intellectual security. Razumov repeats, at a tragic level, what the language teacher illustrates at a moral level: that in its relation to the public realm the life of reason has to be, paradoxically, at once autonomous and dependent. As a spectator, the language teacher retains his self-possession, but he can only reveal an empty lucidity. As a participant, caught in the thick of the fray, Razumov retains a sense of the significance of his life, but he can only achieve a self-destructive intensity. The fates of the two men are complementary; together, they articulate the tragic truth that the critical intellect, in demanding both detachment and commitment of its adherents, imposes conditions that are at once necessary and incompatible.

8

Conclusion

J'ai jeté ma vie à tous les vents du ciel mais j'ai gardé ma pensée. C'est peu de chose – c'est tout – ce n'est rien – c'est la vie même.

(I have thrown my life to all the winds of the sky but I have kept my thought. It is a trifle – it is everything – it is nothing – it is life itself.)

Conrad to R. B. Cunninghame Graham, 8 February 1899

It has been my purpose in this study to try to demonstrate that Conrad's major creative phase rests on a continuous and consistent effort of thought. I began by arguing that Conrad conceived of his own art in terms of insight and vision rather than of laughter and tears; that he founded his values, both artistic and moral, on the hypothesis of a 'spectacular' universe; and that he steadily, even fiercely, resisted every attempt to reduce the significance of his work to its causal or biographical origins. It seemed, right, therefore, to approach the novels with the assumption that their author was in full possession of what he was trying to do and say. The Conrad that this assumption has enabled me to discover is a much more intellectually coherent figure than the one criticism has accustomed us to. From E. M. Forster's notorious verdict that 'he is misty in the middle as well as at the edges'[1] to C. B. Cox's recent more qualified view that 'there is no clear development of ideas throughout [his] work',[2] the mainstream of Conrad scholarship has stressed his power and profundity at the expense of his intelligibility and control. Whether or not my own emphasis is convincing, I can claim at least that if I have eschewed the metaphysics of darkness in favour of the humanly intelligible, it has not been through a desire to minimize Conrad's elemental depths, but because there seemed to me no other way of making them real. However difficult and demanding a writer may be, he must make some sense to himself and to us before we can begin to take him seriously. Moreover, I have not wished to imply, in my

---

[1] E. M. Forster, 'Joseph Conrad: A Note', *Abinger Harvest* (London, 1936), pp. 134–5.

[2] Cox, *Joseph Conrad*, p. 159.

attempt to bring out Conrad's intellectual responsibility, that he is more of a philosopher than an artist. A fictional work is distinguished from a philosophical work not (as a number of modern critics have claimed) by its indifference to ideas, but by the way in which it is interested in them – by the way in which it admits them into itself. The fact that a novel does not make use of systematic proofs and logical demonstrations does not disqualify it as a rational object, nor does it prohibit the novelist from putting into it what is really important in his life.

As an analysis of Conrad's work, this study is of course incomplete. I have not discussed such recognized masterpieces as 'Typhoon' and *The Shadow Line*; nor apprentice works like *Almayer's Folly* and *An Outcast of the Islands*; nor the often undervalued later novels, especially *Chance*, *Victory* and *The Rover*; and I have not considered Conrad's contribution to the art of the short story in collections like *A Set of Six*. But in confining myself to his central achievement, I have at least been able to do some justice to one outstanding question: that of his contribution to the modern movement in literature.

It has become a critical commonplace that Conrad's major theme is the problem of individual identity: the question of what the 'real' self is – where it is located, and how it is to be understood. This problem is not confined to contemporary, or even twentieth-century literature; it is implicit, for example, in the whole of Renaissance tragedy, and explicit in Shakespearean tragedy. But what is modern about Conrad's treatment of it is the form he gives it – or, more accurately, the form it assumes as he struggles to give it definition. A retrospective survey of the novels we have just examined establishes that, for all their variety, they rest on a common assumption: namely, that the real is to be found not in the sphere of the inner and the private, but in that of the outer and the public. This assumption alone would be enough to declare Conrad a modern, for it reflects what is perhaps the most cherished conviction of twentieth-century thought. During the last hundred years, the shift from a Christian, or an Idealist, or even a Romantic concern with individual experience to a behaviourist, or structuralist, or marxist emphasis on its determinants – a move from private intentions to public systems, as it were – has been so radical and comprehensive that it now virtually governs our sense of what is real. Indeed, to the modern mind, an appeal to the public realm is little short of being a criterion of rationality. In most modern philosophy, for example, it has become axiomatic that what counts in establishing the meaning of a statement is not the intention of the speaker (what he thinks he is saying) but the context in which he makes the utterance (what he is actually saying). To this position, which may be termed 'realist', Conrad shows himself profoundly responsive. In *The Nigger of the 'Narcissus'*, what matters is not what the crew may desire or think, but what they actually do – whether they succeed or fail to 'drive the ship'. In 'Heart of Darkness', even a single step beyond the obligations of civilization exposes one to the danger of falling into the 'horror' of the atavistic self. In *Lord Jim*, individual regret or reformation, however sincere, cannot annul the verdict of the facts. In *Nostromo*, the sole test of a moral or political project is its objective consequences. In *The Secret Agent*, the mark of sanity is not passionate commitment, but adjustment to the received routines of socialized life. And in *Under Western Eyes*, individual thought itself is dependent for its intelligibility on received norms and institutions. Conrad's systematic commitment to the 'outer' bears quite unambiguously on the problem of personal identity: the test of what a man really is cannot be what he thinks he is, but what he does – not his individual consciousness but his public role. Hence Conrad's almost obsessive interest in the phenomenon of self-deception. His scepticism of almost all self-descriptions, his doubts as to a man's own view of his relationship to himself, or to society, or to the universe, place him in the forefront of twentieth-century deflators of a naïvely self-confident nineteenth-century individualism.

The modern intellectual to whom the social alone is real is well satisfied to regard the individual as an abstraction, for his assumption has enabled him to deal effectively with a number of previously intractable problems. Conrad, however, is not a philosopher, or an economist, or a sociologist, but a writer – that is, a man for whom felt experience is the very substance of his craft. However valid the view may be that the 'outer' is the sole testing-ground of truth, it must generate a formidable new difficulty, for it condemns the inner self to a condition of irremediable solitude, leaving it (in Iris Murdoch's vivid phrase) 'marooned upon a tiny island in the middle of a sea of ... facts'.[1] Hence Conrad becomes our contemporary in a double sense: not only in his adherence to the modern doctrine of public reality, but also in his registration of the anguish that this doctrine produces.

In the first chapter I referred to the disarray into which criticism had been thrown by its inability to classify Conrad either as a

[1] I. Murdoch, *The Sovereignty of the Good* (Routledge, 1970), p. 27.

realist or as a romantic. What I am suggesting here is that he should be regarded as both: that the 'realist' thrust of his thought (the view that the verifiable alone is real) produces a 'romantic' counter-thrust (the view that the visionary alone has value). In *The Nigger of the 'Narcissus'*, this 'romantic' reaction is not given full expression, but held in check by the special conditions of sea-service. But thereafter it acquires an imaginative force that closely matches the intellectual force of the scepticism it challenges. In 'Heart of Darkness', it manifests itself in Marlow's affirmation, against all the evidence of essential 'darkness', of what I called positive illusion. In *Lord Jim*, it reveals itself in Jim's obstinate search, in the very teeth of an unredeemable disgrace, for the fulfilment of his dream of honour. In *Nostromo*, it is the survival, in the face of a comprehensive historical and philosophical materialism, of Mrs Gould's faith in the value of the moral imagination. In *The Secret Agent*, it bursts out, against all the claims of common sense and moderation, in the intensity of Mrs Verloc's unselfish suffering. And finally in *Under Western Eyes*, it displays itself in Razumov's declaration, defying allegiances on which his very survival depends, of moral and intellectual independence. The stronger Conrad's commitment to the 'outer', the more unyielding his affirmation of the 'inner'.

The most striking aspect of these affirmations, however, is that they do not resolve the tragic dilemmas dramatized by the novels, but constitute them. In Conrad's work, faith and scepticism in the reality of the inner self are not only in conflict, but in contradiction. The inner world is not simply challenged by the outer, but ruled out by it. Conrad's affirmation of the inner world is therefore inherently paradoxical. Since the inner world is inconsistent with Conrad's criteria of the real, his defence of it is that of a man who knows that it must exist yet cannot see how it can. If his novels make a tragic point, it is that man seems capable of discovering the reality of his own values only through their defeat or contradiction.

Failure to grasp the paradoxical form of Conrad's positives helps to explain, it seems to me, the persistence of the two oldest, and perhaps most basic, objections to his work: that it is philosophically pretentious (in the sense that it promises more than it gives), and that it is morally nihilistic. This first charge is, I suppose, understandable enough: Conrad's interest in the 'inner' prompts the conclusion that he is some sort of metaphysician, for the private self or 'soul' has traditionally been the springboard for visionary realities, as the public role has become the testing-ground of the substantial self. Conrad is not offering a metaphysics he can't explain, as Forster alleges; he is dramatizing the need for a metaphysics that can't exist – or (to moderate the formulation) that seems illusory to the kind of thinking he holds rational. Raising the question of whether metaphysics can exist at all must not be confused with proposing unintelligible metaphysical theories.

If the first charge arises out of a failure to grasp the nature of Conrad's commitment to the public and the demonstrable, the second stems from an equivalent failure to understand the nature of his concern with the private and subjective. In her well-known essay, 'The Idea of Perfection' (which seems to reflect an intellectual predicament very close to Conrad's own), Iris Murdoch distinguishes between two concepts of morality, one based on the idea of vision, the other on the idea of action, and puts a case for the former against the authoritarian claims of the latter. An ethic that accords a central place to moral understanding is of course a necessary condition for the production of imaginative fiction; indeed, literature itself would cease to exist in a culture that outlawed the contemplative life as parasitic on the active life. We have seen that Conrad defends the novelist from pragmatist attack on the grounds that his task is as real as 'the conquest of a colony'; but, as we have also seen, he never wavers in his conviction of the primacy of imagination. To remind us that the creation of a significant imagined world is distinguishable from indulgence in merely private reverie does not license the conclusion that writing a novel is *identical with* conquering a colony: it is only, in its own way, *as real*. Conrad never claims that 'life' cannot be differentiated from 'art'. On the contrary, his entire aesthetic rests, as I have tried to demonstrate, on the notion that the novelist's concern is not life merely, but life understood. If Conrad's conviction of the primacy of vision or understanding in the creating of a novel is right, it follows that the novelist's values will be implicit rather than overt – that what he believes will not reside in what he sees, but in the kind of attention he gives it; that it will be found not in the action he depicts, but in the way in which he depicts it. That Conrad devises narratives which turn on cases of suffering and defeat does not permit us to conclude with the modern realist that he is a moral nihilist, or even a moral sceptic. His positives are finally registered not in the mere sequence of represented events, but in the wealth and subtlety of the artistic context from which these events derive their significance.

My argument in this study has been that only an appeal to the tragic will do justice to Conrad's achievement as a novelist. One of the tests of the relevance of a critical concept is that its application should give rise to a reciprocal effect: that it should both illuminate the new setting and itself be illuminated by it. I call Conrad's work tragic because it dramatizes the contradiction between private vision and public action. But does not such a contradiction, in its turn, provide an insight into the nature of the tragic itself, which represents moral catastrophe not in order to deprive us of our values, but to put us in better possession of them?